לזכות Schmukler Family ב"ה

The Heroic Struggle

The Arrest and Liberation of
Rabbi Yosef Y. Schneersohn of Lubavitch
in Soviet Russia

THE
Heroic Struggle

The Arrest and Liberation
of Rabbi Yosef Y. Schneersohn of Lubavitch
in Soviet Russia

Translated and adapted from the memoirs of the Rebbe
by Rabbi Dr. Alter B. Z. Metzger

KEHOT PUBLICATION SOCIETY
770 Eastern Parkway / Brooklyn, New York 11213

The Heroic Struggle

Copyright © 1999
by
KEHOT PUBLICATION SOCIETY
770 Eastern Parkway • Brooklyn, New York 11213
(718) 774-4000 • FAX (718) 774-2718

Orders Department:
291 Kingston Avenue • Brooklyn, New York 11213
(718) 778-0226 • FAX (718) 778-4148
e-mail kehot@chabad.org

Library of Congress Cataloging-in-Publication Data
    Schneersohn, Joseph Isaac, 1880-1950.
    [Selections, English. 1999]
    The Heroic Struggle : the arrest and liberation of Rabbi Yosef Y. Schneersohn of Lubavitch in Soviet Russia / translated and adapted from the memoirs of the Rebbe by Alter B. Z. Metzger.
        p. cm.
    Includes bibliographical references and index.
    ISBN 0-8266-0439-0 (alk. paper)
    1. Schneersohn, Joseph Isaac, 1880-1950--Captivity, 1927.
2. Rabbis--Soviet Union--Biography. 3. Hasidim--Soviet Union--Biography. 4. Habad. I. Metzger, Alter B. II. Title.
    BM755.S285A3 1998
    296.8'332'092--dc21
    [b]
                                                            98-17462
                                                            CIP

Printed in the United States of America

Table of Contents

Preface

The subject of this book is especially significant given the events of the last few years. The still-recent fall of Communism in Russia was followed by a tremendous resurgence of open Jewish religious observance, long driven underground by brutal, systematic repression. This resurgence was not, of course, merely a matter of Russian politics: Had the Jewish underground not survived in seemingly impossible circumstances, no Jewish religious renaissance would have been possible.

The crucial background incident to this remarkable survival is undoubtedly the event whose conclusion is celebrated on the *chassidic* holiday of the 12th and 13th of *Tammuz*—the arrest and subsequent release from prison for "counter revolutionary activity" of the sixth leader of the Chabad-Lubavitch *chassidic* movement, Rabbi Yosef Yitzchak Schneersohn, of sainted memory, in 5687 (1927). Seldom is the will to resist of an oppressed community so bound up in the person of a single leader as that of the Russian Jewish community at this period. Imprisoned by a regime that routinely used murder and terror to crush all opposition, one quite capable of ignoring the world's outrage and murdering a well-known public figure, the Rebbe staunchly endured deprivation and torture, physical and mental, and emerged from his ordeal miraculously alive and undaunted, his defiant stance entirely intact. Although subsequently forced to leave the country, he was able to continue leading the Jewish resistance from abroad. Ultimately, his activities laid the foundation for the current Jewish revival, which took place under the leadership of his son-in-law and successor, Rabbi Menachem Mendel Schneerson, of sainted memory.

The events of the Rebbe's arrest until the beginning of the events of the prison cell itself are narrated in a translation of the Rebbe's autobiographical *Notes of the Arrest (Reshimat Hama'aser)*.[1] Incorporating notes actually taken during the imprisonment,[2] *Reshimat Hama'aser* was written by the Rebbe on 15 *Sivan*, 5688, the first anniversary of his arrest.[3] The Rebbe's future son-in-law and successor, Rabbi Menachem Mendel Schneerson, painstakingly copied the notes from the Rebbe's journals.[4] During the Rebbe's travels in the storm of WWII, fleeing the Nazis, the original was lost. The present work is taken from Rabbi Menachem Mendel's journals, known as "*Reshimot*." Many years later, when Rabbi Yosef Yitzchak arrived in the U.S. he thanked his son-in-law for saving the historic notes.[5] They are an inexhaustible source of rich insight into the many remarkable facets of a singular spiritual personality. The work exhibits a perceptive eye for detail, remarkable insight into the process of terror, and above all, firm courage in the face of captors brutally insensitive to the Divine sanctity of human life. The Rebbe's sustained psychological awareness of his own reactions and emotions illuminates the entire narrative.

The Rebbe's successor said on many occasions that the Rebbe took these notes in order to share his unique *chassidic* heritage of spiritual faith and courage with others, and thus aid them in bridging the ordeal of spiritual or physical crisis.

The events of the prison cell are covered in a translation of a further autobiographical segment composed by the Rebbe and published originally in the journal *Yagdil Torah*.[6] The events of the first interrogation at Spalerno, continuing through the negotiations for the Rebbe's release and the release itself, are taken from *Di Yisurim fun Lubavitchen Rebben in Soviet Russland* (Riga 1930). Other sources drawn upon from time to time are cited as they appear.

The appendices sample the Rebbe's writings and discourses, and those of his successor, on the spiritual significance of the imprisonment as well as his account of some of the events immediately preceding the arrest. Additional material in the appendices includes an extended narrative of the events before and during the arrest, by one of the Rebbe's close *chassidim*, Reb Elye Chaim Althaus, as well as recently declassified material from the Rebbe's G.P.U. file.

RABBI DR. ALTER B. Z. METZGER

BROOKLYN, NEW YORK
TAMMUZ 12, 5759
72nd Anniversary of the Liberation

Notes

1. Printed in *Likkutei Dibburim*, vol. 4, pp. 1222 ff; *Sefer HaSichot* 5687, pp. 179 ff.
2. *Sichat 13 Tammuz, Sichot Kodesh* 5729, vol. 2, p. 262.
3. *Pesach Davar, Likkutei Dibburim*, Hebrew Edition.
4. *Yemei Melech*, vol. 1, p. 217.
5. *Algemeiner Journal*, July 15th, 1977.
6. *Yagdil Torah* vol. 5, Number 54 *(Sivan-Tammuz* 5743): pp. 259-304. It was subsequently printed in *Sefer HaSichot 5687,* pp. 266 ff.

Historical Background

By Dr. William W. Brickman, Ph.D.

The narrative of the imprisonment and release of the Lubavitcher Rebbe, Rabbi Yosef Yitzchak Schneersohn, describes his sufferings for his activities to spread Jewish religious education and observance behind the Communist Iron Curtain. His stubborn efforts contributed immeasurably to the perpetuation of Yiddishkeit in the former U.S.S.R. and ultimately to the current revival in the post-Soviet era. This was accomplished in the face of the Russian regime's perennial policy of atheistic indoctrination and forcible prevention of the exercise of religious freedom. The enormity of the task and the significance of the achievement is especially evident given the history of Judaism in Russia.

To speak of the U.S.S.R. as a country where anti-Semitism has prevailed throughout its history, in spite of its own declared tradition, is to say nothing new. More than this, over the decades it has maintained a vigorous campaign to eliminate Jewish observance.

But this policy did not originate in the minds of the Communist overlords. Historically, anti-Semitism and anti-Judaism, or anti-*Yiddishkeit*, is a continuous process dating from the early nineteenth century.

The accession of Czar Nicholas brought about a series of anti-Jewish actions by the Russian government. The general policy constituted the Russification, assimilation and compulsory "enlightenment" of the Jews. The regime also conducted a series of ritual murder trials. Perhaps the most damaging development was the imperial decree in 1827, instituting the conscription of Jews aged 12-25 ("cantonists") for 25-31 years of military service. The goal was the alienation of the adoles-

9

cents and young men from their religion, and their conversion to Christianity.

Alexander II, the "Czar liberator" of the serfs, introduced in 1856 the "benevolent" policy of training the "*Kazyionnye*," or Crown Rabbis in official rabbinical schools for service as government-paid functionaries in Jewish communities. Torah-loyal Jews did not accept these Russian rabbis, as they did not accept the campaign against the traditional *cheder* (primary school) and the *melamed* (teacher).

The government's "refined" attitude toward Jews gave way to systematic oppression after the assassination of Alexander II. Under his successor, Czar Alexander III, a policy of massacres, or pogroms, of the Jewish population commenced in April, 1881, in Kiev, Odessa, Warsaw, and other cities. The Russian regime, identifying radicalism and nihilism with the entire Jewish people, instituted repressive laws and regulations, resulting in an exodus to Western Europe and the United States.

The policy of government-inspired pogroms continued under the last czar, Nicholas II. The massacres at Kishinev and Homel in 1903, and in Minsk, Lodz, Brest-Litovsk, Bialystok, Odessa, and other towns in 1905, shocked even the non-Jewish world. Finally, the notorious trial of Mendel Beilis in 1913 for the alleged murder of a Christian boy for ritual purposes made it clear that Russia and anti-Semitism were synonymous.

However, despite anti-Semitism and anti-Judaism, *Yiddishkeit* persisted in the *shtetl* and in larger Jewish communities in the Russian empire. The *cheder* and the *melamed* continued to flourish. *Yeshivot* increased in number and in impact. Rabbinical literature flourished and helped instruct Jews not only in Imperial Russia, but far beyond its borders as well. Torah-Jewry survived in the face of Russian repression and growing Jewish secularism.

Then came the February Socialist Revolution of 1917. The Provisional Government at once eliminated Jewish disabilities in religion, culture and education. The promise of spiritual security proved to be short-lived when Vladimir Ilyich Lenin and his Bolshevik brigades overthrew Alexander Kerensky's government in the October Revolution.

Once the Bolshevik Revolution was in full swing, the new government, on the basis of its anti-religious policy, immediately turned to questions of nationality and religion. On November 15, 1917, the Declaration of the Rights of the Peoples of Russia, was co-signed by V. Ulyanov (Lenin) as Chairman of the Council of People's Commissars of the Russian Republic and I. Dzhugashvili (Stalin) as People's Commissar for Nationality Affairs. It proclaimed "the abolition of any and all national and national-religious privileges and disabilities," while upholding the principle of "the free development of national minorities and ethnographic groups inhabiting the territory of Russia."

Not long afterward, in January, 1918, the Council of People's Commissars decreed that "the church is separated from the state" and that "the school is separated from the church." "The teaching of religious doctrines in all state and public, as well as in private, educational institutions in which general subjects are taught, is forbidden," the decree continued, "Citizens may teach and study religion privately." Seemingly, schools exclusively devoted to the teaching of religion, such as *yeshivot*, were permissible under the decree. Yet, the final sentence suggests that religious education must be confined to the house. In any event, a subsequent regulation specified a maximum of three pupils in any type of private religious instruction.

The first Constitution, July 10, 1918, of the Russian Socialist Federated Soviet Republic reiterated that "the church is separated from the state and the school from the church," so as "to ensure for the workers' genuine liberty of conscience." It went on to add that "freedom of religious and anti-religious propaganda is assured to every citizen." This apparently states that public religious demonstrations and publications are on a par with atheistic activities. The provision for religious propaganda was radically modified in the U.S.S.R. Constitution of 1929 as follows: "Freedom of religious worship and of anti-religious propaganda is recognized for all citizens." Under the new basic law, religion was confined to houses of worship, but any public manifestation was forbidden. Even this minor measure of leniency, whether a concession to internal protest or an attempt to project a facade of tolerance to foreign nations, was very much mitigated by anti-religious forces in the state structure and the societal hierarchy.

The Communist war on *Yiddishkeit* is as old as the Bolshevik Revolution. In order to encourage Jewish acceptance of Communism, Stalin's People's Commissariat for Nationality Affairs set up in 1918 the Commissariat for Jewish National Affairs (*Yevkom,* as abbreviated in Russian), plus Jewish Sections (*Yevsektzia*) of the Communist Party. In neither case did the term "Jewish" carry any religious or even traditionally cultural connotation. The first head of the *Yevkom,* Semyon (Shimon) Dimanshtein, made it abundantly clear that "Jewish National Affairs" actually meant Communist National Affairs by and for Jews. This faithful functionary of the Bolsheviks was not an ignoramus by any means; in his youth he had received a thoroughly traditional Jewish education. In 1918 his policy was summed up in the statement that "there is no salvation for the Jews on any road other than Communism."

But the actual application of Communist power in the Jewish community ("on the Jewish street") was carried out by *Yevsektzia,* particularly the assault upon the beliefs and practices of the Jewish religion. Although these Jewish Sections of the Communist Party regarded all religions equally as despicable and detrimental to society, an especially jaundiced eye was focused upon Judaism, the faith of their fathers and fore-fathers.

The Jewish Communists began their anti-Jewish activities in 1918 by rejecting a proposal for the control of Jewish schools by the *kehillah* (Jewish community), the traditional religious body which was later abolished by a decree signed in July, 1919, by Samuel (Shmuel) Agurskii, a deputy commissar of the *Yevkom,* and endorsed by Stalin, proclaiming "the dicta-torship of the Proletariat in the Jewish street." The *Yevkom* and the *Yevsektzia* were empowered "to undertake measures for the liquidation of the bourgeois institutions." This directive provided the basis for the abolition of the *kehillah,* as well as for considering as illegal the *cheder,* the *yeshivah,* other educa-tional institutions, and all non-Communist social, philan-thropic and cultural organizations. The war on *Yiddishkeit* was well under way.

Both the *cheder* and the *yeshivah* now went underground. The Jewish Communist campaign to uproot *Yiddishkeit* took on several forms of feverish activity. They were responsible for the confiscation of synagogues and schools, harassment and arrest of rabbis and other religious functionaries, the ban on ritual slaughter (*shechitah*) and circumcision (*milah*), the clos-ing of the ritual baths (*mikveh*), and the spurious trials of ele-mentary religious schools, *yeshivot,* holidays and rituals. They printed the anti-religious publications *Der Emes* (1918-1930) and *Der Apikoires,* and administered a Yiddish language school in the same ideological vein. But, they were surprised that many Jewish parents preferred their children's exposure to compulsory Marxism-Leninism in the Russian language in a Russian school rather than anti-*Yiddishkeit* through the medi-um of the "holy" language of Yiddish in a Jewish Communist school.

Contributing to the complication experienced by religious Jews was the law in 1922 establishing Sunday as a day of rest. Even worse was a decree, in August 1929, by the Council of People's Commissars mandating no cessation of work and no common day of rest.

The "*Yevseks*" were very much aware of the persistence of piety among Jews despite their activities. Nor were they to be more successful, in 1928 and later years, in persuading the Jewish masses to migrate en masse to a new promised "homeland" in Birobizhan. Neither the establishment of that Jewish Autonomous Region in the Far East nor the authorization of Yiddish as its official language constituted a magnet to move Jews far eastward.

The "*Yevseks*" fought *Yiddishkeit* with extreme fervor. Dimanshtein, mentioned above, and Agurskii were heads of the *Yevkom*. Moishe Litvakov, a Hebrew cantor who became a fanatical foe of Hebrew and a staunch supporter of Stalin, served as editor of the daily *Der Emes*. By no means a religious ignoramus, he possessed a large collection of Hebrew books, among them many writings on *Chassidism* in general and on Chabad in particular.

One activist in the assault upon *Yiddishkeit* was Maria Yakovleva Frumkina, more familiarly known as Esther, a leader in the *Yevsektzia* and in the program of political indoctrination. An influential speaker and writer, she was the granddaughter of a rabbi, and had been married to a rabbi. She wrote a work in Russian entitled *Down with the Rabbis: An Outline of the Anti-Religious Struggle among the Jewish Masses.* Esther assured her Russian readers that the *kampf* against the Jewish religion within the Jewish community was being waged "more energetically and stubbornly, above all, more systematically, than in the non-Jewish environment." That this was no mere boast was clear from the perennial persecution of the pious Jews by the "*Yevseks*" during the 1920's: the repeated arrests of rabbis, *mohalim*, and *shochatim* on the spurious charges of espionage and Trotskyism; the show trials of traditional holidays, rituals and schools; the anti-*Shabbat* campaign; the restrictions or prohibitions of the baking of *matzot*; and innumerable other measures.

Esther explained the vicious attack upon adherents of *Yiddishkeit* to an American Jewish visitor, Boris D. Bogen: Better for the "*Yevseks*" to fight *Yiddishkeit* than to entrust the process to the tender mercies of the Russians: "The danger is that the masses may think that Judaism is exempt from anti-religious propaganda and, therefore, it rests with the Jewish Communists to be even more ruthless with rabbis than non-Jewish Communists are with priests." As an example of "*Yevsek*" mercy, Esther mentioned approvingly the use of armed violence by Jewish Communists in the ejection of Jews from a synagogue in Vitebsk, the scene of one of the notorious trials of the *cheder*.

The Communist careers of Dimanshtein, Agurskii, Litvakov, Frumkina, and others of their stripe fulfilled the prophecy of Isaiah: "Your destroyers and they that made you waste shall go forth from you." It was an irony of history, but not of the Soviet experience, that the reward of these renegades was not a plaque on the walls of the Kremlin, but liquidation during the Stalin purges of 1936-1938. Tragically, the evil that these individuals achieved during their tenure as terrorizers of the Jewish community continued in various forms after their execution. The removal from the Hebrew alphabet of the final forms of five letters and other changes gave Soviet Yiddish a bizarre appearance. The exclusion of Hebraic-religious terms from the Yiddish vocabulary was part of the process of De-Hebraization, or of excising the "clerical reactionary" element from the language. The fanatics were disappointed in their efforts in 1930 to bring about the Latinization of the Hebrew-Yiddish alphabet. The elimination of the traditional vocabulary and orthography from the Yiddish language is a fact of life today in the Soviet Union.

The year 1921 marked the inauguration of the anti-Jewish trials by Jews. The *cheder* of Vitebsk was pronounced illegal and ordered closed following a "judicial" proceeding. In the same year, the Lubavitcher *yeshivah* in Rostov suffered a similar fate. These decisions not only failed to liquidate religious education, but on the contrary, they influenced the growth of underground instruction in various towns. Even the arrest of the Lubavitcher Rebbe in 1927 and his liberation and departure from the U.S.S.R. the following year, did not result in the diminution of the drive to spread *Yiddishkeit* by education.

A wide array of Yiddish anti-religious literature appeared. One notorious example is Altshuler's *Hagode*. This work derisively begins with a page on "*Bedikas Chometz*," equating the search for leaven with the expunging the enemies of the revolution or turning them over to the G.P.U.; the *seder* order is now satirically the revolutionary order; the *Kadesh*—the blessing over the first cup of wine—is replaced by "*Kaddish*," the prayer for the deceased, to be recited for the entire capitalistic order; and in the place of *Hallel*—thanksgiving to G-d for liberation from Egypt—the author jeeringly introduces the communist hymn of the "Internationale."

The intensity of the attacks against religious observance indicated the sustained dedication by many Jews to their historical heritage of Jewish faith.

In the midst of the relentless war on Judaism carried on by the non-Jewish and Jewish Communists, it was still possible for resistance to flourish. The underground *cheder* and *yeshivah* were responses to the forcible closing of educational institutions. Imprisonment, as in the cases of the Lubavitcher Rebbe and many of his *chassidim*, did not at all diminish the determination to overcome the obstacles to the teaching and practice of *Yiddishkeit*. The Lubavitcher Rebbe, of blessed memory, and his influence were fully recognized by the G.P.U. and the *Yevsektzia*. As narrated in *Sefer Ha-Toldot*, Moishe Litvakov remarked in 1927 that "the G.P.U. is aware of Rabbi Schneersohn's crime, and we have decided to uproot him. We already have a collection of the necessary evidence to accomplish this." The repeated surveillance by the "*Yevseks*" finally provoked the Rebbe during his Purim address in 1927 to attack the informers present by frequently mentioning the *Yevsektzia* and adding immediately, "*Yemach shemam!*" ("May their names be blotted out!")

When the Soviet regime made *Shabbat* observance virtually impossible, religious Jews managed to get jobs as night watchmen so that they were not required to perform physical labor. In 1960, the present writer met in the synagogue an Ashkenazic Jew who did not desecrate a single *Shabbat* during the 43 years of Soviet power. This he was able to accomplish by exchanging days off with non-Jewish fellow workers.

In one area, publishing, it was extremely complicated to counter the Communist campaign. The last religious book to be published in the U.S.S.R. was a commentary on Maimonides in 1926. The last *luach* (calendar) and Passover *Haggadah* were issued in 1928. Thereafter, calendars appeared in manuscript form only for over three decades. In like manner, scholarly works were prepared and circulated in manuscript form. Although neither a Hebrew Pentateuch nor a Talmud was published in the Soviet Union, Jews continued to study the tomes published in Czarist times.

As for the Jews who fought fanatically against pious Jewry, history provided its own irony and they were excruciatingly impaled on the spearhead of their own communistic ideology. The leadership was hounded, burned and buried by Stalin and his stalwarts on the basis of transparently false accusations of political heresy, deviation and treason. Many of those who survived suffered traumatic disillusionment. Perhaps the most eloquent expression of this disappointment was articulated by the well-known Yiddish writer, *Der Nister* (Pinchos Kahanovich): "We have been left with nothing …we have no G-d and we have no Torah. All we have left are the letters of the Yiddish alphabet." And even these were almost taken away by Jewish–Communist zealots.

In conclusion, the Soviet Communist war on *Yiddishkeit* took a terrible toll in Jewish souls. Nevertheless, and in the face of fanatical ferocity on the part of atheistic Jews, Judaism managed not merely to survive, but also to flourish, not only in large cities, but in small communities as well. *Yiddishkeit* did not yield to the *Yevsektzia* and the *Yevkom*. Perseverance by the pious, in the society dedicated to their destruction, resulted in the preservation and perpetuation of the Jewish religion in Soviet Russia.

The above essay, condensed from Dr. Brickman's original and lengthy historical overview, was first published in the *Ufaratzta Journal*, Spring 5740 (1980): pp. 7–11.

Prologue

In the era subsequent to the Russian Revolution, great fear fell upon the Jewish religious community. Cruelly persecuted by the government and particularly by the *Yevsektzia*—the Jewish Communist group—many Rabbis and educators withdrew from communal involvement motivated by fear of economic privation, imprisonment, and even death.

Only a small minority were willing to assume the perilous role of leadership in this spiritual vacuum. At the vanguard of such efforts stood the sixth Lubavitcher Rebbe, Rabbi Yosef Yitzchak Schneersohn, of blessed memory.

Events had been progressing towards an ultimate confrontation between the Rebbe and the *Yevsektzia* for a number of years.

In *Tammuz* 5680 (1920) the *Yevsektzia* had already begun to stalk the Rebbe. On one occasion three agents of the secret police entered the Rebbe's synagogue with pistols drawn to arrest him. When he stood before the interrogation committee, the Rebbe stated: "I have already declared that I will not abandon my principles. No man or demon has been born, nor will be born that will make me budge even slightly."

In 5682 (1922) an organization called the "*Va'ad*" was created, with the Rebbe at its head. Some of the activities of the *Va'ad* were as follows:

1) The organization of a jurist legal advisory board. Through their legal efforts many attempts at hindering religious practices were thwarted. In many towns the synagogues had been turned into workmen's meeting places; thanks to the intervention of the *Va'ad* through its committee of jurors, many synagogues were restored to their former use.

2) In the city of Gomel the Jewish cemetery was expropriated and stables erected on the grounds. One report stated that "two hundred coffins had already been removed." The grave diggers had arrived at the grave of the famed Chabad *chassid* Reb Izak Epstein, better known as "Reb Izak Homler," and the jurist committee intervened, with the result that Trotsky himself sent a telegram prohibiting such activities.

3) The *Va'ad*, in its struggle against the legal prohibition of religious education, mounted an intensive petition campaign throughout the land pleading for permission to provide religious education. Despite the intensity of religious suppression at that time when many religious parents were very much afraid to let their names be known, this effort resulted in the supposed concession of permitting religious education with the significant restriction that "No teacher could have more than three students."

4) The *Va'ad* funded the education of 5,000 children, but "some 16,000 children had to be refused admission for lack of funds."

5) The *Va'ad* established a small number of *yeshivot* which would provide room, board, and clothing for the students.

6) The *Va'ad* set up an advanced house of study to train Rabbis and *shochatim* (ritual slaughterers).

7) A program of night classes known as "*Tiferet Bachurim*" was also maintained thanks to the *Va'ad*. These classes instructed workers and professionals in all matters of Judaism.

The *Va'ad* continued its underground activities after the Rebbe's departure from Russia until 5694 (1934), when three of its members left Russia and settled in Israel and England. The willingness of the members to carry on during this final phase had been conditional upon the Rebbe's acceptance of responsibility for directing the *Va'ad* from outside of Russia. In *Iyar* of 5681 (1921) a libelous campaign produced a decree to close the Rebbe's *yeshivah*. To penalize the

Rebbe, all his property was confiscated, including inherited property.

At the beginning of 5683 (1923) government enactments against Torah and Judaism intensified and children's Torah education was outlawed. With a viciousness that surpassed the strictness of the government decrees, the *Yevsektzia* hunted down, suppressed, and plotted against every attempt to strengthen Judaism.

The Rebbe traveled to Moscow and called a council of many Rabbinical and communal leaders to evaluate the situation. The Rebbe advised them of a practical course of action, and an organization was created that would remain to perform its work in Moscow. After consultations with prominent lawyers in Moscow, and a great effort of emissaries to the government, the Rebbe was able to obtain ambiguous permission to teach Torah to five or six children in one house, and a clearer statement of permission, to teach classes of three children, as mentioned above. The Moscow organization decided to publicize this latter permission in all places. Similarly, they strove to restore *mikva'ot*, synagogues, and supervision over all religious needs, by sending representatives who traveled from place to place.

At a meeting in Moscow in the month of *Adar* 5684 (1924) the Rebbe was elected leader of the organization formed previously, and also while in Moscow he made a binding "covenant" with nine dedicated *temimim* (students or ex-students of his *yeshivah* (Tomchei Temimim Lubavitch) to work to strengthen Judaism with self-sacrifice, "even to the last drop of blood."

On the journey back to Rostov, the Rebbe was met by his secretary, Rabbi Elchanan Dovber Morosow, who told him that agents of the local G.P.U. were waiting to imprison him and send him into exile for his work to strengthen religion. The Rebbe turned around on the road, and stayed in a small village near Moscow until the fury subsided. On the 11th of *Nissan* the Rebbe returned to Rostov, and on that very day he was visited by soldiers, who put a search on his house and proposed that he accompany them voluntarily to prison. A determined effort succeeded in preventing his imprisonment, and after much negotiation, it was agreed that he would be allowed to leave Rostov of his own accord and travel to Leningrad.

In *Sivan* of 5684 (1924) he settled in Leningrad and toiled there in the strengthening of Torah and Judaism: Rabbis, children's education, *yeshivot*, ritual slaughter, advanced classes in Talmud, and *mikva'ot*. He also formed a special council to help manual laborers to observe *Shabbat*.

In 5685 (1925) the terror weakened somewhat, and accordingly the general work for Judaism proceeded more systematically, so that the Rebbe was able to devote himself more to organizing the teaching of *Chassidus*. He was able to begin establishing *yeshivot* to teach *Chassidus* in many places, and he also recited *Chassidus* briefly on every *Shabbat*. These conditions continued during the year 5686 (1926) until, on *Rosh Hashanah* 5687 (1927), the number of visitors was more than the rooms of the Rebbe's home could hold.

In the meantime the *Yevsektzia* had begun to reintensify its efforts; in one account the notorious *Yevsektzia* official Litvakov complained to an acquaintance of two incidents resulting directly from the efforts of the Rebbe.

In one instance, a young man traveled about Russian Georgia in many areas where the synagogues, religious schools, and *mikva'ot* had been completely shut down, and delivered inspiring addresses to the communities about loyalty to the Jewish faith, including citations of various passages of Russian law permitting religious observances. His words had a profound effect and brought about a resurgence of religious observances in many cities and villages. Once, the local officials mistook him for an emissary from the government and actually spent communal funds to restore the *mikveh*. There were also cases in remote areas where the vested *Yevsektzia* council was deposed and driven from the villages by young men claiming they had the legal right to practice their Jewish faith.

Litvakov concluded: "After extensive investigation we have discovered that the Lubavitcher Rebbe was the primary cause of all these activities and that his agents were involved in all of them." Despite the protestation of his acquaintance that these activities were legal, Litvakov stated: "We are fully knowledgeable of his actions," and concluded angrily: "We will tear him from his roots and have already commenced gathering the necessary evidence."[1]

Though informed of the above conversation, the Rebbe continued his efforts, even publicly condemning his harsh adversaries.[2]

The period in which the Rebbe's arrest took place was particularly dangerous for those likely to be targeted as enemies of the state.

The headlines of the *New York Times* of Saturday, June 11th read "Executions Spread Terror in Russia, Europe is Shocked …Police Activity Continues."

The Soviet minister to Warsaw, Pierre Volkoff had been assassinated. There was a "bombing at a communist party meeting at Leningrad, and the wrecking of a trolley car en route to Minsk, which resulted in the death of a Russian official, who was transporting an alleged Polish spy."

Subsequently, in retaliation, the Communist government began executing members of the previous regime's nobility, military, and ministers and other political prisoners.

A G.P.U. press communique of June 10 stated "In view of the open transition to terrorism and destructive struggle by monarchist and White Guardist elements, acting from abroad on instructions and with funds from foreign intelligence services ...the Collegium of the State Political Department passed death sentences at its session of June 9 on twenty persons, and the sentences have been carried out." [3]

On June 14th, the day of the Rebbe's arrest, the headlines of the *Times* read "Moscow in Panic Under Mailed Fist; Foreigners Leaving." According to a Riga press dispatch cited in the article, "twenty-eight more ex-Czarist officers have been arrested and shot in Moscow...while in Odessa the [G.P.U.] announces that eleven former merchants and officers have been executed on a charge of spying for Rumania. The reprisal shootings now number more than one hundred."

According to a continuation of the headline, the "Soviet Army Commissar, blaming Britain for the assassinations, says War is Inevitable," and subsequently the training of 300,000 army reservists in the Ukraine was lengthened, a move "considered in Warsaw...as masked mobilization" according to the *Times* correspondent. The article continues that "extensive war training of children, including girls in Soviet schools" was also taking place: "All girls in secondary schools and colleges [were to] devote at least two hours daily to rifle practice, 'gas drill' and hand-grenade attacks."

The world, shocked by the terror and horrified by the communist paranoia, prepared for war. In fact Berlin had already announced that they would side with "foes of the Reds."[4]

The sentencing in Warsaw of the assassin, Boris Korenko, 19, from Vilna, on June 15 to only 15 years in jail caused further concern by the international community of a Communist backlash due to the lightness of the sentence.[5]

Korenko said at his trial only that he was carrying out "the order of a White Russian secret organization."

The stage had been set for the arrest of the Soviet Union's most outspoken Jewish leader: The Lubavitcher Rebbe.

Notes

1. From a "Letter from one of the Rabbis," *Sefer HaMa'amarim* 5711, p. 197.
2. See also *Sichat Purim*, in *Sefer Hasichot* 5687, pp. 159 ff.
3. "Executions Spread," *New York Times*, June 11, 1927, p. 1.
4. "Executions Spread," *New York Times*, June 14, 1927, p. 1.
5. "Volkoff's Slayer Gets 15-Year Sentence," *New York Times*, June 16, 1927, p. 95.

CHAPTER ONE

The Arrest

The date[1] was Tuesday night, the 14th of *Sivan*, 5687 (June 14, 1927). It was already twelve o'clock at night, shortly after I had concluded receiving people for private audiences. It was my custom to receive people for these audiences three times a week—Sunday, Tuesday and Thursday. The meetings were scheduled for the hours of seven until ten at night, but usually extended for an hour or two more, particularly during the summer months, due to the many visitors. This particular night these sessions extended until half past eleven.

The prayers were scheduled for three fixed times during the course of the day. After the morning prayers we would recite a segment of the Psalms as divided according to the days of the month. I had established this recitation on the basis of a personal unrevealed reason and had requested all members of the Chabad movement throughout the world to adopt this practice in their respective synagogues. Thus, by following this recitation every day, they would finish the book of Psalms once monthly. After the daily recitation they were to recite Mourner's *Kaddish*. Praise G-d that this practice was widely adopted, and fortunate is their lot both materially and spiritually. For those following this practice my request persists to the present day; in the morning there should be a regular study session in *Mishnayot*, between *Minchah* (the afternoon prayer) and *Ma'ariv* (the evening prayer) a study session of *Aggadah*, and at night, a class in Talmud.[2] On this occasion many people had come. I began the audiences with the *chassidim* at the regular time and concluded at 11:30.

I then prayed the evening prayer with a quorum group that assembled in my home thrice daily for public prayer. I was weary and exhausted from my tasks and also deeply distressed because of my recent communication with Rabbi Dovid Tevel Katzenelenbogen [the Chief Rabbi of Leningrad], in which I opposed the "General Assembly" planned by Leningrad's communal leaders.

Various anti-religious Jews, scheming to undermine traditional Judaism, had scheduled this meeting and deceived the Chief Rabbi of Leningrad into siding with them by creating false issues of personal conflict.[3]

Thus weary, I washed my hands in the traditional manner for the evening meal with the members of my household, a few moments after twelve o'clock. About twenty minutes had passed when the doorbell rang forcefully. The door was opened, and two men burst into the dining room shouting: "We are representatives of the G.P.U.[4] Who is Schneersohn? And where is he?" As they spoke, a contingent of armed men entered after them and stood in a line awaiting their commands.

I answered calmly and clearly: "I do not know which Schneersohn you seek. If you enter into someone's home, surely you know in advance who dwells there, and this drama is pointless. Deliver your message and clearly state your wishes. The building superintendent, who knows the identity of all the people in this house, is here with you. What need is there for this clamor and disruption?"

"I am not shouting," said the spokesman, "This is my normal manner of speech. It seems that you are not familiar with the methods of G.P.U. representatives. Show us through your apartment so that we can place an appropriate legal guard, and as master of the household, come with us to observe the search."

"True," I replied, "I am not fully aware of your methods, and I have no desire to know them.

"Either you are completely in error, or someone has fabricated a libel against us. In any event, it makes no difference to me. As for the emissaries from your organization, I have not feared, I do not fear, and I will not fear them. The building attendant can direct you about my quarters, and you may search as you wish in ostensible accordance with the law that you invoke." I then calmly added, "I am certain that you will not disturb me from my evening meal."

My words, spoken evenly and without any betrayal of emotion, had a strong effect on the callous officials, and for a brief instant their wings drooped. They gazed at me with surprise, as silence prevailed in the house.

Among the intruders was a young Jewish G.P.U. official by the name of Nachmanson. He had received a Jewish education in his childhood in his hometown village of Nevel, and his father had actually journeyed to Lubavitch as a *chassid*. His commanding voice broke the silence as he instructed the armed men to take guard positions at the various doors of the house. Anyone desiring to enter the house was to be admitted, but they were to prohibit any movement from room to room or any oral communication. He stressed that his instructions were to be followed strictly.[5]

He then turned to his companion, a short dark-haired Jewish man named Lulav, from the family of that name in Riga, and stated that they should begin their work. He concluded by addressing me and saying that, if I could eat, I was at liberty to do so. They would not disturb me, but he had instructed a guard to remain in the room with us.

They first went to search the room of my daughters Chaya Moussia and Shaina and asked them: "Which party do you belong to?"

They answered that they were "members of our father's party, apolitical Jewish women who hold dear Jewish traditions and despise the new trends."

"Why?" inquired Nachmanson, astonished.

"Why?" replied Shaina, "this we are not obligated to answer you. You asked regarding our beliefs and I replied. As to the question 'why,' this we are not obligated to explain, for you are not here investigating my letters and documents for discussion's sake. What we were, we still are; and we declare this openly, regardless of whether you find it acceptable or offensive."

Nachmanson answered: "You must consider the authority and power of the G.P.U., which we represent. The G.P.U. can force even the silent tongue to speak and tell what is hidden within the heart. Our interrogators are remarkable craftsmen. To them all is revealed, willingly or otherwise. There can be nothing hidden. There, everything melts; even stone speaks and divulges its secrets."

"The entire tragedy," answered my daughter, "is that you wish to accomplish everything by power and coercion. This is unethical and repugnant, attempting to intimidate intelligent and informed people with the power of the fist and the threats of the gun."

I will not deny that it was gratifying for me to hear these words spoken with logic and composure—albeit feigned—and in a firm voice. Nevertheless, I was very much concerned for her fate, lest Nachmanson, who prided himself on his power, would think of arresting her also.

The men remained in the house for another hour and a half, proceeding from room to room and searching thoroughly, but it was clear that this was not their actual intent. They then prepared an official form and handed it to me for my signature. I scrutinized the document, which stated that the search had conformed with all the pertinent regulations and that I had been informed of my prisoner status.

Upon reading the document, I replied that I was unable to sign a form in which it is stated that everything was executed legally. "To me the entire visit and search is suspect," I said, "Everyone knows who Rabbi Schneersohn is and what his activities are." Surely, one of two possibilities must have occurred: error or libel—on account of either I could not sign.

"As to arresting me," I continued, "it appears that the pleas of my family are of no avail; however, I would also like to respond on my own behalf as to why you want to imprison me.

"It is clear to me that the entire matter is either an error or a fabrication, either of which will be clarified within a day or two. Everyone is thoroughly aware of my identity and actions: I have not used secrecy. I live in one of the largest cities in this country, and my home is in its center. I have a synagogue and deliver *chassidic* discourses there on the Sabbath and Jewish holidays. This means that I have not acted covertly.

"I believe that the arrest will result in highly negative publicity, and you should proceed with caution until the truth is clarified—if you are actually seeking the truth. However, if you mean to conceal this error or libel with lies and falsehood, I am certain that you will regret it. Do as you will, but Schneersohn will not be arrested with a web of deceit."

Nachmanson roughly interrupted me: "The G.P.U. is responsible for its actions and is wholly unafraid of criticism. If the order has been given to arrest you, then I am confident that there is full authority to follow it. I am amazed at your words. Be fully aware that you are now a prisoner."

"I do not understand," I replied, "why you interrupted me and didn't allow me to finish my request."

Infuriated, Nachmanson exclaimed, "What! You wish to request something? That right is yours, just as it would not be denied any other prisoner. But why this insolence? Do you not understand your situation? We have not come here for conversation, nor to hear the requests of your family." He turned to my daughters and declared: "Leave this room. If you speak one more word, then you, too, will be arrested." He raised his revolver and said: "I will speak with this and silence your elegant words, your *krasivorechivosti*."

"We," answered my daughter, Chana, "speak in the language used by people who retain their humanity under all circumstances, not in the tongue of those who have just emerged from the slime, unable to speak forthrightly and capable only of waving a revolver and threatening imprisonment.

"Permit our father to stay with us—do not take the apple of our eye! I and my sisters will gladly go in our father's stead. Our father is weak; the doctor has instructed that he should not go out. Bring a doctor—let him be examined—let him remain under guard until the physician will determine that he can go out. After all, you too are a human being—you must also have feelings and emotions. You must surely have what the world calls ethics and decency." She burst into tears.

"*Ach!*" I exclaimed, "Only wishful thinking could imagine that pleas and tears could help."

"My daughter," I turned to my daughter Chana and to my wife and two other daughters, who stood white as snow, their eyes streaming with tears, and stated: "A barbarian and pleas for decency are two contradictory things."

"Why," I continued, directing my words toward Nachmanson, "do you not permit me to conclude? We can discuss all your methods of terror, and your lecture on ethics and how to speak, in prison. But here in my own home you must listen to my words. I am still within the walls of my own home, and I desire to speak in the presence of my family, in the presence of trustworthy witnesses whose testimony you cannot contradict."

Nachmanson replied: "Your words are infused with venom. You do not approve of the laws of the present regime—*nu,* we will yet discuss this. Now speak as you wish 'in the presence of irrefutable witnesses,'" and with a smile he winked to his accomplice Lulav and the other armed G.P.U. men in the room.

"I demand permission to put on *tefillin* and pray, and also that kosher food be made available to me from my own home," I stated.

"You may take your *tefillin*, religious books, paper and pen, and I give you my sincere assurance that no one will disturb you from your prayers, from reading and from writing. This very day you will return home. You will just be asked a few questions by the director of the prison and then be permitted to return home," Nachmanson replied.

The lengthy exchange had ended, and as they awaited the vehicle to take me to the notorious Spalerno prison, my mother the *Rebbetzin* [Shterna Sarah], who had been in her own room and oblivious to all that had occurred, abruptly entered. Nachmanson, the leader of the search party, had himself given the order that she should not be awakened. She had awakened nevertheless; I don't know why.

Upon seeing the uninvited visitors, she cried out in a frightened voice: "What is this? Why have they come? Shall they extend their hands against innocent people, against my son who strives to help others? No!" she called out powerfully, "I will not let them take my darling. I will go in your place. Take me," she entreated of the leader, "take me. Do not disturb my son, my only son, who responds to others in their hour of distress. Will you even subject a person of such integrity to so severe an ordeal? Woe! Imprisonment! Woe unto us, my dear departed husband...! They are taking our son Yosef Yitzchak—your only son who sacrifices himself for others—your one and only son—he who heeds your instruction with actual self-sacrifice—bandits have come— slayers of innocent people. And for what purpose? Holy ancestors, they desire to extinguish your soul-flame. Come what may, I shall not permit them to take you."

Nachmanson turned to me and said: "Please quiet her. Take her to her room, and put her mind to rest. I am not responsible for her emotional outburst. We were quiet and did not desire to cause her any unrest. Please calm her."

At that moment, it glimmered within my mind that there is a spark of good even in the depth of evil. These words did not seem to emerge from a cruel, blood-stained person. Was it possible that this stone-like man also possessed a heart and was capable of morality? Did he too have a conscience awakening within him a feeling of mercy? Or perhaps he realized that the woman standing and weeping before him was none other than the famed *Rebbetzin* of Lubavitch. Perhaps he had for that moment repented and regretted that it had been his fate to be a G.P.U. agent.

I went with my mother to her room and there discussed some matters which I could not speak of in the presence of my "guests," though they did not disturb me at all. For they had gone outside for a walk, leaving in my home a group of armed guards, awaiting the arrival of the vehicle.

I found it difficult to determine the cause of this event or those responsible for it. I could speculate, but it seemed most likely that they were taking me hostage. I could not pinpoint the specific reason, but this was my impression.

I shared my speculation with the members of my household. "But for what?" asked my son-in-law Rabbi Shmaryahu Gourary.

I responded, "I do not know for what, but this is clearly the case."

My mother exclaimed, "An informant with false accusations," and my wife and daughter repeated the words, "A false accusation."

"No," I answered, "I do not believe that they will accuse me falsely, and I have done nothing that they could use as the basis for such an accusation. I am certain that are taking me as a hostage."

"What should we do?" my son-in-law inquired.

"What should be done?" I responded, "First let emissaries be sent to the graves of my father and my ancestors, in Rostov,[6] Lubavitch,[7] Nyezin,[8] and Haditz,[9] to inform them of my plight. Also, ask all of the *chassidim* to recite Psalms during the first days."

My family repeated my words "the first days" in astonishment, asking me what I anticipated. I answered that this we would eventually see with G-d's help. I told them not to raise a clamor, as word would be known very quickly all over.

I instructed that the *chassidim* here and abroad should not be hindered from whatever avenue of effort they would pursue. The members of my family, however, were to seek out confidential contacts to intercede for me—but first and foremost, I stressed that the entire network of educational activities should be maintained. Henceforth, the task of fundraising would certainly be formidable because all of those involved in these activities, willingly or compelled by circumstances, would be deeply shocked and frightened by my arrest.

"Therefore, you should know my firm instructions, that despite my present debt, you should try to obtain more money through loans and to immediately forward the required aid to every educational group. And you all must assume the responsibility for properly administering this effort till G-d shall return me to all of you."

According to what I had heard from one of my daughters, I was certain that my secretary, Mr. Chaim Lieberman, was already aware of the happenings in my apartment.[10] I was certain that he had already destroyed all documents that might have incriminated him as my secretary. It would also be good if he would move out of his apartment until things quieted down. Why should he suffer as well? Moreover, he was the sole individual with the knowledge to continue the work, for he was totally knowledgeable as to what was to be done. I was certain that they would find nothing incriminating in his possession. For this I was grateful to G-d.

Their faces white as plaster and their eyes filled with tears, my mother, wife, daughters and son-in-law stood shocked. At that moment, no words were to be found. They gazed at me with wonderment, hope and longing, mercy and supplication, not uttering a word.

Amazing, I thought: in just a few precious moments I would be taken to the Spalerno prison! "Spalerno" is known to all. Everyone knows that it is dreadful, and its very name evokes fear and terror in everyone, no matter what religion, nationality or party. This prison on Spalerno street, or as it is referred to, "Spalerka," is well-known even to children, and it is common knowledge that being taken there is no laughing matter, and that one's stay there is never for merely a day or two. When one is sentenced to be taken to Spalerno, it is for one of two reasons: either judgment has already been rendered, or for questioning—and particularly for investigation.

The reader may wonder, what is the difference between "questioning" and "investigating"? It is difficult for me, however, to dwell on this. Briefly, questioning is oral: questions, answers. Investigation is quite another matter. It is the coercion to speak. As Nachmanson stated: "There, one talks; there, the mouth opens—you speak and speak!" Mere questioning is done in any facility, but Spalerno is different. So I awaited the military vehicle that would take me, in a few precious moments, to this Spalerno.

At such a critical moment, there is much to say, much to request, much to mandate and settle. Yet the mouth does not speak and the mind does not control the heart. The emotions overflow, restricting the capacities of thought and speech. Thank G-d, I didn't lose control. I spoke out, briefly, yet laden with instructions on the successful continuation of our work. I said to my family:

"Surely they have spun an intricate web of accusations in which to ensnare me. They will try to force me to confess to actions of which I am wholly innocent and which are wholly irrelevant to my efforts for the strengthening of Torah and Judaism.

"But I will only tell them: 'I am involved in the promulgation of Torah and its *mitzvot.*' I will assume the entire responsibility and incriminate no one else; and G-d forbid, if any one else will be arrested and informed that it was done by my word, then I forewarn you now that it is an absolute falsehood. No power in the world will make me yield.

"It is also clear to me that this arrest has been elaborately planned, for they would never have taken so major a step without adequate preparation. Nachmanson's face reveals his intent. They most certainly anticipate causing great harm to the whole Jewish people by imprisoning me. But I have profound faith that the G-d of our sacred ancestors will liberate me from their hands, and I will return and continue my work. Please obey my words carefully and do not despair, and G-d will aid us."

I then warned them to take all of the correspondence in the house and to distribute the documents in various secure places.

I had barely concluded when Lulav entered, stating that the vehicle was waiting for me and that it was necessary to hurry.

I responded: "The conditions in this country at present make it a matter of certainty that no one will be late. Even those who today concern themselves with the imprisonment of others may be certain that their turn, too, will come. There is no reason to hurry, nothing will be lost."

I put on my overcoat and received a departing blessing from my mother and my daughters Chana, Chaya Moussia, and Shaina. I also went to give my departing blessing to my grandson, who was sleeping in his crib. . .

I then blessed my domestic helpers, who upon hearing and seeing that I was to be taken to the awesome Spalerka, bowed their heads, gazing downward, unable to look at my face—for they were frightened and distressed at the entire spectacle. In the beginning they had no knowledge of what was taking place, because the guards separated us and they were confined to the kitchen. They were emotionally powerless to express any response to my departing blessing.

I kissed the *mezuzah* on the door and sat on one of the benches. The official Lulav and his subordinates, armed soldiers, surrounded me in the manner of prison guards and in accordance with prison regulations.

My belongings, *tefillin*—*Rashi, Rabbeinu Tam, Shimusha Rabbah*; a *talit*, a *gartel* (prayer sash); my religious books—*Siddur* (prayer book), Psalms, *Tanya*, and my other personal effects: change of clothing, a handkerchief, food, valerian, a small pillow, were all placed in one package—in a travel bag.

The cover of the bag was inscribed in Roman letters "S.S.";[11] my father, of righteous memory, had purchased it and used it during the course of his journeys from the year 5673 (1913)—a plaid blanket was also given to me.

I did not want to carry my belongings myself, so I gave them to one of the armed guards. Lulav leapt forward and took the bag from the soldier and said in Yiddish: "Give the bag to me, I will carry it. *Chassidim* remain *chassidim*; my grandfather carried the bags of your grandfather and I, too, will carry your belongings."

I removed the bag from Lulav's hand and replied: "Your grandfather was a *chassid* of my grandfather, so he was privileged to carry those bags to the place of my grandfather's choice, whereas you desire to carry my bag, G-d forbid, to a destination of *your* choosing. No, this cannot be. In your way I will not go. *Chassidim* certainly do remain *chassidim*."

I reclaimed my possessions and restored them to the guard who held them originally. I kissed the *mezuzah* and departed with armed guards in front of me, to my right, to my left, and behind me.

As we descended the stairs, I could hear the voices of my family pleading to accompany me to the vehicle. I turned about and saw an armed guard physically barring their way. I called out to Lulav inquiring as to why they were obstructed and if he had authority for such action.

My confident tone and clear words had the desired effect on Lulav. He commanded the guard to move away, and he permitted my family to accompany me as a group. I was thus able to speak a few words with my son-in-law.

In the courtyard all was quiet, no one was there, aside from the members of my family, the contingent of guards and their officers, Nachmanson and Lulav.

Nachmanson stated with a smile: "You can kiss and take leave of each other here in accordance with all of the etiquette of the aristocracy because I will not let you go out into the street."

I turned to Nachmanson and said: "It is not befitting for a highly placed official—so concerned with propriety, who asks for a signed document corroborating that his visit and search accords with the law—to prevent members of a family from accompanying one dear to them."

"Go!" Nachmanson answered, enraged, "it appears that you are still unable to adapt to the present situation. You are a prisoner and obligated to obey the command of an authorized official."

"Who is the official," I inquired, "and what is the command? You can clearly see that despite all of your efforts, you will not frighten me." I continued: "Please grant my family's request!"

Nachmanson turned aside, and all the members of my family and I went out to the street. The vehicle stood surrounded by armed soldiers. Within sat a prisoner, obviously a foreigner of prestige, approximately forty years old. He was dressed in traveler's clothes, his face snow white; his eyes conveyed deep bewilderment, his face an expression of deep anxiety and fear. Facing him, on guard, sat an armed soldier.

As I emerged onto the street, my glance fell upon the large clock hanging in the window of the clock store across from my house. The face of the clock was as white as the faces of my household members, may they live, and the hands—indicating that it was twenty minutes after two—as black as ravens.

During this period of two hours and ten minutes, how much pain, suffering, fear, and anxiety had the members of my household endured! And for what reason? Because of false libels, because of malicious informants—because of my effort to strengthen Judaism, because of strengthening the Torah.

We stood together for a few moments, and then, with the help of one of the soldiers, I climbed onto the vehicle and sat in the place indicated for me. Facing me, as a guard, Lulav sat holding only a revolver, for Nachmanson sat with the driver, most certainly in conformity with prison regulations.

"Be well and strong," I called out to my family, "and may G-d help us to be reunited soon in good health."

At that moment the vehicle moved and commenced its journey to the notorious Spalerno prison.[12]

I looked out and saw on the corner our good friend Rabbi Eliyahu Chaim Althaus, his face contorted with fear. I nodded silently to him as an indication of blessing and leave-taking, but I perceived that he stood uncomprehending. He appeared as though he would, in a moment, burst into intense weeping or anxiety. A moment passed, we turned left to Litaina Street and Pinchas, Rabbi Althaus's son, suddenly appeared. I was jolted by the sight of his white face, his black bulging eyes, and his figure, buckling over. He peered intently, trying to see who was in the vehicle, but he did not seem able to perceive clearly.

We then quickly turned to the street on the right, Spalerno Street. At number 24 stood the massive edifice, the notorious prison: Spalerka.

The prison doors were sealed. Nachmanson and Lulav instructed the guards to maintain strict security with the "distinguished guests" in the vehicle, myself and the other prisoner. They themselves hastened to the gate keeper, but to their astonishment they did not receive entry clearance. The outer guard did not reply to these newly arrived officials; the guard within opened the small inquiry-gate. I could not hear his question, but I did see that Lulav and Nachmanson were talking to each other in distress.

Lulav approached our guard while Nachmanson exerted every effort to gain access to the prison, but the guard closed the opening. Nachmanson, humiliated and agitated, stood, one hand on the door bolt and the other wiping away the sweat on his inflamed face with a handkerchief.

There are many kinds of human sweat: the cleansing sweat which removes human sin, the sweat caused by the performance of a *mitzvah*, the sweat of intense effort in the study of Torah, the sweat generated by work sincere and honest, the sweat of intense physical toil. In stark contrast to these is the sweat of anger and murder, the sweat of the hangman, the sweat of the bandit and the murderer.

Lulav called out to his comrade Nachmanson: "We are late. May gloom take A! He tells *us* thus, while he idly sleeps. Official B should be informed of this. He will take the situation into his hands: then A will either no longer sleep or he will slumber eternally."

Suddenly the sound of the opening door bolt was heard, but Lulav told us to wait and not go forward without orders.

The prisoner next to me was disintegrating mentally. The soldier assigned to him stared at him fixedly, a bayonet in his left hand and a rifle in his right. His eyes were riveted on the prisoner and not distracted even momentarily. The prisoner's face was snow white with fear and his body was quivering. His clothing was European tailored; he seemed to be a person of means and was even wearing silk gloves. He looked, however, terrified, as though he would succumb to sudden death.

Notes

1. Starting here the main narrative is taken from *Reshimat Hama'aser (Sefer Hasichot* 5687, p. 177*)*. The Rebbe is narrating in the first person.

2. A note regarding this request is quoted in Appendix 7. It was found on the Rebbe's table after his arrest.

3. The *Yevsektzia* supported the proposed meeting, and the Rebbe's opposition was one of the immediate causes of his arrest. See Appendix 7.

4. *Gosudarstvennoye Politchezkoye Upravleniye* ("State Political Administration"), a precursor organization of the K.G.B.

5. The Rebbe once related that since his home was the subject of frequent searches, and he was aware that the *Yevsektzia* had every intention of harassing him until his activities ceased, he was somewhat prepared for this search. He had prepared in his office various manuscripts and letters that had no value. As they were searching, he placed these papers on top of the incriminating documents. Due to these preparations, the *Yevsektzia* missed a large amount of evidence that would have been helpful to their case against the Rebbe (*Sichat 12 Tammuz, Sichot Kodesh,* 5718, p. 29).
   Elsewhere, the Rebbe writes details of the search:
   > The search was only a cover, and was relatively mild compared to their usual conduct. Also, their words were respectful and polite. They spent a half hour inspecting the bookcases in the large room where we usually prayed. They spent an additional two hours in the other room, where they randomly selected several books from the bookcases. The bookcases with manuscripts from the holy Rebbes they did not open, but inquired as to whose writings they were. I answered them briefly. They were interested in the bookcase containing the rare manuscripts, such as *Livnat Hasapir* [date unknown] handwritten by Rabbi Avraham Sava of blessed memory and the *Shemoneh She'arim* [c. 1649], handwritten by Rabbi Shmuel Vital of blessed memory, and additional books written on parchment such as *Sefer Mitzvot Gedolot* [c. 1545], and various books of Kabbalah. They showed special interest in the various incunabula prints, such as *Ralbag on the Torah*, from the year 5246 (1486), *Ramban on the Torah* from the year 5249 (1489) and others.
   > Their full attention, however, was directed to my desk, and the papers and books that were lying on it. They also asked me to

open the drawers for them, and they inspected each paper thoroughly. Yet, they only took several papers of no value. But when they found the catalog of letters which were in my library, they were quite interested. These included some eight hundred letters of the Baal Shem Tov and his disciples, of righteous memory; letters of the Alter Rebbe, the Mitteler Rebbe, the Tzemach Tzedek, the Rebbe Maharash and especially the letters of my father the Rebbe; a large collection of 2,000 letters, journals, and minutes of all the meetings that were held over tens of years; the records of the founding of Yeshivat Tomchei Temimim; a detailed report about the founding of Yeshivat Torat Emet; reports of the directors of the *yeshivot*. Also: reports on the founding of Tomchei Temimim in Warsaw; reports of the directors of the *yeshivot*; copies of public letters of encouragement; epistles and letters to individuals from the year 5681 until 5686 (1921-1926), contained in some five binders, some of them 300 to 400 pages. (The binder of 5681 (1921) was taken during the search of that summer at my dwelling at 44 Brotsky Street in Rostov, and the binder of 5683 (1923) was burned during the search at the above dwelling in 5684 (1924), after which I was compelled to move my residence from Rostov to Leningrad, thus only five binders were left.) With great effort, and through various excuses, I was able to convince them not to take them. (*Yagdil Torah*, vol. 5, p. 288ff.; available in *Sefer Hasichot* 5680-5687, p. 264.)

6. Resting place of the Rebbe's father, Rabbi Shalom DovBer, fifth Rebbe of Chabad-Lubavitch.

7. Resting place of the Rebbe's grandfather, Rabbi Shmuel, and great-grandfather, Rabbi Menachem Mendel, third and fourth Rebbes of Chabad-Lubavitch.

8. Resting place of Rabbi DovBer, second Rebbe of Chabad-Lubavitch.

9. Resting place of Rabbi Schneur Zalman, founder of Chabad-Lubavitch.

10. The memoirs of Rabbi Eliyahu Chaim Althaus (Appendix 7) state, "One of the daughters of the Rebbe [Rebbetzin Chaya Moussia], while in a room by herself with a window open to the courtyard, managed to give a message to Rabbi Menachem M. Schneerson [the Rebbe's future son-in-law and successor] through the open window, saying 'Schneerson: guests have come to visit us!'" He understood and ran to notify others (including the Rebbe's secretary, Mr. Chaim Lieberman, as noted later) of what was taking

place, and of the necessary precautions.

11. Presumably for "Shalom Schneersohn."

12. The Rebbe's successer, Rabbi Menachem Mendel Schneerson appointed people to stand at various intersections to determine where the Rebbe would be taken. (Rebbetzin Chaya Moussia, quoted in *Kfar Chabad*, 29 *Shevat* 5748 [#322], p. 37.)

CHAPTER TWO

Arrival at Spalerno

"**S**tand and descend from the vehicle 'distinguished citizens,'" was the command. The guards abruptly formed a path from the vehicle to the gate. My neighbor descended first, for he had sat to my right and was closer to the door. I noticed that I had been wise not to hurry, for when he descended, they took his personal belongings, which were in a large trunk on which a guard had perched during the journey. It was a handsome trunk, with finely carved details and of foreign make, for such elegant objects are not seen nowadays.

I then realized that he was indeed a foreigner and unable to speak Russian. The guards gestured to him to proceed to the gate. Two men came out of the gate and carried in the trunk, and afterwards, Nachmanson signaled to his comrade Lulav from within the gate. Lulav turned to me and with subdued joy said, "Now would you please exert yourself to proceed. I will take your bag if you wish or if you do not. You are now a guest with us, and you are obligated to submit to our orders."

"Yes, this is a great victory, but I hope that it will only be a brief one," I replied patiently and with confidence.

"Speaking is forbidden!" shouted an armed guard. It seemed that he could no longer suppress his cruelty and his hatred for Jews, especially a Jew respected by his religious brethren.

Nachmanson went before me. There were now two new armed guards accompanying me, for the earlier ones

47

remained outside. One was on my right and the other on my left, and Lulav walked behind me.

We passed through a large courtyard within a building, six stories high and extending to all four sides of the courtyard. On each side there were two or three entrances. No one else was in the courtyard except for the guards at the entrance. Nachmanson walked quickly, but he was compelled to wait for me because I walked with unusual deliberateness. This was because my legs were in pain and, in fact, I was not in any particular hurry. Even before I entered the gate, I began requesting that Nachmanson keep his word about restoring my *tefillin* and letting me pray.

I walked step by step with occasional short intervals to rest as I moved from one level to the next. With difficulty I climbed upon the rungs leading to the administrative head-quarters, as Nachmanson went before me. He turned to me, his face red with rage, and said: "Even before entering the administrative headquarters to be informed of your obliga-tions, you are already badgering me with such demands. This is astonishing. Are you oblivious to your situation? Are you unaware of the rigorous discipline of prison? First you will be brought to the administrative headquarters. There you will fill out the required questionnaire. Only later, when you are brought to your cell, can you pray. I think that in a short while you will forget your present concerns and realize the seriousness of your situation. You will no longer be preoccu-pied with these foolish matters. Forget that you are Schneer-sohn, the distinguished *Bogamolnik* (one who prays to G-d). You are now a simple person who is being punished with imprisonment or other punishment for your flagrant acts against the proletariat. Now you will pay for everything."

I did not respond but gazed at him intently, and I per-ceived that this had a far more piercing effect than any words.

Nachmanson turned to Lulav, "What do you think will happen to this distinguished citizen, who has waxed and thrived for many years in the affluence and luxury of bourgeois life, when he comes to his new apartment—Spalerka Salon? The simple fare of black bread and kasha will not rest well with him. There he will leave behind his pride. There, at the interrogation table, he will speak, declare, answer all the questions put to him. Right, distinguished citizen?"

As though oblivious to Nachmanson's conversation with Lulav, I pursued my former inquiries: "Where are your assurances in your official capacity as a representative of the G.P.U. that I would be permitted to put on my *tefillin* and to pray? Why didn't you reveal to me while I was still in my home that you would not let me pray? What prevents you from being truthful? Whom did you fear? Why did you give me such firm assurances? Is this the normal conduct of a representative of the G.P.U.?"

Nachmanson laughed sardonically, with a mixture of pleasure and vengeance. I saw then that I was dealing with a totally different person. This was not the Nachmanson who was in my apartment, nor the man in the courtyard. This was a G.P.U. official, whose primary task was to frighten the prisoners, to confuse them and render them submissive—ultimately to extract confessions and admissions about imaginary events.

At that moment I recollected the text in *Reishit Chachmah*[1] at the beginning of the Tractate *Geihinom*: "It is written, 'Who can stand before His anger? And who can be upright before the fierceness of His wrath?'[2] Rav Zeira commented, citing the verse from Proverbs,[3] 'The leech has two daughters who cry out, Give, give.' Rabbi Elazar commented further, 'Two groups of angels stand at the gates of *Geihinom* and cry, Give, give, bring, bring.'"

We advanced a few more steps. Nachmanson opened the door to the corridor of the administrative division. He whistled, signalling to one of the guards, "Take this citizen," he ordered, handed him a paper, and said, "Here are his documents. Escort him to the administrative office and give this to official X."

He turned to me laughing, "Now you will begin to understand where you are." Even before he had finished the sentence, he hastened to descend and run after Lulav, who had already gone down. They were obviously in haste to accomplish important tasks. Apparently their night's work was still incomplete.

The guard led me and indicated with his finger that I should walk the length of the corridor to the wide open door. He told me that I would then be given a questionnaire by one of the secretaries and that I should answer all the questions in writing.

This corridor was a long room, more than 150 feet long and twelve feet wide. On both sides there were many closed office doors, and at every 30 feet was a small burning candle suspended from the ceiling. Along the length of the room stood ten or twelve armed guards, each armed with a Cossack pike at his back, a polished sword in his left hand, and a rifle in his right. They stood like marble pillars, unmoving, yet their eyes attentively surveyed the entire area.

The dreadful, bizarre scene would inevitably frighten any normal person, who could not begin to comprehend the reason for the elaborate display of weaponry and the intended targets of these instruments of destruction. Indeed, where could people be found so callous and corrupt as to be capable of wielding such weapons? Could a person be such a wild animal that such things must be used to tame him?

The enveloping silence, the darkness, the blackness of the walls, the small candles, the malevolent statue-like soldiers with massive powerful figures, their height, the broadness of their shoulders, the harsh outline of their features, their uniforms of stark red and black, the excessive display of weaponry—pike, sword, rifle—all merged into one composite image that terrified the eye of the beholder and made the heart shudder.

Through the two rows of soldiers in the frightening dimness and in death-like stillness, I walked to the end of the corridor. In my mind the question arose, "Where am I going and for what purpose? What is required of me and how will this all end?" As if in internal dialogue with my soul, I responded clearly, excluding all doubt: "I shall shortly arrive at the open door, exactly as the guard told me. Did he not give me clear instructions that I must write out the answers to the questionnaire?

"And what then? Later, surely Nachmanson's promise will be fulfilled, that I will be brought to the place where one 'speaks willingly or unwillingly.'" I advanced slowly and thought:

Tractate *Geihinom*—First Section.[4]

Whether inadvertently or deliberately I do not know, but apparently because of my intense inner reflection or the agitated confusion of my thoughts, I veered to the right. As I approached the open door I perceived another hallway extending to the right. It seems that without any forethought I had turned in this direction.

The corridor was exactly as long as the one through which I had just passed. But aside from this there was a stark contrast: here the walls were plastered, and there were many windows. There were no armed guards, and long benches extended along the entire length of the room. In this area there were also many doorways, but they were white, with numbers written on them, and signs printed with thin, sharp words. I did not pay attention to them, however, because I was very much shaken by the incredible contrast between the first corridor, coarse and dark, with its intense security, and the present environment, so normal and civilized. Somehow, under the influence of these new surroundings, I walked with longer and more confident strides, and no one challenged or directed me. As I advanced I realized that I had erred in my movements, for I had been instructed to go forward up to "the door open for all prisoners." How had I somehow turned and arrived here? Would this magnify my supposed violation of the law? Perhaps now they would accuse me of intruding into an area prohibited to prisoners, thus enabling them to bring harsher and more perilous accusations: that I was now attempting to ferret out knowledge of the ins and outs of the Spalerno Prison.

Nevertheless, I did not hurry back. Had I been aware originally, I would not have ventured in this direction; but since I was already there, I had already crossed the line, though without conscious intent. And indeed, this is the way of Divine Providence. Were my actions any less significant than those of the wind-buffeted wisp of straw, or a wind-driven swirling leaf? Rabbi Yisroel Ba'al Shem Tov[5] had taught that even these seemingly minor incidents were all due to G-d's exalted Providence.[6]

I noticed a bench standing a few steps away, approached it, and sat down to rest a while. I suddenly remembered that I did not have my bag. I was surprised at my forgetfulness—where might I have lost it? I concentrated and recollected that I misplaced it when I was separated from the second escort group, from the "angels of *Geihinom*," namely Nachmanson and Lulav, and transferred to the guard who had escorted me to the dark corridor. Apparently I was so concerned and preoccupied that I had forgotten it.

Like myself, I thought, my bag is also here in this section. Whatever the circumstances, no one would steal it. If Lulav had taken it to the administrative headquarters, it would certainly be there. If he had entrusted it to a guard of the dark corridor, it would be there. At any rate, it was most certainly secure. At this time, I must use these precious moments to prepare myself for the "room open for all prisoners."

"What is happening in my home right now?"

This thought possessed me: Conscious of the different personalities in my family, I could imagine their reactions and behavior, and the composite scene. I pictured the sobbing of my mother; the white, apprehensive face and the deep inner anguish of my wife and her shocked muteness; the shattered hearts and the confusion of my helpless daughters; the apprehension and concern of my son-in-law. I also thought about my future son-in-law, Rabbi Menachem [Schneerson], who had gone to the home of my secretary, Mr. Lieberman. I hoped to G-d that he was not also ensnared in this net of intrigue. What of all my dear friends and my *chassidic* disciples? What were they doing at this very minute? This vivid panorama excited me, and my eyes flowed with hot tears. I was deeply agitated and my entire body trembled: G-d forbid, was it possible that the sacred *chassidic* manuscripts and writings were also taken? I now realized that they were attempting to exact revenge from me. The angry words of Nachmanson, his conversation with Lulav, clearly indicated that I was dealing with people set on vengeance, on weaving lies, improvising dangerous charges against me. Who knew if they had not touched the core and apple of my eye, the sacred *chassidic* manuscripts and writings. And if, G-d forbid, this had actually occurred, how awesome was this situa-

tion. How incredible the catastrophe that these sacred manuscripts would also be swept into custody and imprisoned![7]

I felt the need to still this surge of thought. Like a flash of
lightning there gleamed within my mind, "And what of G-d?
Who has done this? Who has generated this entire sequence
of events? Everything has its source in G-d. True, I am indeed
a son, a husband, a father, a father-in-law, one who loves and
is beloved. They are all dependent upon me, but I and they
in turn are dependent upon G-d Who spoke and created the
world. I have done all that I am capable of doing, and G-d
will do according to His will, may He be blessed." At that
moment I emerged from the mire and constraints of my situation, and ascended to transcendent spiritual heights, with
thoughts beyond the confines of finite, physical existence. I
was bolstered by pure faith and absolute trust in the Living
G-d, secure in the merit of my holy ancestors.

*The Rebbe interrupts his narrative at this point with a sequence
of periods and the phrase "letters of thought," connoting either feelings too intense or personal to express, or ones so profound as to be
inexpressible.*

These thoughts sustained my soul and strengthened me
greatly. I was unconcerned with the present situation and sat
in absolute peace.

Then I began to readjust: "I am a prisoner in Spalerno, I
do not know for what cause. In the interrogation room they
will subject me to a barrage of questions: some normal
inquiries for information and others startling and totally
unanticipated. From my answers they will attempt to weave
a net of false accusations or provide a match to ignite a blaze
of revenge."

I took a cigarette and then began to formulate a general
outline of response. I resolved to be strong and not yield to

fear, to speak clearly and in no way to be affected by the intrigue in which they sought to enmesh me.

This strong personal resolve caused a sense of inner exaltation and a sense of self-worth, as though I was sitting in a garden or strolling on a sunny day. This specific feeling was evoked by the rays of the sun that shone upon the white wall opposite me. I was on the verge of retracing my steps and returning to the "door open for all prisoners." But then I reflected: What need was there for haste? Would I miss anything due to my delay? Indeed, I felt the need to organize my thoughts once again. It was my custom that, prior to publicly delivering any *chassidic* discourse, I would review it once again, even though I was wholly conversant with the concepts involved. I felt that I had now returned to my usual frame of mind, thank G-d.

How great is the inner faith, the perfect faith, which is transmitted through our heritage to all Jews, a spiritual inheritance from our patriarchs. How great is the power of absolute trust in G-d. These are not only the foundation of our Jewish faith, our holy faith, but the foundations of life itself, normal everyday life, the material existence of every Jew.

"Give thanks to G-d for His great kindness," that He had caused the seeming error of my turn into the corridor.[8] For it provided shelter and respite from falling into the web of fright and confusion prepared for me by Nachmanson and Lulav. G-d's Divine Providence had led me like the strand of straw or tree leaf thrust by the driving current of the wind.[9]

I was like them, but my situation was more significant (for those possessed of human speech are above objects of vegetative existence,[10] this is even truer in the case of pure and holy [i.e. Jewish] souls who surpass mortals who are capable solely of human speech). I was fully conscious that I was in the hand of G-d's Divine Providence, may He be blessed and exalted.

I was still sitting in my place when I heard the clamor of voices in one of the rooms behind the wall opposite me— not the sound of outcry or anguish, but the sound of laughter, of people secure in their existence and fortunate in their lot. A few moments passed, one of the doors opened, and three people emerged. The sight of a strange man sitting with a confident spirit smoking calmly, took them aback. For a moment they stood on the threshold startled, hesitating to emerge and scrutinizing me closely.

I remained sitting with the same serene composure of the past ten minutes as though unaffected by this new occurrence, but my heartbeat intensified. I feared they would ask me why I was on the bench in the corridor.

After gazing at me for a few moments, they continued toward the left, to the wide open door which I have already mentioned a number of times. However, one of them retraced his steps and entered one of the rooms. I paid no heed as to which room and I was sure that someone would shortly appear to question me. I decided, therefore, to wait there and not proceed to the administrative center until the arrival of this person.

My presumption proved accurate. The person who had returned now came out of the room accompanied by someone else, who in turn approached me, inquired about my presence, and asked for whom I was waiting.

"I did not come here," I replied, "I was brought here and I was told to go to the administrative center. I am waiting for my *talit* and *tefillin*, for the man who brought me here assured me while I was yet in my home that he would provide a place to pray. He also said that I was being brought here merely for a few hours to answer some questions."

It appeared that the fluency of my answer, my sincerity, and my dispassionate composure took my questioner aback. He stood without uttering a word, scrutinizing me from head to toe in amazement. I could not tell for sure, but it seemed to me that he was a gentile, not a Jew, a Russian from the regions of Vitebsk, Smolensk, or Mohilyev; a calm, deliberate person, though young, not more than twenty-five. His eyes glimmered with inner feelings, the emotions of a toiling farmer.

He stared at me and I gazed back at him. There was no word or communication between us. I took out a cigarette. He, too, took out a cigarette from his container and hurried to offer me his lit match. He turned aside to sit on the very same bench with me.

I now realized that being in this corridor was in no way a trespass of prison regulations. However, who knew what Nachmanson and Lulav could make even of this—to stir up a cauldron of intrigue, a thick morass of hearsay and hatred of religion in order to denounce me? But in any event, my fear had passed.

"It is only half past three and they have already brought many people here tonight. They are bringing in unusually large numbers," the man told me. He spoke reflectively, as if speaking to himself: "Our comrades are working tonight far beyond their duty, and I also have been here four hours overtime already."

"Where are you from?"

I replied, "I come from a small city—I do not know if you have ever heard of it. My birthplace is Lubavitch. It is bounded on one side by the train station Rudnia, located between the cities of Vitebsk and Smolensk, and on the other side by the train station Krasnoya, situated between Arsha and Smolensk."

"Lubavitch," he replied, "Yes, I know it well. Even from early childhood I knew of it. It is not small at all. There was a big market place and two houses of prayer." He asked me, "Gusin—would you know of that town?"

I knew Gusin, and the station and surrounding villages. Many of my acquaintances lived there, obviously Jews. However, I had no knowledge of the landowners and peasants in that area, for I had no contact with them.

I thus ascertained that my guess that he was not Jewish and from the South was correct.

"In Lubavitch," he continued, "dwelled the family of a saintly man. They lived in a large courtyard close to the marketplace. There was a well in their courtyard, and whenever I would come with my father to the market place, I would go there to drink water. We would also lead our horses there to drink."

"Yes, yes," I answered, and my heart began to pound from great emotion and the awakening of many memories and associations. At the same time I was surprised by this unusual encounter. I could not determine if it could affect me favorably or adversely, and I was on the verge of deciding to proceed to the administrative center.

I began, "I am required to go to the administrative center," and arose from my place.

"Yes," he answered, "I will accompany you and show you what is to be done and with whom to speak." He continued, "Were you ever here before? Are you aware of what is required? Can you write?"

I replied, "No, this is my first time here; I do not know what is required of me, nor what must be written."

He told me, "Stenographers will question you and transcribe everything you answer. After you have answered the questionnaire, they will take you to the search room. They will take all those things not needed by a prisoner: your money, watch and other belongings. They will then hand you over to one of the orderlies to lead you to the administrator of a prison division, and you will be placed in a cell under his custody."

I listened attentively. I was gratified by G-d's kindness, that He had strengthened and fortified my heart so that these words did not cause me fear or panic. I sensed that I had adjusted to the current situation. I hoped that I could sustain my present stance with G-d's help, not to allow Judaism to be trampled underfoot. I could not permit any coercion to affect my firm resolve; I had to remain staunch and unwavering.

"Through which corridor were you brought here?"

"I was brought here through the corridor to the left of this one. I was weary from my trek on the stairs, and seeing that there were benches here, I sat on one of them to rest."

"That corridor?" he asked in great anger. He stopped walking, his face glowering with astonishment. "Who are you? Where are you from? How long have you lived in Leningrad?"

"I am Rabbi Schneersohn from the city of Lubavitch. In 1915 we fled from the Germans when they advanced toward our borders. We traveled to Rostov and dwelled there till 1924. In May of that year we came to Leningrad."

"Why were you brought to that corridor?" he asked incredulously. "Where were you arrested? Were you in the company of traitors? Who was with you at the time of the arrest? Did they find in your possession subversive propaganda or other kinds of literature? Who brought you here?"

I answered with equanimity, "I was arrested in my dwelling on 22 Machovaya Street, Apartment 12. I was with my family eating supper, and no one else was in my house aside from my family. I had no literature nor any form of subversive propaganda. Thus, there was nothing to be discovered. I was brought here by two officials named Nachman-son and Lulav."

He exploded in rage: "May darkness take them! And why through that corridor? Have they brought a traitor? Have they begun using that corridor?" He muttered to himself as he scratched his brow.

"No," he said, "what you are saying is untrue. Undoubt-edly there was some serious violation of the law. They would not lead you through that corridor unjustifiably. Tell me the truth, comrade, or you will make the situation even worse for yourself."

"There is nothing to reveal," I stated, "I have already spo-ken the truth. Nachmanson and Lulav brought me to the door of the corridor. Nachmanson whispered something into the ear of the guard standing by the door and transferred me to his custody. The guard directed me to proceed into the large room through the open door. However, I was very weary, and seeing benches to sit in the corridor, I sat down to rest. And there is basically nothing more to relate."

"*Ach*, not true," he said, "something is irregular here. You speak falsely. For this you will be placed in solitary confine-ment with an increased penalty of three or four months of additional imprisonment, perhaps even more, unfortunately for you. Speak the truth, what is your actual crime?"

We heard a voice calling from behind, "Chimka, what is all this chatter? Come here quickly and stop the foolish talk there."

He responded, "Yes, wait, I will be there shortly. I need something in the office."

Turning to me he said, "No, this matter must be clarified."

From Chimka's astonishment I understood that the dark cor-ridor through which Nachmanson had directed me to proceed to the administrative center was for serious offenders. Anyone led that way was obviously quite a criminal.

Actually, his words had no effect on me, and I turned toward the administrative center, the room with the open door, the place, as described by Nachmanson, "where one speaks either willingly or through coercion."

Notes

1. An ethical work containing a description of *Geihinom,* Purgatory.
2. Nahum 1:6.
3. Proverbs 30:15.
4. This phrase is used on page 63 as a kind of chapter heading and is followed further on by a "second section" and "third section," thus suggesting a parallel between the description of the prison and the levels of *Geihinom* described in *Reishit Chachmah.* The insertion of the phrase here is evidently meant to suggest a similar idea.
5. Founder of the *Chassidic* movement, hereafter referred to as the "Ba'al Shem Tov."
6. See the *Ma'amar Tiku,* 5688.
7. Rabbi Menachem Mendel, the Rebbe's successor, busied himself all night with depositing the writings in the homes of various *chassidim.* One of them was Rabbi Schneur Zalman Duchman. (As related by Rebbetzin Chana, *Di Yiddishe Heim, Sivan* 5724, p. 6; see *Igrot Kodesh* of Rabbi Menachem Mendel Schneerson, vol. 3, p.11.)
8. The Rebbe's successor attributes even more significance to this "mistaken" turn into the corridor, describing it as a miraculous event, which spared the Rebbe his life: "Special clearance had been given from Moscow for the execution of political prisoners that night, but by the time the Rebbe was processed, several hours late, the permission was withdrawn. The reason for this was in revenge for the assassination of a certain minister outside the country." (*Sichat* 12 *Tammuz, Sichot Kodesh* 5730, p. 399). See Prologue.
9. This is a reference to the teaching of the Ba'al Shem Tov, cited in many *chassidic* sources, that Divine Providence is related to all cre-

ation, even to animal life, vegetation and inert matter. There is G-dly reckoning and judgment about how many times a leaf or strand of straw will be swept about and in what specific place. The Rebbe states in a talk, "From minor matters we can derive insight into ones more significant. If Divine Providence exists even regarding something as trivial as a plucked leaf or a strand of straw, whether it should remain in its present location or be transferred someplace else, how much more does it encompass everything related to the existence of a Jew." (*See Sichah* 19th *Kislev* 5694, section 3, and *Hayom Yom*, 28th of *Cheshvan*.)

[The following footnote that appears in *Reshimat Hama'aser* was written by the Rebbe, Rabbi Menachem M. Schneerson]:

My father-in-law, the Rebbe, related: "In the discourse of *Rosh Hashanah*, 5687, I interjected a comment regarding the opinion of the Ba'al Shem Tov about Divine Providence affecting even the inert vegetative and animal levels of creation and applying to every detail, though this was not actually related to the discourse. If not for my uttering this statement, I do not know if I would have had the strength to undergo the extreme ordeal and suffering of imprisonment."

10. The Rebbe refers here to the well-known concept in *Chassidus* of the division of existence into four categories of beings: inanimate, vegetable, animal and articulate (human).

CHAPTER THREE

Tractate Geihinom, First Section

I stepped across the threshold and gazed into a room approximately 36 feet square. Along three walls of the room sat some 20 women, most of them writing and smoking. They faced the center of the room, and on the other sides of their tables stood the benches where the "guests" were brought in to sit.

The room had three doors: one, open wide for the prisoners who were brought through the dark corridor; a second door, to the right, seemingly for petty prisoners who came through a different corridor (through which Chimka thought I was led); and a third door, leading to the next section. On the right side of the entrance from the dark corridor, I saw my bag lying on the floor, together with the plaid blanket.

It was a strange sight: there were approximately forty people in the room: the twenty secretaries writing on long forms and the twenty prisoners answering their questions, either willingly or because of the force of circumstances. Nevertheless, absolute silence prevailed; a deathly stillness. The questions and answers were exchanged very quietly. Only the scratching of the pens on the sheets could be heard.

In the open center of the room stood a group of people. It appeared that their task was to supervise the interrogation procedures, for they did not speak to each other. No detail was lost upon them as they peered at every side of the room and at each person. They were armed, and although they wore simple military garb, their very appearance was frightening. Their faces were red and sullen with rage, their eyes glimmered, their buttons were of burnished copper and they were of massive build.

My general impression was that here the web was woven. Here the prisoner would begin by giving basic information: his name, age, birthplace, family, religion, residence, etc. But by means of the innumerable questions, the person was transformed from one stating simple information to one admitting matters that he never dreamed of. The sensitive manner of the secretaries, and their soft speech, together with the confused thought and crushed state of the prisoners, served to elicit answers for the questionnaire that would later provide ample basis for the prosecutor's accusation that the prisoner had, in fact, already acknowledged his guilt.

As I stood viewing and assimilating all that was taking place in this first section of *Geihinom* itself, one of the officials lifted his arm, indicating that I was to proceed toward a table to my left. An interrogation place was now available for me, as the secretary had just finished with a prisoner.

I saw the secretary hand over to one of the escorting guards the papers and documents of the prisoner and his *yarlik* number. The term "*yarlik*" is to be encountered under various circumstances. A customer coming to a large department store to buy merchandise from the different departments proceeds to the cashier and is there given the *yarlik* package number of his purchase. A package is dispatched through railroad mail, express or regular, and a receipt is given with the *yarlik* number.

But in Spalerno, *yarlik* numbers are imposed on human beings. Customarily, the *yarlik* number is pasted on the merchandise package, but this *yarlik* number is not actually affixed to the body of the prisoner; rather it is impressed upon his very soul. His personal identity is lost. He is transformed into a number.

Up to this point, the prisoner is addressed by his actual name, but from the point that the questionnaire is signed and sealed, he is addressed by his *yarlik* number. I do not know if the *yarlik* is a reference to the month, day, or some other numerical sequence, but I am aware that the person preceding me, in whose place I sat, was designated as *yarlik* 26803.

His clothing was of medium quality, and he seemed to be about 60 years old. He had a kindly face and appeared to have some white-collar profession—bookkeeper or director of a business; he was mild mannered and spoke quietly and politely.

As he stood up, he was approached by the escorting guard, who upon reading his form exclaimed: "Aha! So much is written here!"

The face of *yarlik* 26803 turned green, his eyeglasses slid off his nose and his whole body trembled.

"Follow me!" commanded the guard. "Don't be so agitated, in a short while you will rest upon bedding of straw and stretch out on thin, narrow planks . . ." (I could not hear anymore, for they had left the room).

"Sit, Citizen," said the stenographer. "Here is a sheet of questions. Answer each question clearly, and answer each question in the correct space."

"I have nothing to write," I replied, "this does not relate to me, and I have nothing to answer."

"What?" inquired the secretary, "you do not wish to follow the official procedure? It is an established law that each individual arriving here must fill out this answer sheet and clearly respond to all the questions."

"I did not come here to visit," I stated. "I was taken here. The persons who brought me know who I am and what I am. Why do something utterly pointless?"

"Do you forget where you are? Or is your mind confused? Do you mean to institute new procedures in this department? What is your name?"

"I know very well that I am a prisoner brought to Spalerno, and my mind, thank G-d, is in good order. I do not seek to institute new procedures. My name is Schneersohn. I live at 22 Machovaya Street, Apartment 12. I will not write any answers to the questionnaire, and you can enter the information just given."

The secretary took the form, entered the facts given, and then continued: "What is your title?"

"I am an 'Honored-for-Generations-Citizen.' "[1]

"That title no longer exists."

"I do not know if it does or does not exist, but my title is Honored-for-Generations-Citizen."

"What is your vocation?"

"I am involved in studies, the study of the knowledge of G-dliness known as *Chassidus*, and the study of Jewish Law and its observance in accordance with the Jewish religion."

"Religion! G-dly knowledge!"

"Yes! The knowledge of G-dliness. One G-d has created and formed all existence, and His Divine Providence extends over all creations: the crawling creature in the sea and the small creatures in a desert wasteland, and mankind in civilized society."

"How can I possibly write such answers on the questionnaire?"

"Who compels you to write? As far as I am concerned, you need not write anything. If you want to write, then write, and if you don't want to, then don't."

Suddenly three men appeared at the threshold of the Second Section and gazed into this one. Their eyes searched the room, and upon perceiving me, the expression upon their faces indicated that they had found what they sought.

I recognized one of the three as the driver of the arrest vehicle which had conveyed me to Spalerno. They were all young and dressed in normal civilian garb: breeches, silk shirts of different colors of either English or American make, and red knee button boots. Their thick belts had holders for watches on the left side and holsters for guns on the right. Their hair was finely combed, and a look of pleasure could be discerned on their stoic, frozen faces.

Their entrance cast a chill throughout the entire room. Though the guards in the center of the room and the secretaries made no sound or additional movement, a definite change of atmosphere could be sensed in the room.

The three stood silently, but their entrance seemed to instill a deathly fear that affected even the prison workers. Each secretary tended to her task with greater intensity and rigidity; the faces of the sentries in the center of the room changed perceptibly from flushed red to pale white, their eyes moving about and scrutinizing all within their gaze, driven like violinists in an orchestra following the baton of a raging conductor.

One of the three took out a gleaming silver holder filled with cigarettes and offered it to his companions. They all looked toward my table, and I was certain that they sought a plausible reason, any slight pretext to approach.

I understood that they wished to know what was being written in my questionnaire. I was certain that they knew of me and my work. I did not know whether they were of the Second or Third Section, but be that as it may, they were officials of high station who did not customarily visit this department. And this was the cause of the fear which had gripped the entire room.

I surmised that they wanted to involve themselves in my questioning and to augment the explicit questions already on the form, to pound in pegs on which they could later suspend false accusations.

But how could this be done—that high officials should dabble in the tasks of a simple secretary? This itself would reveal their devious intents.

"What am I to do?" said the cigarette-smoking secretary, as though speaking reflectively to herself, "I cannot write such answers. It is my responsibility to ask every written question and to transcribe the answers. I am unable to write of such things as G-d, religion, and G-dly commands."

"Is it possible," I asked, "for a prisoner to smoke, too?"

"Yes," she replied, "it is not forbidden to smoke in this room, although the prisoners do not customarily smoke. If you desire to do so, I will request permission from one of the officers standing in the center of the room."

She spoke in such a tone that the newcomers who stood nearby could hear.

With a light smile upon his lips, one of the three high officials approached and with simulated surprise inquired, "Does this citizen desire to smoke a cigarette?" And turning to me, he declared, "Here it is not forbidden to smoke. You may take a cigarette."

I took a cigarette, while the official offered me his cigarette for a light. I thanked him saying that I had matches.

The secretary complained to the official who had approached the table, "I am unable to fill out this citizen's questionnaire since he does not provide any responses. He asserts that this is completely unrelated to him, and he refuses to answer anything but his name, address and family title."

The official took the form, scrutinized it for a few moments, and then turned to me: "You have not answered

any of the questions in this form; you must fill it out completely. There is no other alternative."

He spoke calmly, like an administrator scrutinizing a
report written by a subordinate. He added, "I am sure that
the citizen knows where he is at present. This official division has special laws and regulations, and all who come here
must comply with them. The officials of this department
expect their demands to be fulfilled immediately and precisely."

I responded, "I wish to take this opportunity to clarify
whether the assurances of those authorized by your agency,
or more precisely, the representatives of your agency, are
trustworthy, and if one may rely that their assurances will also
be observed meticulously."

The official replied, "I do not understand what you are
saying, citizen?"

"A representative of this agency who came to arrest me
tonight assured me that I would be allowed to put on *tefillin*
and to pray. It is already an hour and a half that I am here and
his word has not been kept. He told me on his own initiative that I would be here merely for a matter of hours and
that upon my arrival, a number of high officials would ask
me a few questions and then permit me to return home.

"I do not know why he said this to me. I do not know if
his motive was solely to calm the members of my household
or whether it was his malicious intent to perpetrate this
bizarre jest.

"Frankly, I am totally unconcerned as to the rationale for
his conduct. But I am a religious Jew. I desire to put on my
tefillin and pray. No one on Earth has the power to disturb
my service of G-d. I demanded this at the time of my arrest,
and I was given this assurance by the representative of the
G.P.U. His final words to me were 'Though I am a Communist'—this was with irony—'I will not lie.' These were his
words and I now demand that they be fulfilled.

"As to the questionnaire, I have already stated that I did not come here of my own free will; I was brought here by the emissaries of the G.P.U. I am certain that those who arrested me, as well as the high administrative officials, know who and what I am.

"All I have to state is as follows:

I am Rabbi Schneersohn, son of the famed Rabbi Schneersohn of Lubavitch. I bear the hereditary title of 'Honored-for-Generations-Citizen.' My birthplace is Lubavitch; I studied there at the *yeshivah* and I subsequently lived for eight and a half years in Rostov and three years in Leningrad. My primary preoccupation is religious study. I am involved in the philosophical system known as *Chassidus* and also concern myself with clarifying the laws and statutes of the Jewish religion. I, like all other religious Jews, have no link with politics. I have nothing else to write."

The firm answer, the clear response, my cold composure and the equanimity reflected in my smoking calmly were all "natural vessels for that which transcends nature," and the official, as though reflectively talking to himself, said, "What is written is adequate." He turned to the secretary and with light laughter, but with burning eyes, said, "Write as the citizen states."

Directing my question to the official, I asked, "And what of prayer?"

He answered majestically, "You will receive an answer from the prison administrator of the division where you will be escorted for confinement."

He left with restrained rage.

The secretary took a new form and wrote my statement with great care and handed it to me for my signature.

I took the questionnaire and read it carefully. I drew a line through all of the blanks of the remaining questions to clearly indicate that these questions were unanswered. After I had finished reading it, I signed the document.

During these last few moments, the three officials conversed with each other, and attempting to conceal their primary interest in me, they glanced around the room and then left.

"Wait here a few moments," said the stenographer. She took the form and went to the second room. She returned and took a piece of paper the size of a postcard upon which was written in large black letters thus: "*yarlik* number.... ." I perceived that in a moment, I would also be transformed into a *yarlik*; I did not yet know the number, but in a moment I would know this also. She was still writing in books: large thick books, of which there were many.

All the secretaries wrote in these books. I did not know what she wrote, but after writing, the secretary placed a seal on the form that I had signed.

I will not deny that the placing of the seal pleased me. I would have been far more pleased if the entire arrest incident had not occurred. But since I had been brought there and had been compelled to sign, it was much better that it bear the official seal so they couldn't substitute a similar form or one totally different. Who knew the mentality of these officials capable of creating something from nothing? But hopefully, the seal would prevent this.

Her entries into the four thick volumes were completed. She wrote on the dotted line of the card next to the word "*yarlik*" my number, 26818. At that moment I was transformed into a *yarlik*. I thought to myself that most certainly in another few moments a guard would come to escort me to the Second Section, or, as I had been previously told by Chimka and the senior official, directly to the head of the division where I would be imprisoned.

"Yes, everything is prepared," said the secretary, and glancing at the form, she said, "Yes, little is written, but its content is highly significant." Her face assumed a compassionate expression and she whispered, "Perhaps you wish to send a message to your household. Tell me and I will pass it on immediately after work."

I did not reply at all. I merely awaited the escort, for I had already begun to experience the painful anguish of this ordeal. I wished that the matter would be brought to a head. I suffered emotional turmoil from these unnecessary preludes.

The secretary gathered all the documents and told me to follow her, for she had been instructed to do this personally and not to use the customary escort.

As stated, I was agitated. The clock struck half past four, and I had already undergone innumerable painful experiences—the talk with Chimka, the memory of the market in Lubavitch, with the farmers bringing their horses to drink the well water, the argument with the stenographer, the talk with the senior official—all of which disgusted me. I hoped that something concrete would occur, to speak to an authoritative interrogator or to finally be in a cell, but in any event to be released from this psychological manhandling.

With strengthened heart and a regular stride, I proceeded on.

I passed through the second room, which I had taken to be the Second Section when I sat in the first. Now I saw that I was mistaken. We passed through a third room, and I came to a dark corridor, but not the one that Nachmanson had brought me through at first. Here, there were a few burning candles and no armed guards, and in this corridor we had to descend on iron steps in four or five ladders.

"My traveling bag," I said, "I left it in the room where I wrote the form. Can I return later to obtain it? It is in the area between the entrance door to the dark corridor and the threshold to the second corridor, a reddish sack wrapped in a cover with a green, plaid blanket resting on it."

"Why didn't you take all your belongings?" she answered. "Now you cannot return. It will be necessary to write a special request form, which cannot be done now. The only choice is that I go and bring them to you, or even better, when I go back, I will be able to bring them or send them to you. Perhaps they will permit me to send it with one of the escorts. You should know that the security here is very strict. The slightest infringement of the rules through unnecessary speech or the slightest sign of communication with one of the prisoners can result in a punishment of imprisonment for three or four months. It is better, therefore, that upon arriving at your destination, that you inform them of having forgotten to take your belongings, and they will certainly let me bring them here.

"You should know that they are preparing very serious charges against you. I know that they have gathered much evidence. Now I know who you are, for I have been informed by officials B. and R. They intend punishing you severely and the situation is very dreadful. Among the three officials was R. himself."

We climbed from ladder to ladder as she spoke. My feelings alternated between fleeting moments when it appeared to me that her words were lies intended to frighten me and then for brief instants to the impression that she spoke the truth. Who knew, perhaps there existed, even within this secretary, a drop of human feeling. I will not deny that these moments were intensely difficult. My thoughts blurred, my head pounded very rapidly, my feet stumbled, and an inner tremor passed through my entire body.

Nevertheless, I did not inquire where I was being led, though I was certain the secretary would tell me. I feared it would exert a strong adverse effect upon me and make my spirit fall. I felt stronger not knowing.

She related: "Twelve people were brought here tonight, the majority of them clergymen—Russians, Lutherans, Germans, Poles, a Moslem and only one Jew—yourself. A Russian, a Georgian and a Pole were brought through the dark passageway with armed guard directly to the third room (it appears that this was one of the doors in the dark passageway) and from there to the sub-cellar under the building, where they were shot to death without any interrogation. We were only told to make an entry in the book—unlike the case of those instructed to answer the questionnaire; in all probability you will remain in the fortress for a few days and then be interrogated.

"I was instructed to bring you this way to the first story inspector—"control." All of the prisoners brought to Spalerno are led through there."

At this moment I realized that the entire procedure was meant to frighten. The darkness, the ladders with their iron rungs, the dark walls, stale air—all evoke intense emotions and the dread of being led to a fearful place.

I am certain that sensitive and talented authors would find much material for lengthy works on the nature of human feeling and conduct by merely depicting the range of my experiences during the past two hours from my arrival in the prison until my arrival in this place where they brought ordinary prisoners.

The secretary knocked on a door and the guard, an armed soldier, opened it and asked in great amazement, "Where is the escort guard?"

"There is no guard," answered the stenographer. "I was ordered to bring this citizen prisoner to Room 4; permit me to proceed."

"And the password?" asked the guard.

"I do not know it, please call Comrade C."

"Go out to the vestibule," answered the guard, "and I will call the official. He will give you the authorization to enter; I cannot permit you to stay here."

She said: "What heavy security! Every step is guarded with sword, spear, guns and bayonet."

This transparent charade was abhorrent to me. For it was obvious that causing fear and confusion was the primary goal. This was the means for implementing their evil intentions. I moved to the side, leaned on the wall, and waited.

A few moments passed; the door opened and there was a dark-complexioned face, black as a raven with long wild hair. This person, dressed in a green tunic without a belt, appeared at the threshold of the structure.

"Good morning, Comrade," said the secretary. "Official D. ordered me to lead the prisoner this way to the Fourth Investigation Division through this corridor. Please permit me to obey this command because I have a message for the comrade investigator which I must give orally."

The comrade with the coarse features scrutinized me from head to toe. I sensed the animosity he bore me and my mode of dress—I was dust to him.

He scratched his forehead, spat profusely and yawned. Then, sharp, pungent words came out from between the teeth of this lion: "May darkness take all the prisoners! I worked a double shift tonight. It is less than an hour that I lay down to rest. And behold, the black wind brought this refuse! Was he then sick and unable to be brought through the entrance where all the prisoners go? And why did he come by way of this specific entrance? Through this entrance they are led to the basement dungeon to rest in eternal sleep."

"I have no time," answered the stenographer, "tell the comrade guard to let me obey the command. In the administrative section there is much work, and I cannot wait too long."

"Go," said the eloquent comrade. He opened his mouth in an extended yawn, emitting a strange sound. He spoke but his words were unclear. Only the final phrase of his triple benediction was understandable: "May darkness take you and all the prisoners together!"

We came to a small dark corridor and then turned right into a clearly-lit corridor. We took a few steps and entered a large room approximately 24 feet square. There were four writing tables with chairs. Two tables were empty, and two officials sat at the other tables; they were both immersed in their work, and there were open ledgers and papers resting on the tables.

The stenographer hastened toward one of the officials and said, "I have brought *yarlik* 26818," and placed the papers on the table.

The officials conveyed the image of stereotypical functionaries accustomed to sitting at a desk. They apathetically shuffled the pages of the thick books and lazily picked away at the many accumulations of documents and papers scattered on the table.

It appeared that these officials, too, were extremely exhausted and that their presence here was either voluntary overtime or a function of administrative requirement. From moment to moment they lapsed into sustained yawns. They scratched their backs and heads lethargically, and they list-lessly lifted papers and put them down again.

The stenographer whispered some words to the official which stimulated him to the effort of overcoming his weari-ness and sloth. He turned to me, saying, "Wait in this room," and pointed toward the door to the right of the entrance.

"Very well," I answered, "but my personal belongings are in the area where I filled out the form. How can I obtain them? Is it possible for someone to bring them?"

The official responded with rage, "We have no servants to concern themselves with the personal belongings of prison-ers. What need do you have for your belongings? There in your prison cell belongings are unnecessary. What exactly do you have there?"

"There," I answered, "I have my travelling bag; I have some things I need, *tefillin*, *talit*, siddur, a book of Psalms, other objects, and a thick green silk blanket. If you instruct one of the attendants to bring them, I will pay him for his effort."

"Bourgeois customs!" exclaimed the enraged official, "give them servants! The prisoners are too sick to carry their bags! It is forbidden to bring any kind of religious garments within the walls of the prison. In any event, the division head, in whose custody you will be placed, will confiscate all clerical garments and religious books. What difference will it make to you if they remain where they are now or in the storage chambers of the head prison official? Forget this nonsense: You must understand that you are a prisoner."

"During the two hours that I have been here," I answered emotionally, "I have heard repeated dozens of times that I am a prisoner. I do not know if I alone am a prisoner or if all the officials here are also prisoners. We are identical to each other. You are not allowed to move from your guard post. Just as I must obey prison discipline, similarly you must fulfill your obligations. Stop your abusive diatribes regarding religious matters which are holy to me. The law authorizes me to request my belongings and that you permit me to pray."

My emotional outburst had a strong enough effect to awaken the other official, and he stared at us with eyes of intense astonishment. My official, with smoldering anger, stroked his moustache and delved into the piles of paper resting on his desk.

It appeared that they were unaccustomed to hear someone speak with such self-assertion. For a moment I had actually poured out all the rage that had welled up within me when I was in the First Section. The official rose from his chair, approached me, opened a door, and said, "Sit in this room till I call you." He left and closed the door.

Notes

1. In recognition of the activities of Rabbi Schneur Zalman of Liadi, the first Chabad-Lubavitch Rebbe, on behalf of the Russian Government during the Napoleonic War, the family was given this official designation.

CHAPTER FOUR

Tractate Geihinom, Second Section

I entered the enclosed room, which had only the one door which I had used. It was a small room, nine feet in width and eighteen in length, and its walls were painted red. The one large window had been enclosed from the outside with iron bars, the normal prison practice, particularly in Spalerno. A table stood in the center of the room with a number of chairs around it.

I sat down on one of the chairs and noted that the time on the room clock was twenty minutes to five. "What is my family doing?" I thought. By now, word of my arrest had surely reached my friends and even those in the new suburb adjacent to Leningrad. I sighed deeply.

I thought: "It is not appropriate, nor can I permit myself at this time to yield to thoughts that will cause me despondency. This is not the place for sadness or anxiety. This time and place require G-d's Divine mercy and His sustenance to be resolute in spirit, with an uplifted heart. Yet, at the same time, I must be fully aware both intellectually and emotionally of the details of G-d's constant Providence, a consciousness of the Divine that can only be evoked by bitterness of soul and retrospective reflection upon the sacred countenance of my father, the Rebbe of blessed memory,

The Rebbe interrupts his narrative again at this point with a sequence of periods and the phrase "letters of thought" (See page 54). He then writes the words:

"Father, sacred father," *followed by more periods.*

For a few moments I thought that this would be my place of imprisonment and that I would be confined here. But was it imaginable that they would put a prisoner in such a room, and not a common prisoner, but a prisoner upon whom revenge must be taken, one subject to false accusations, to coerce to reveal information?

I thought, "I must not dwell on these thoughts. I must prepare myself for a totally different mode of conduct in response to a totally new situation: the circumstance of being a prisoner. I must prepare myself for an experience, similar to the ordeal of the Alter Rebbe in the *Petropavlovskaya Krepostj*—Peter-Paul Fortress, and his questioning by the *Taini Soviet*—the Secret Commission. I must condition myself not to be panicked nor frightened, so that I can maintain a firm composure and not yield in the slightest to the right or left from my original firm intent, so that the dignity of the Jewish people should not be trampled underfoot. G-d will strengthen me."

Only three hours had passed and I was already weary. No limb was without pain. I had an intense searing in my head. My heart pained me and I sensed a sharp piercing on the left side, and in addition, my throat hurt intensely.

"At this moment," I thought, "I should not be concerned with the suffering of my body as compared to the anguish of my soul. And indeed my soul endures profound anguish. I plead with You, G-d, look down and see the suffering of Your nation. This was not an arrest of merely one prisoner, nor do they seek to punish me as an individual. For in my own right, who am I? They only persecute me because I am a descendent of my sacred forebears, one of the stones that support the pillars of the 'courtyards of G-d,'[1] the courtyards of Torah. I plead with You, G-d....

"In another five minutes it will be five o'clock. How gratifying it would be if they brought me my bag and permitted me to pray in this very room. And who knows, perhaps it was for this very reason that I was brought here. For G-d 'Who spoke and created the world' has specifically decreed that in the light-filled corridor—the place where I sat to rest immediately upon my arrival—a Jewish man should come on that specific day and hour. He would recite the morning blessings and the special prayer beseeching G-d to protect him from all harm. Perhaps G-d, may He be blessed, decreed that in this place a Jew should pray, so that an exalted and concealed Divine purpose should be brought from the potential to the actual. Any other rationale is inconceivable."

At that very moment I thought that every Jew who believes in G-d with pure faith and in accordance with the Torah teachings of the Ba'al Shem Tov, his successors, and my illustrious forebears would view this event with clear faith and certainly perceive that a dew of reawakened spiritual life was caused by the walking of just people on these stones or beams of wood, on this very floor, these dark corridors, and the ladders with steel rungs. This, despite the fact that the entire structure was built from the very beginning for the purpose of torture, to impose an oppressive yoke on the necks of human beings, to stifle and crush all those who enter within its confines.

Thus, a Jew entering this prison must fortify his mind and heart to recite verses of Torah and verses from the Psalms, to reflect upon the absolute, all-pervasive unity of G-d, Whose glory encompasses the entire world, pervading even this abode of the violent and the dungeons of those lusting for blood.

Suddenly in my mind there flashed the recollection of a splendid scene from nature pointed out to me by my father in my early childhood, when I was five or six years old:

We were traveling in the Crimean mountains between Sevastapol and Yalta in a covered wagon harnessed to a team of four horses, as is customary in that area. The travelers were my father, the Rebbe, of blessed memory, and, may she be designated for a long life blessed with spiritual and material goodness, my honored mother and teacher, the Rebbetzin, and sitting on the side of the coach, our cook, who also cared for me.

The journey was between tall mountains, an area abounding with boulders, and we traveled a circuitous path below the mountains; to our right were the mountains and to the left the sea.

We passed through one resting station located on a mountain and from there we journeyed through the mountains. At one point between stations we stopped to rest in a field where traveling coaches permit their animals to graze. We sat upon one of the boulders. My father turned to the side below one of the tall boulders, or more precisely, entered a small enclosure between two boulders, and recited the afternoon prayer, though it was only two o'clock in the afternoon.

My mother set out some food, for we still had to journey four to six hours. And though I wanted very much to be among the coachmen tending to the four horses, an intense concern weighed upon my mind. My father had told me that upon our arrival in Yalta, a special person would come to be my tutor. I did not yet know his appearance or his nature or habits, or how he would compare to my previous teacher, Reb Yekusiel.

Reb Yekusiel the teacher was an elderly man, seventy years old, if not more, but he had remarkable insight into the thought and behavior of small children aged four or five years old, and he could elicit their love for him and for the subject he taught them. Reb Yekusiel was an unusually gifted educator, and I cannot discern if he inherited this talent or if G-d had specifically singled him out and bestowed it upon him. Be it as it may, he was highly gifted, an utterly unique teacher.

The ingenious illustrations and examples used by Reb Yekusiel to explain the form of Hebrew letters would stimulate the interest of his students, and his lessons were impressed upon their minds and seared in their memory.

Thus, an *alef*- א - is comparable to the burden of the water carrier: a bucket on each side joined by a stick in the middle. Similarly, the form of the letter *alef* consists of two letter *yuds*, one on each side with a line joining them. Whenever we would see a water carrier we would immediately picture the letter *alef*. Our teacher provided such evocative depictions and illustrations that every occurrence in our lives reminded us of something we had learned.[2]

When we decided to journey to Yalta, my father, of blessed memory, himself started to learn with me, and I had already commenced the study of the *Siddur* and knew the meaning of a number of words. During the course of our travels we spent two weeks in Kharkov, where the doctor wished to perform tests on my father and monitor treatments. During this period my father himself learned with me, not entrusting me to a teacher. He also assured me that if I behaved properly, he would personally learn with me. However, when we left Kharkov, he told me that the doctors had instructed him to avoid the strain of speaking excessively, and he would therefore obtain for me a private teacher, and from time to time, my father said, he would learn with me himself.

I had matured enough to realize the obligation of a child to be concerned for his parents' well-being, and I was deeply pained by my father's fragile health. However, my intense desire that my father should himself learn with me prevailed on all other considerations, and I thought to myself that through my good conduct I would cause an improvement in my father's health.

So closely concerned was I with my conduct that, from the time of our Kharkov departure, no aspect of my behavior was done without forethought so as to be most appropriate. In this spirit I took a prayer book, sat upon one of the small stones, and reviewed the lesson on the chapter in Psalms, commencing, "The heavens relate G-d's glory."[3]

We sat down to eat. My father pointed out to us an area in the distance on the heights of a very tall mountain, and from afar we could see a large opening in a boulder standing on its top.

My father related that in the year 5644 (1884) he journeyed with his brother, Rabbi Zalman Aaron along the same route. They left the resting station at night; they stopped to rest in this field at six in the morning. From the distance it appeared that there was only an opening in the stone. Reaching it, they found a long cave, and within it, small boulders providing comfortable places to sit.

At that time my father explained to me that G-d created the world so as to enable each Jew's fulfillment of G-d's commands. Thus, a traveling Jew may realize that it is time for prayer. According to Jewish Law, he should not pray in an open field, but in an enclosed area. It was for this very reason that G-d created rocks formed in this fashion, similar to the shelter of a house, so that a Jew could pray in a proper way even in this remote area.

"Yes," I thought, "perhaps I will pray in this room. I still do not know what my fate will be, and whether it will be possible for me to pray today at all. For who knows what G-d's Divine Providence has decreed?"

Suddenly, the door opened and the official called for me to come forward. He inquired angrily, "Is this your bag and blanket?" A soldier stood near the door holding a glittering sword in his left hand and a rifle in his right. Two knives dangled from his belt.

"Yes," I answered, "these belong to me. Would you permit me to pray and to put on *tefillin* in this room?" Taking my *tefillin* out of the bag, I said softly, "Please, give me fifteen to twenty minutes to put these *tefillin* on as my religion requires, with the guard watching."

"No," replied the officer harshly. "What is this? Do you wish to make a synagogue even *here?* What do you have in your possession? Money, a watch, objects of gold or silver? Whatever you have give to me; a prisoner has no right to have precious objects. Your belongings will be well protected; personal belongings are returned to released prisoners. For those exiled, the valuables are sent to the place of exile, and for those executed, the valuables are given to the heirs."

I handed over all that I had with me. He counted and documented it all. He then gave me a receipt for everything I had given him: a simple watch and 58 rubles.

The officer turned to the soldier and said, "I now entrust you with prisoner 26818. Take him to the head of the Sixth Division. He already knows the prisoner's room. I have been ordered to tell you to carry his bag, for he is ill and has been promised assistance."

"Yes," answered the soldier, "but how will I carry his blanket?"

The officer replied, "I grant you permission to place the sword in your scabbard and the rifle in his case, for he will most assuredly not flee. Surely with two fingers you can crush such a fragile insect."

The *tefillin* remained in my hand, and the soldier rearranged his weapons and stared at me with smoldering arrogance. He opened the door and we proceeded through the dimly lit corridor till we reached an iron gate.

The gate guards, armed soldiers both inside and outside, stood like marble statues with their weapons. Their task was to guard the prisoners caged in the six sections, each section said to contain one hundred cells.

At the sight of my guard walking proudly with the bearing of one distinguished in rank accompanied by a Jew with a reddish beard and a Rabbinical hat, mocking smiles flickered across their faces. The senior guard read the confidential memorandum sent to the head of the Sixth Division and placed his seal upon it and the *yarlik*-prisoner document. The gate was then opened and we entered the "Third Section of *Geihinom.*"

Notes

1. An expression describing the Temple precincts, but used here in a broader sense to convey the entire Torah heritage exemplified by the sanctity of the Temple.
2. For more on R. Yekusiel, see *Sefer Hasichot* 5700, p. 161.
3. Psalms 19:2. (*Siddur*—included in daily morning prayer.)

CHAPTER FIVE

Tractate Geihinom, Third Section

We proceeded along the right side of the gate to a dim corridor lit by small candles. I began, not merely to ask but to entreat, in the profoundest sense of the word, my guard to permit me to put on my *tefillin*. I also told him that it was difficult for me to walk quickly. His answer was a curt "no," and he warned me that if I persisted, he would place me in solitary confinement.

I persisted in my request, asking for five minutes, or at least three minutes. I explained to him that I was a religious Jew and that donning the *tefillin* would entail only a very brief interval. The guard was smoking a cigarette; he answered that he knew full well what *tefillin* were. He had lived in a small city not far from a synagogue, and he was familiar with Jewish worship, but he would not grant my wish.

We proceeded, he in front and I behind him. Realizing that he would not relent, I decided to put on my *tefillin* as I walked. I placed the *tefillin* on my hand, and barely managed to place them on my head, when the guard saw what I had done. He struck me and pushed me toward the left to the ladder leading downward, and I fell down all the ladder steps. It is only with G-d's aid that I did not break a hand or leg. With great effort I managed to climb a few rungs; my pain was great.

I realized that the metal buckle of my belt had broken and that it had apparently cut a gash against my stomach. My heart contracted with pain; I felt that in another instant I would faint.

My guard screamed at me, "You will soon see the fine treatment which will be granted to you by the head of the Sixth Division: then you will forget all about your requests and your prayer. When you lie three or four days in the darkness with the mice in slime and mud, you will understand that you cannot transform Spalerno into a Jewish prayer house."

We came now to a broad corridor, with three ladders remaining before the third platform, where the office of the head of the Sixth Division was located. There he would judge me for my infraction of prison regulations.

I felt compelled to sit on one of the rungs to rest, for I felt an intense pain and I sensed blood flowing from my wound. I found movement very difficult, and I tried to repress my pain.

I gripped the iron rail of the ladder and climbed with great difficulty from rung to rung. My guard had already reached the third ladder, and I crawled forward like a broken old man.

The head of the Sixth Division stood on the landing to welcome his "distinguished guest." It appeared that he had already received word from the central administration. It was impossible for me to tell if he had been told to be lenient or strict, for his face was expressionless, like stone.

"Prisoner 26818," called out the soldier, extending his documents to the head of the Sixth Division.

"Good, good," barked the official, "hand over the merchandise. It is tedious sitting here with folded hands." He looked down and saw that I had still to climb up the third flight. "Hurry up, old man, why the slowness?—time is precious!" I reached the landing with the *tefillin* in my hand.

"Proceed for the search," shouted the officer, taking his leave joyously, whistling a melody. As he walked a few steps, he called out a command: "Petia, take the merchandise *yarlik* 26818 and get to work," meaning that he should receive me from the accompanying guard and bring me to his room, the administrative room of the Sixth Division.

The man, or beast, called Petia emerged from one of the cubicles or holes at the top of the landing, and approached me. When he finally reached me, he scrutinized me closely and murmured to himself, "Astounding, the rags that they have begun to bring here. Words are useless. A real parasite, a Jew with a long beard. Proceed, old man, to the search! Don't worry; we will clean you out as you deserve. We'll pull you apart bone by bone."

This specimen, Petia, was in charge of storing the belongings of the *yarliks* brought to Spalerno.

Petia was not armed, nor did he carry any kind of weapon, but nevertheless he resembled a destructive demon. He was of average height, but his face was livid and his voice like a lion's. He was cross-eyed, and he was unable to look directly forward like a normal person.

Petia proceeded before me to show me the way, leading me to the office of the head of the Sixth Division.

"Why do you limp?" Petia called out to me. "Has the Spalerno air affected you? Isn't the air good here? Like a scent, like fragrant scents. For parasites such as you we have such pleasant odors that prisoners on their very first day here collapse to the ground as though gripped by illness. They lie for two or three days in such a state, until the doctor comes. Sometimes he arrives late and all he needs to do is write the death certificate."

The wound made it difficult for me to walk. I needed to rest after every step. I felt the blood oozing, I was in intense pain, and my heart contracted within me.

"Why is your face so white," Petia asked, "Are you ill? After the search you can die. Things here are quiet. No one will disturb you, and no one in your family will know. The doctor will write a certificate for the office, the official will sign, an entry will be made in the office ledger. They will erase your file and throw your body into one of the dungeons below the building."

I cannot claim that his words did not affect me, yet I also considered what spiritual lesson could be derived from them.

All are fully aware of the teaching of the Ba'al Shem Tov that every utterance and breath, everything one hears and sees, contains guidance in the service of G-d.

Even one not endowed with superior intellect can easily understand how such words as Petia's can awaken a feeling of repentance, a feeling of fear of Heaven, a feeling of Divine Providence, a feeling of faith and trust. But even in such a situation the Evil Inclination can be found. There, too, Satan dances and tries to mislead with his guile and deception. Even in such circumstances, evil intervenes and tries to prevent an individual from being what he should be.

The pain overwhelmed me, and it was impossible for me to take another step. I rested for a moment.

"Why are you so slow?" he cried out, "Shall we bear you on a stretcher to the official for the search? Jew-face, cease your arrogance!"

"Petia!" the head of the Sixth Division called out, "where have you gotten lost? Where is prisoner 26818? Bring him immediately. I am waiting!"

"I am coming right away," Petia replied, and turning to me he said, "See, his patience has worn thin. The demon! A dog's carcass."

With G-d's help we reached the official's office, a small room approximately nine feet square, without a window, lit by candles, and with an iron door.

"Here he is," Petia said to the official, "This rag belongs to you. This is also merchandise? In a short while he will expire."

The official, hearing Petia's eloquence, smiled and with obvious delight responded, "What can be done, brother? If nothing else is available, this, too, will suffice. We cannot be without work."

"Very well, then," he said turning to me, "let us proceed with the search. What is it you have in your pocket?" He searched me briefly, finding nothing. He then looked through my bag and found the Rabbeinu Tam *tefillin*, the *tefillin* of Shimusha Rabbah, my *gartel*, and the books; he took them all. I was still holding my Rashi *tefillin* in my hand. He turned to Petia: "Return to your place. When I am through with the search, I will call for you."

Only one broken chair stood in that room, and I sat on it. The official continued with his search of my bag. I turned to him with a plea that he permit me to pray.

"No," he answered, with intense rage.

Since I was sitting behind him and held my Rashi *tefillin* in my hand, I did not wait a moment and placed them on my head and hand, recited the *Shema*, and commenced the silent prayer of *Shemonah Esrei*. At that very moment he concluded the task of searching and examining my belongings and turned to find me wrapped in *tefillin*. For a moment he stood astounded, gazing at me wide-eyed with eyes of bewilderment and panic; and at that moment he was transformed into a wild beast. The blood rushed to his face—with his two hands he grasped at my head *tefillin*, screaming, "Jew-face, I will place you in solitary confinement. I will pulverize your face, you demon...!"

As I concluded the blessing "And reign over us, You, G-d alone, with kindness and mercy,"[1] I was compelled to remove my *tefillin* for fear that he would tear the straps.

"Petia!" called the official, roaring like a lion, and then he said, "I pity you, old man. Even if I do nothing, you will die quickly. Your white face and black lips tell us clearly that we will not be busy with you for long here. What is your disease? Tell me."

I did not answer. I understood clearly that the single purpose of the officers and orderlies was to frighten and confuse the prisoners. They attempted to manipulate the prisoners the way a small child would play with cards.

"So, what do you wish?" asked Petia angrily, his eyes to the floor.

"Why do you ask? Don't you know what you need to do!" answered the official.

"What? To remove the refuse? Has he been registered already?"

"Not yet, I will shortly enter him into the large registry of the newly-arrived prisoners. Give him a number, then attach his file. Everything will be done according to rules and regulations."

Petia said, "Why are you so preoccupied with this refuse? Hand him over to be taken out. It doesn't really matter. He won't last for long anyway. A day or two and then he will die."

"No, things are not done in that way. Everything must be done strictly according to regulation. The file must be prepared properly and numbered in proper sequence. If he is ill, we will enter it in the necessary registry and send a certificate for the doctor. What is today, Wednesday? If I can manage to send it off today, then approximately by Saturday or at the latest, Monday, there will be a medical examination. Who knows? Perhaps before then he will be completely released from all his illnesses."

"One puff of smoke from a gunbarrel and it is done," commented Petia radiantly.

The officer replied, "That is a decision reserved for the upper levels. If I receive an order to dispose of the merchandise, I will do just that. Petia, you are thoroughly aware of the procedure. You have a good deal of experience."

Petia responded: "I know, I know full well. I love watching the prisoners quivering in their agony for two or three hours. There are, however, some who are so frail that when you lead them in, they walk like the dead. You just begin to remove their clothing and they die from fright; that's not satisfying. But when blood flows, it's a pleasure to watch. We sometimes need to wait five or six hours till it's all over. Then, only then is it gladdening. It's delightful for me to see them then—it's sheer pleasure!"

The officer commented: "I have already finished. Everything is prepared, file 26818. He should be taken to room 160, number four."

Turning to me the official said, "Now, old man, your name is 'number 160/4.' Go! Petia, receive number 160/4. Sign that you received 160/4, and that's it."

Petia wrote and signed. The officer stood nearby, looking on with a proud air and beaming face, and concluded, "Good, everything is in order."

Petia said to me, "Now you're all mine. Come, now you can rest. Take your belongings."

I extended my hand to take the *tefillin* resting on the table because they were all tangled. Thank G-d, that the officer had not opened the boxes. I picked them up and arranged them properly. I hoped that perhaps I could have them with me in my cell.

I pleaded with the officer that the *tefillin* be given to me because I had been promised them. The officer laughed and said, "Old man, forget everything. You must realize that you are a prisoner. Forget your nonsense. You will get nothing except what has already been given to you: your underwear, handkerchiefs, and nothing more.

"If it really means so much to you," continued the officer, "then you can write to the higher officials: if the order will be forthcoming, I will give you everything you want."

"Here," I said to the officer, "you are my officer. I have no need for superior officers in the higher echelons. I plead only with you to do this one act of mercy for me. Give me the *tefillin* and the religious books. My underwear, handkerchiefs and food are unnecessary."

How remarkable is the effect of a humbled self and soft words, so great to soften even a heart of stone. For a brief instant it seemed that the officer had been transformed from a tyrant into a human being. He stood reflectively scratching his head.

"Forbidden," Petia said, "it's forbidden. Stand and proceed!"

"Forbidden," repeated the official, "I cannot grant your request without authorization. If you wish, make a written request. Here is some paper; you may write."

Sitting in the office, I had noticed a bulletin board with a page of printed prison regulations. It stated that every prisoner who had money entrusted to the prison administration could submit his request or communication by telegram. It was only necessary for him to state in writing that the expense for dispatching the telegram should be deducted from his money, which was in the custody of the prison authority.

Invoking this privilege, I requested that I be allowed to communicate my plea by telegram. Petia petulantly protest-

ed that I could write it in my cell, for in a very short while
he had to wake the prisoners. Nevertheless, the official granted my wish.

I wrote three telegrams, all with the identical text:

I HEREWITH REQUEST TO IMMEDIATELY ORDER THE HEAD OF THE SIXTH
SECTION TO GIVE ME MY *TEFILLIN.*

RELIGIOUS RABBI, Y. SCHNEERSOHN,
SIXTH SECTION, CELL 160

I sent the telegrams to: 1) the chief prosecutor; 2) the
chief administrator of Spalerno; 3) the investigator, Nachmanson.

The prison official nodded his head after reading the
telegrams and commented: "He has great aspirations—look
how he writes to the chief prosecutor, the chief administrator and the investigator!" Then he burst out in loud, echoing
laughter.

I understood that I needed to ask for a receipt verifying
his acceptance of the three telegrams, with the assurance that
they would be immediately transmitted.

Petia asked, "Are you finished? Have you calmed down
already? Let us proceed."

I, however, turned to the official and asked, "And where
is the receipt for the telegrams?"

"What receipt?" he replied.

"The law states that an official must give written confir-
mation permitting, and then verifying, the transmission of a
telegram," I answered calmly.

My citing legal obligations compelled him to yield, and
he immediately took a sheet of paper and wrote a receipt. He
placed his seal upon it, then affixed his seal to each individual telegram and placed them in a large envelope, apparent-

ly used for collecting all documents and papers that were to
be transmitted to the administrative office.

Prior to my leaving the small room of the chief official of
the Sixth Section, I asked him the time, and in his kind gra-
ciousness he permitted me to look at the watch on his left
hand, which showed five minutes to six.

Thus I had concluded "Tractate *Geihinom*, Third Section."
I walked beside Petia, who was cursing me and all humanity, trying to terrify me with mortal fear.

I did not take Petia's harsh words to heart but looked around
at the huge structure of the Spalerno Prison. I marveled at
the unusual skill of the architect of this remarkable edifice; it
was built to provide for all prison matters. Moreover, there
were special areas in which to oppress, persecute, torment,
and torture human beings.

Spalerno was a building within a building. An outer wall
enclosed the entire area on all four sides, with dimensions of
approximately 300 feet by 300 feet. The inner wall was like
a square box, and within the wall there were cells with iron
doors.

Between the inner and outer walls extended a corridor
some 18 feet wide, and there were large windows in the
outer wall approximately 24 feet high. There were three levels within these 24 feet; a lower platform, above it a second,
and above it a third platform.[2] From the sides of the inner
wall there extended a walkway somewhat more than four
feet wide. Iron ladders led up to it, providing access to the
rooms and cells. The space between the outer and inner walls
on ground level was like an alley from which one could go
up to the first walkway which provided access to the second
floor and also to a ladder leading to the second walkway,
which is the third floor of the prison.

I proceeded on the walkway from the office of the head official to room 160. I did not know its exact location but followed Petia, who spoke continually, trying to frighten me with his many recollections, describing his great pleasure at witnessing the execution of rich people and clergymen. Once he waited for one of the executed to expire because it was his task to cast the cadavers of seven slain victims into one of the pits under the second dungeon in the subterranean section of the building. He had already disposed of them all, except for one who continued to shudder and "refused to die."

He continued: "He was like you, pale and large in build. Though he was the fifth victim executed, he outlived them all. He kept twitching his hands and feet the whole time.

"My comrade went to receive his payment. He was well rewarded for his labor, receiving 420 rubles (the payment for each execution was 60 rubles) and three bottles of vodka. My job was to bring them from the cell, prepare and separate them, and when it was all over, it was my responsibility to remove the corpses and clean the blood from the floor and walls of the room.

"That prisoner had still not died and I decided to drink some tea. When I returned he was still quivering. It was so pleasurable for me to gaze upon this scene that I drank the tea without sugar! My patience finally ran out. I kicked him twice with my foot and he lay there lifeless. Blood began to flow from his throat and his color immediately changed to the black of a beetle."

Although his words didn't frighten me, they nevertheless made a strong impression. I shuddered at his long, detailed story.

"Actually, you should have been placed in a cell all by yourself," said Petia, "for you are among those scheduled for execution. For those prisoners there is a special room for solitary confinement. But apparently all the rooms are full, so you were assigned cell 160.

"Here is your room." He took a large key and unlocked the latch of one of the iron doors. Then he took another key which opened the lock within the door itself. When the door was ajar he told me to go in and lie down on the floor. Before I could enter, he grabbed me sadistically with both hands, threw me into the room, and flung my bag after me. This greatly intensified the suffering and pain from my earlier wound.

He hastened to close the door, saying, "Sleep on the floor till the order comes to give you a bed, a container, a bowl, and spoon." I was disoriented and did not understand his references to the eating utensils. Petia closed the door and left.

Notes

1. *Siddur Tehillat Hashem* p. 55.
2. It seems likely that the Rebbe means that the third floor began at the *top* of the 24 feet.

CHAPTER SIX

In the Cell

The room was 2½ *archin*[1] wide, five *archin* long and 2½ *archin* high. The walls were of stone and one *archin* in thickness. The door was of iron. High on the wall close to the ceiling and facing the courtyard was an opening for a window. This opening was one *archin* in length by half an *archin* in width, covered by vertical iron bars and one horizontal iron bar, forming an intersecting barrier. The window was imbedded in an iron frame; the glass itself was only a handbreadth by a handbreadth.

Three thick iron chains, one on each side and the third in the middle extending from above, made it possible to open the window by suspending it on these iron chains. On the outside, an extended iron railing blocked the prisoners' view of the outside and prevented them from communicating with prisoners in the cells across the courtyard.

The room contained an iron bed fastened to the wall and an iron table, approximately three feet square, also fastened to the wall, and a water faucet. In a corner of the room there was a hollow vessel for the hygiene needs of the prisoner, an electric light, and a hot water pipe passing through the cell to provide warmth. This cell was normally for one prisoner, but with the increased number of prisoners, two, three, and even four prisoners were placed in such rooms.

The thickness of the cell door was approximately the size of a handbreadth, but I could not discern if the door was totally made of iron or merely iron-plated on both sides. The door was approximately six feet high and and three feet wide. There was a small opening the size of an egg in the middle of the door with an iron cover, to enable the guard to scrutinize and supervise the actions of the prisoners in the cell at any time. Approximately ten inches below this opening, there was a small square window through which the prisoners received food and drink. This window in the iron door was shut, locked with a latch.

There[2] were three men in the room whose identity I did not know. Two of them reclined on boards supported by wooden frames, and one reclined on the metal bed attached to the wall. One of them was a Jew and the other two were gentiles.

The first one, K.,[3] had been here for six months, and it was already nine weeks since he had been informed of his death penalty verdict. When his time would arrive, he would be given twenty-four hours notice.

This one-day advance knowledge was the law. He could use this period of time to request clemency and mercy through either a telegram or an express letter (which must be delivered within two hours) to be submitted to the superior official—or he could agree to be an informer or worker on behalf of the G.P.U. to purchase his life.

The second man was a Jew, Sh., who had been there for two months and had been called for interrogation only once.

He had been asked many questions about his business and about a number of specific business people. To the answer that he had no knowledge of them, the interrogator stated that he would sit in prison until he remembered. And if he found remembering difficult, the cold air of Siberia would refresh his memory. All he needed to be allowed to return home and eat his fill of bread was to agree to be an informer.

The third man was a gentile, S., a farmer on the Finland border, who it was decided, was a Finnish spy.

When I entered the room, the first man to give me a place to sit was S. He folded over his mattress (a sack of straw) and arranged my possessions.

I felt a flow of blood caused by the blow from the guard's ruthless push. I removed my garment, took wet handkerchiefs, and placed them upon my wound. The flow of blood, along with my pale white face, was an enigma to my fellow prisoners, and they questioned me although my clothing indicated that I was a Rabbi.

The Jew Sh. recognized me. Trembling, he cried out, "Rebbe, has the hand of the G.P.U. touched you also? In Heaven's name, what has happened to this country. Has there been a revolution? It is already more than a week now that hundreds of prisoners are led down the corridor outside our cell to their death, and we hear their groans and outcries." He said that he had been here over two months and it was only recently that such upheaval had set in.

He questioned me about the time and reason for my arrest. How had I received such serious wounds on my stomach and knees which appeared to have been caused by an iron bar, a wound from which the blood continued to ooze?

He spoke to me in Yiddish, as K. and S. stared open-mouthed. I did not reply for two reasons. Firstly, the pain was so excruciating that I was unable to speak. I also feared I had been placed among informers who would make false accusations. I had heard from experts on these prisons that when the prison authorities wished to elicit confidential information, they would place the prisoner with seemingly congenial and friendly cell-mates, and as time passed he would be lured into revealing his secrets.[4]

Suddenly an announcement was heard, "Awaken, it's time to get up."

At the sound of this announcement the prisoners hastened to get out of their beds, for the guard peering through the peephole would punish those who still lay down.

A short while passed, and then the announcement was made: "Prepare to receive bread." Each call was repeated three, four or five times with an intense effect on the prisoners. A clatter was heard in the outer corridor, for the locks on the cell door windows were being opened to give the food to the prisoners.

The same occurred in our cell: A guard accompanied by an attendant bearing bread called out to the prisoners:

"Prisoner one, take bread!" K. approached the opening and it was handed to him. "Prisoner two, take bread!" Prisoner Sh. also came close to receive his bread. "Prisoner three, take bread!" and prisoner S. repeated the ritual.

"Prisoner four," he addressed himself to me. I sat in my place with the wet, bloodstained cloth upon my knees and stomach. "For you there is no bread. When we receive the order, we will provide it for you."

I responded, "I do not need bread. Give me a pencil so that I can write a request."

The official answered, "You have already sent three telegrams. Enough. What more do you want? You have generated enough headaches for the administration with your foolishness. I will not provide a pencil for your message."

"In accordance with the law, you are obligated to fulfill my request. This is my privilege. If I so wish, I can dispatch a hundred telegrams every day."

I spoke to the prisoners and to the bread-bearing attendant: "Gentlemen, you are witnesses that this official has denied me that which the law allows."

Upon hearing the honorary title "*Gospoda*"—"Gentlemen" (a pre-revolutionary term of respect which was now forbidden to be uttered even in the gardens and parks in the U.S.S.R., to the extent that it was now used as a derisive term for the prison orderly while he fulfilled his tasks), his eyes flashed, his face reddened, and he said trembling: "Do you see this counter-revolutionary! He should be shot on the spot... without any... demon! Here is a pencil! Hurry, take it!"

I replied, "I am unable to stand. Give it to this gentleman (and I pointed toward K, who was sitting by the door) and he will hand it to me."

"No," answered the prison official, "That is forbidden according to the law. Every prisoner must personally receive the object given to him by the prison official. Stand and accept it."

"I cannot. I am ill."

"If so, then never mind. If you want to follow the law, then let's follow the law."[5]

He attempted to close the opening in the door, and I cried out: "According to the law, I demand to see the section head immediately." And he closed the window.

An announcement was sounded: "Prepare to receive hot water!" and each prisoner prepared his container.

Suddenly, we heard the door locks being opened. Terrorizing fear fell upon the three prisoners. They all remained seated in their places, their faces white as chalk. I did not understand the reason for their fright. I didn't know why, but I was also shaken. The door opened and the division head entered. His eyes fierce, his face livid, he called out, "Who asked for me?"

"I did," I replied.

"What is your wish?" he asked angrily.

"I want you to give me my *tefillin*, my prayer book, and my religious books as assured by the agents of the G.P.U. I also wish to be seen by a doctor."

"I will give you neither the *tefillin* nor the religious books. A doctor will arrive no sooner than tomorrow, morning or evening. You will not lose all your blood in the course of one or two days from so minor a wound."

Seeing that drops of blood were falling to the ground, he shouted to hasten and clean the cell because the cleanliness and sanitary condition of the cell was the responsibility of the prisoners. He turned to leave in a fury.

I said: "In the name of the law, I am addressing myself to you, the director of the Sixth Section, to inform you that I am commencing a hunger strike until my request for my *tefillin* and my religious books is fulfilled. Here is my protest written in accordance with the law."

Upon reading my protest, he became enraged. He approached me and raised his hand to frighten me, but did not touch me. Petia, who was also present, said that I should be taken down to the chambers, and there I would find peace from my distress.

"Yes," said the division head, "I will tell the upper administrator who hates overly-sensitive prisoners." Petia commented that I would then stroll on the Sabbath in Paradise.

The division head was pleased by this and then warned me that I should not presume to call him again and disturb him from his rest, for he had the authority to penalize me harshly. As for my hunger strike, he would adhere to the law and forward my request to its destination·either tomorrow or the next day. And they closed the door behind them.

The official's appearance in the cell made an intense impression on the prisoners. When his footsteps could no longer be heard, they began to whisper to each other; and because of my great pain I could not make out what they were saying.

A few hours passed, my pain diminished, and I wrapped myself in my *talit* and prayed at length. I also recited Psalms by heart. During the course of my prayers the time arrived for the daily outdoor walk. However, when the official saw that I was praying, he did not disturb me.

The time arrived for the hot water served at night to the prisoners.[6] I obviously took no water. A short while passed and the officer supervising the outdoor walk came to the cell. He called me to go outdoors, for it was a prison regulation that even those guilty of the most severe crimes had to briefly participate, although they would walk alone under guard. However, I declined to go.

At this time the doctor arrived, accompanied by the division head. He examined me and gave me a dressing for my wound, inquiring as to its cause. I did not reply but addressed myself to the official, requesting my *tefillin* and religious books. He ignored my inquiry.

The day passed, night cast its wings; a call was heard: "It is now time for bed; lay down and go to sleep." The Jewish prisoner Sh. gave me his place, saying he would sleep with either S. or K. He also gave me a pillow and urged me to hurry and go to sleep, for in another hour the clamor of those being led to the dungeons would begin, and the shrieks and outcries agitated and frightened all who heard.

The prisoners were already asleep in their places, yet I still sat. Petia the guard peered in through the door opening, and seeing that I was still awake, admonished me to sleep. I answered that I was waiting to say my evening prayers at 11 o'clock[7] and then I would sleep. I asked him if that time had already arrived.

He did not reply at all, but closed the viewing crevice and left. I remained seated and repeated those texts that I knew by heart. A short while later, Petia once again peered through the hole and informed me it was already 11 o'clock.

I prayed the evening prayers. As I was yet in the midst of the *Shema*, the sound of heavy footsteps could be heard, and then the opening of a door not distant from our cell.

Suddenly the cry of a man begging for mercy was heard, and then an officer's voice in Russian, commanding, "Place your hands on his mouth to silence him. Then a heavy silence. My hands and knees trembled. In a moment I would faint. From the courtyard I suddenly heard a bizarre cry *"Ay, Ay!"* and the sound of rifle shots.

A wellspring of tears flowed from my eyes. I felt incapable of uttering a single word. Fear gripped me upon hearing footsteps approaching our room. Once again a door opened. For a brief instant, a shriek could be heard, and then it was abruptly stifled. This was immediately followed by rifle shots and the scream of a human being crying out in intense pain. There was a second and third rifle shot. And it was silent once again.

I fortified myself and prayed, and when I was reciting "Hear our voice," a great tumult could be heard from the other side of the courtyard, the sustained screams of the slain and volleys of gunfire. This lasted until dawn—I obviously could not sleep.

A cool breeze wafted in through the window. The oppressive silence of death prevailed in that place of wanton murder. My pain had diminished somewhat, fear passed from me, an exalted spirit steadied me, and my thoughts merged into meaningful order.

My first thought was "It is written, 'the world abounds with G-d's glory,'[8] and this includes Spalerno also." The image of the *Petropavlovskaya Krepostj* and the imprisonment of my grandfather the Alter Rebbe, our first father, of blessed memory, stood before my eyes. I beheld this vision while fully awake.

How powerful is the faculty of thought and the quality of imagination, enabling man to envision mental imagery as if it were authentic experience. At such a time one can entirely transcend the wasteland of the physical and the material. The eyes blur, one's thoughts surge as though ascending within the realm of soul and spirit, man's pain-ridden flesh is alien and distant from him.

The sound of "Awaken, it's time to get up" roused me from my sleep. For I, too, was a prisoner and the fear of the guard affected me, too.[9]

"We are all alive," Prisoner K. said, "after so fearful a night, thank G-d that we are all alive."

He continued, "Every time I heard the approaching footsteps, I thought the end was near. In a moment they would open the door for me to follow them. There were moments when I trembled and instances when I actually thought that it was far better to perish than to endure the pain of agonizing uncertainty for so long. But when night passes and day arrives, it is possible, once again, to pour out your heart to the Almighty."

This was the first time in my life that I had been in such an environment, among such simple people who were removed from any kind of intellectual concern. The simplicity and sincerity of K. made a profound impression on me.

The twenty-five hours of my imprisonment had already stamped upon me the identity of a prisoner. I had to become accustomed to these circumstances, because I was a prisoner. All of my material and spiritual needs were within the narrow confines of this cell containing four men.

Initially, I could not comprehend how four people could coexist in this room with its stifling rancid air. How could they function and cope with simple bodily needs?

In these twenty five hours I experienced things of which I had never known. I saw ruthless people, callous, capable of shedding human blood. I heard the screams of the dying and the derisive laughter of bloodthirsty sadists.

I will never know the identity of those slain this night, whether Jews or non-Jews, businessmen, intellectuals, or clergymen. But one thing was clear: that those slain were totally undeserving of the bitter penalty imposed upon them. They were family people, fathers to children, sons to parents, husbands to their wives, breadwinners providing food and clothing for those dependent upon them. Who will care for their survivors?

"Who knows," I reflected, "if at that very moment, as these individuals are being taken to be slain, shrieking and pleading, at the very same time, their wives, sons and parents are in deep slumber with visions of hope, unknowing that at this very instant their husbands, fathers, or sons are being led to slaughter.

"How tragically unfortunate is the man who in his last moments is denied the opportunity to express his last requests to his survivors—to have a last glance of those dear to him, his beloved and his friends, to bless his children.

"Life in this prison is dreadful. Even more terrifying is death itself."

Possessed by such thoughts, I sat bent upon the boards vacated for me by prisoner Sh. I could find no rest from my pain. At that instant, I realized that I had been oblivious to my pain the entire night. Spontaneously, I let out a deep groan. At the same time I thought that such a groan was still far better than the lot of the people whose blood-drenched bodies were strewn in mounds in the subterranean chambers of this massive fortress.

My thoughts were suddenly interrupted by the announcement "Prepare to receive bread!"

Hearing this call, the faces of the prisoners lit up. They looked at each other with joy and beaming expectation.

I had not yet been apprised that the orderlies were changed daily and that there were three different ones. The first was Petia, with his usual expression of rage constantly on his face. The second individual was young, a good (!)[10] man, ethical and concerned about the welfare of the prisoners. The third man was elderly, neither good nor bad. The shift of the young guard was a good twenty-four hour period. He responded to all questions, providing pencils and cigarettes for those requesting them. Sometimes he would even bring old newspapers, and he was not begrudging in distributing the daily portion of hot water. Sometimes he would open the viewing hole in the door (when he was certain that the supervisory control would not pass) and chat with the prisoners, telling them of what was occurring in the outside world.

Thus, it was quite understandable that an upbeat mood prevailed in the cell when his voice was heard.

"You can talk to this guard," said prisoner K., "you can ask of him to request that the prison administrator provide your religious garments and your holy books."

"Indeed," said prisoner Sh., "he is a fine person; he will do for you whatever is possible. I will speak to him and ask him for a cigarette, but I do not have money."

During the search they took the currency that I had in bills, but not my coins. The section head in his later search also permitted me to retain my bag, which also held some coins. I counted them and found the sum total to be seven rubles and thirty-five kopeks.

This large sum astonished my cellmates, for according to the official regulation one could have no more than two rubles in coins.

I gave fifty kopeks to prisoner Sh. on the possibility that he could acquire a cigarette or at least some tobacco with cigarette paper.

I then learned that prisoner Sh. had four rubles, also on account, whereas K. and S. had nothing at all, although prisoner S. received a food package every week. Prisoner K.'s relatives, moreover, were in another city; so he truly had nothing, and his garment had withered away more than a month ago. He was a habitual smoker, but during his entire stay in the prison, he only could smoke the remnants from prisoners Sh. and S. His hair had grown long during these four months, for he did not have the ten kopeks necessary to pay the barber who came once every ten days to this section of the prison.

I loaned K. a complete ruble and to S. forty kopeks. Prisoner Sh. declined the coins, saying he would accept them only if something was available for purchase.

The time for bread distribution arrived. The guard opened the slot in the door and my cell-mates stood ready to say good morning to the guard and to receive their daily rations.

The crevice opened. The guard addressed the prisoners by their first names, first prisoner K, then Sh, and finally S. S. stood for a few moments in conversation with the guard, who abruptly ended the conversation, closed the opening, and moved on.

One hundred and thirteen prisoners had been taken from the sixth section last night. Some of the judgments were as follows: sixteen had been freed, thirty-two were transferred to Narim, one to Solovaki, six to Siberia, two to Kresty (a hard-labor prison in Leningrad), seven to Ural, nine were shot to death. Also, one hundred and eighty-three new prisoners had been brought in last night.

Prisoner Sh. was white as chalk. "Who knows," he speculated, "what will be the end of all the prisoners. It would be far better to go insane, to be confined in a mental institution, than to be here." He added reflectively to himself, "Perhaps the fate of those slain last night is far better than our present existence. They no longer live. They are at rest and we face an uncertain fate."

Prisoner K. protested this train of thought. He said that this brief respite was still far better than death because there was still hope for survival. "It is quite possible that the mercies of He Who is Above all things will shine upon us. A living person can hope to pass away with dignity amongst relatives and friends, and not like a beast or animal savagely torn apart in the depths of a forest, never to receive proper burial. No! G-d has created man that he should live and die with dignity."

The cell became very hot, and the prisoners all took off their clothing and went undressed. Sh. and S. were in their underwear, while K, who had no underwear, walked about as though on the day of his birth.

The air was suffocating and I sat fully clothed, actually experiencing cold. My cell-mates looked at me in amazement. I was obviously ill.

My heart intensely gripped me. The last distribution of hot water for the day had taken place and I still had not received my *tefillin*. It was already forty hours into my fast—not even a single drop of water had entered my mouth. Hours of physical pain and torture, but above all, torture of the soul: *tefillin, tefillin.*

The announcement was heard, "Lay down to sleep." I had already recited the evening prayers and was lying in my bed.

We suddenly heard footsteps approaching. We were gripped by fear. A few seconds passed. The locks were opened. The ray of a flashlight shone into the cell. We looked at each other with astonishment, confusion, and the very fear of death.

The door opened, three people entered, all of them with rifles; four stood outside with drawn swords.

Someone asked, "How many people are here?" "Four," answered one of the officials.

"Prisoners! What are your names? Answer in order."

"One!"

"Kutainik!"

"Two!"

"Sheftelevitch!"

"Three!"

"Saitin!"

"Four!"

"Rabbi Yosef Yitzchak Schneersohn," I answered.

One of the officials stared at me with an expression of contempt. They conversed for a few moments. We were so overwhelmed with fear that we did not comprehend what was being said.

One of them spoke in a low voice to me, "You, come with us."

All during this time I sat on my bed and a piece of wet cloth rested on the wound dressing provided by the doctor. I wore my *tzitzit* and my Rabbinical hat. I arose from my bed, removed the cloth, and prepared to go with them.

They awaited me and I could see that my cell-mates Sh. and K. were crying, tears streaming from their eyes. S. stood openmouthed like a marble statue, white as lime.

Without saying a word, I walked out into the corridor. One of them turned to me and asked that I show my belongings. I pointed them out and he looked at them from afar.

I proceeded a few steps behind them. One of the three led the group. Two of the sword-bearing soldiers walked in front of me and two of them behind me, and two of those who bore rifles and who had entered my cell were behind this retinue.

"Remove your hat and button up your clothing so that your fringed garment cannot be seen."

"No, I will not remove my hat," I answered.

"I hereby order you to remove your hat, and if you refuse you will have a bitter end."

"I will not remove my hat, and I want to know if you know who I am."

"Who are you?"

"I am the Lubavitcher Rebbe."

He asked, "So?"

I replied, "The Lubavitcher Rebbe is not frightened nor taken aback by your attempts to intimidate him."

He commented that the G.P.U. could overwhelm even the most obstinate person during the first forty-eight hours of his imprisonment. But he no longer insisted that I remove my hat.

Upon descending one ladder, the group of three dispersed to different corridors, taking with them two of the officials with swords, and now only two individuals with swords accompanied me.

Once again we descended a ladder and I proceeded slowly because the pain had returned with even greater intensity. I let out a deep groan and stood because I could not advance any further. Then one of my escorts told me that I would soon be in the interrogation room and I could rest there.

This had a twofold effect upon me: I now knew that I was being taken for questioning (the entire procession had given the impression that I was being led to the firing squad—may G-d protect us). I also sensed that even here, amongst such callous individuals, there could be awakened the fleeting emotion of human compassion in response to the groan of a prisoner.

I stood for a few moments and summoned up my remaining strength to go further.

"Here!" said one of my escorts, gesturing with his left hand. "We must wait here until we receive a command."

Since standing without support was difficult for me, I leaned on the wall to brace myself.

Seeing my frail condition, the second escort commented, "I do not envy you. Within a day or two they'll give you 'beans'" (a Slavic expression for the bullets of the firing squad).

"Comrade," responded the other person, "why say such things? Can you really anticipate the verdict of the judges? We must perform our duties and not go beyond that."

The first one answered, "I heard Comrade M. saying that the decision would be rendered within three days, well before the wealthy people can possibly influence our national leaders."

These words affected me profoundly, and I prayed from the depths of my heart that G-d should endow me with the fortitude to speak during the interrogation session without succumbing to fear.

While I yet reflected on these thoughts, the door opened and a resonant, authoritative voice called out assertively, "Bring the prisoner here. Give me the document of prisoner 3/160/4 (these identifying numbers indicated the number of the section—3[11], the room number—160, and the number of the prisoner in that room—4) to sign and you can leave."

Upon entering the room, I was gripped by a sense of deep apprehension. Three men were sitting, a gun resting in front of each. Clusters of weapons were arranged in all corners of the room. Their faces all had an expression of rage, and their eyes glimmered with animosity and anger.

The room was about 24 feet long and 15 feet wide. There was a table and a number of chairs. The room had a large broad window whose panes were painted over so as to prevent any viewing.

As I approached the table one of them spoke ...[12]

The Rebbe's account of his imprisonment includes the following incident, narrated by prisoner S. in the cell. The Rebbe describes S. as unable to falsify, completely unsophisticated and accustomed to relate what he knows without embellishment or exaggeration. S. is the speaker:

It was the first day of my imprisonment and I was unaware of the prison regulations. I was the only person in this cell at that time, and when they ordered me to go to sleep, I was not really tired, so I sat and smoked a cigarette. The guard glanced through the cell window and angrily ordered me to lay upon my bed. I answered with an abusive word of refusal. I hadn't yet finished my cigarette, when the door opened abruptly and the guard commanded me to follow him. I did. We descended ladder after ladder until we were in the corridor of the basement of the building. The guard opened one of the doors and instructed me to enter. I went into the cell thinking that he would follow me, but in an instant I heard the shutting of the cell door.

I took a step and found myself in oozing slime. The stench was suffocating. I lit a match. The size of the room was ten square feet. The walls were wet with moisture, and all kinds of creatures were crawling up and down the walls: white, black, long and large, and very frightful. The mud reached my ankles and I stood there all night. From time to time, I would have to push away the huge rodents that leaped at me with fearful, terrifying shrieks.

It seemed to me that a day had already passed.

["What about food?" asked K.] There, a person has no desire to eat, nor even to smoke; you lose your desire for anything in that frightening cell. I heard the door being opened and I thought, "Now they will take me to be shot."

I heard a whistle and the harsh command: "Come here."

I replied: "I can't see anything. Where should I go?"

The official lit up the room and I saw a steel bed, just as here, but the sight was terrifying!

"Leave!" shouted the official, and immediately I left the room.

"Go up the stairs," he commanded, and I thought to myself—Thank G-d, I will not die at the hand of the firing squad.

"Now," said the officer, "you will know how to address an official. It is forbidden to speak offensively to prison author-ities. You are a prisoner and I am your officer. I am taking you to sleep—will you sleep?"

"Yes, your Excellency, I will sleep."

Instantly he hit me several times across my cheek. I was confused and unsure of the reason for his blows.

"What sort of 'excellency' am I to you?" he raged. "You vile being, slave of the White Russians, spy. I will confine you to the cellar for three days, not just for the three hours you were locked in!"

I began to cry and plead, "You are my father, my dearest, my lord and master; I will obey."

In quick succession he struck me three times. The blows were painful; my teeth shook and blood flowed from my nose. I maintained my self-control and tried to stand at respectful attention as appropriate before a person of rank. I still remembered the discipline of the army in the old days. I was a man! I served my Czar four years. I fought in the Russo-Japanese war. I have seen generals, and I know that order is order—discipline, not games. You remain a faithful soldier until your last breath, not like the youths now who sing prattle commands of "Right" and "Left," and act like confused puppets.

"What sort of 'master' am I to you?" said the officer. "You must call me '*Tovarishtch*'—'Comrade.' There are no longer any masters; now we are all comrades."

"Very well, so be it, Comrade," I answered, "I will no longer address you in that way."

Again he struck me with his fist and said, "What sort of 'Comrade' am I to you? That is not the proper way to address an official. You must constantly remember that you are a prisoner and that I am your officer. You must say 'Comrade Officer.'"

Weak and broken, I walked forward. I wanted to sleep, I wanted to smoke. My teeth hurt and I felt pain in my sides. As I walked, I kept repeating to myself, 'Comrade Officer.' I must not forget it, I thought, woe to me if I forget! How pleasant it would be to sleep once again on the bed in my cell.

Notes

1. A former Russian measure, equivalent to twenty-eight inches.
2. Beginning here until p. 114 is from the Rebbe's additional memoirs published in *Yagdil Torah*, Vol. 5, Number 54, pp. 259-304. (Printed in *Sefer HaSichot* 5687 pp. 266 ff.)
3. Further on, their names are mentioned: Kutainik, Sheftelevitch and Saitin.
4. Later on, after he became acquainted with his cell-mates, he began to advise them and encourage them, in order to lift their spirits. He also gave them food; (*Sichat* 12 *Tammuz, Sichot Kodesh 5734*, vol. 2, p. 265; *Yisurim*, p. 50.)
5. Somewhere in between, the Rebbe received a pencil. While in prison, he also wrote a *chassidic* discourse and several other notes on cigarette paper, until the pencil was once again confiscated. (*Yisurim*, p. 23.)
6. "One of the prisoners asked for some more warm water. The reply was: 'Why do you need water, you'll soon be shot anyway!'" (*Yisurim*, p. 27)
7. Nightfall is quite late in Leningrad during the summer.

8. Isaiah 6:3.
9. "That morning, the guard opened the little window and called in happily, '130 pieces of meat were shot last night!'" (*Yisurim*, p. 26)
10. In the original text, the Rebbe occasionally notes an ironic detail by wryly inserting parenthetical punctuation.
11. This probably refers to the major section of the prison referred to by the Rebbe as: "Tractate Geihinom, Third Section," not the divisions mentioned earlier, as the Rebbe was in the Sixth Division.
12. The continuous narrative in the Rebbe's memoirs ends here. The balance of this chapter and the next consist of out-of-sequence passages of the Rebbe's memoirs. Details of the interrogation are in Chapter Eight.

CHAPTER SEVEN

A Prisoner's "Handbook"

The Rebbe includes in his account the following enumeration of the prison rules and regulations:[1]

1) The officials were prohibited from chatting with the prisoners; 2) All the cells were to be under double lock; 3) The prisoners were required to go to sleep and awaken at the scheduled time; 4) It was forbidden to sleep during the day; 5) It was prohibited to cover up the observation hole; 6) It was forbidden to look out of the cell window (though it was impossible to see anything anyway); 7) It was forbidden to throw anything through the window; 8) It was forbidden to smoke at night; 9) It was forbidden to light a candle in the room; 10) It was forbidden to converse at night; 11) From the hour of eleven at night until seven in the morning one could not request anything, this being the period between going to sleep and awakening; 12) It was forbidden to break the utensils in the cell; 13) Every prisoner was obligated to wash the floor of his cell (?); 14) Every prisoner had to submit himself to the authority of the prison guard; 15) If a prisoner defied the instructions of the guard or violated any of the above regulations, the guard was authorized to punish him according to his judgment by withholding food or hot water for a day or two. He could also refer this to the division head and recommend punitive punishment in a solitary confinement cell for a day or two, and in some instances, even for a week.

The daily schedule of the prison was as follows:

1) In the morning the prisoners were woken with the command: "Awake, awake, it is time to get up." Upon hearing these instructions all prisoners were obligated to get out of bed. The guard peered through the door opening, and woe to the prisoner whom the guard found reclining on his bed or stretched out on the floor after the morning call!

2) An announcement was heard, "Receive bread; prepare to receive bread." At that time someone opened the lock on the small window in the cell door, but there was yet another lock. The prisoners stood waiting for the second guard, who opened the second lock and who was in turn followed by the individual distributing the bread.

3) A kilo of black bread was distributed to each prisoner for the entire day, and usually each prisoner left over large chunks of it.

It was a source of joy for the prisoner, at the time of the door crevice opening, to see another human being, whoever he might be. Then the prisoner could also see the outer wall and enjoy inhaling the cold air from the balcony suddenly piercing through the gap. A moment after the bread distribution, the opening was closed with one lock.

4) A short while later, the announcement was heard, "Prepare to receive hot water." Each prisoner, upon entering his cell, received a wooden spoon, a bowl, and a large aluminum pitcher-like cup. Then the prisoners stood in readiness to receive this sweet gift—hot water.

5) An announcement was heard, "Prepare for lunch." Each prisoner cleaned his plate and spoon in anticipation of receiving his meal. There was lively speculation among the prisoners about what the fare would be that day.

6) Again the call was heard to prepare to receive porridge for the evening meal. Once again, there was animated movement within the room, one prisoner stating that he would take the food but not eat, another saying he would accept and eat, and the third asserting he would refuse the food. The

gap in the door opened and the orderly filled the dishes with black porridge.

7) The call was heard, "Prepare to receive hot water." Twice during the day a pitcher of hot water was given to each prisoner, but no more than one pitcher. Usually the pitcher was received by its handle; however, sometimes the orderlies apportioning the water instructed the prisoner to grasp the pitcher itself, not by its handle, with the intention of making the prisoner hold the burning hot utensil. Also, each prisoner was obligated to receive his own ration.

When I declined to arise from my place to personally accept my portion of food and my cup of hot water (on Friday the seventeenth day of *Sivan*, because on Wednesday and Thursday, and until the second serving of hot water on Friday, I fasted), I remained without water. Only later was it brought especially for me.

8) A call went out: "Room Number such-and-such, prepare for your stroll."

This announcement was received gladly by the prisoners, who waited for it all day—a full twenty-four hours—for it is a legal requirement to provide fifteen minutes of walking daily for each prisoner—to walk outside under the surveillance of a special group of guards.

This walk enabled the prisoners to be briefly freed from the cell enclosure, to breathe fresh air and gaze upon the sky; to walk two hundred yards, and to descend the steel ladders. Moreover, it provided an even greater opportunity: to see people and perhaps, discern a familiar face. The prison held thousands of people from varying backgrounds, many of them eminent and distinguished: skilled doctors, engineers, lawyers, advocates, businessmen, clergymen, people of different faiths, the aged and the young, middle aged, people of different skills, and many, many more.

The prisoners gave much thought to this "outing." First-ly, they reflected on how to derive some personal advantage, in addition to breathing the fresh air. At times one could suc-ceed in seeing a friend, and if opportunity smiled, commu-nication could occur through a subtle gesture, despite the rigorous supervision.

The stroll gave the prisoner something to look back upon when he returned to the cell. Sometimes he would return more broken than he left for having seen certain people, and sometimes, it bolstered the spirit, but whatever its effect, it was of great significance to the prisoners.

There was no fixed time for this stroll, and it could occur at any time during the twelve hours from the time of awak-ening until seven o'clock in the evening. Upon hearing the number of their cells announced, the prisoners prepared for the anticipated pleasure. Each brief moment of waiting seemed like a long time.

There was a special regimen to this interlude. After the announcement to prepare for the walk, a special person came to peer through the door opening to see if the prisoners were ready. Shortly afterwards, the door opened and a special orderly appeared with a contingent of armed soldiers, who accompanied the prisoners.

The commander of these soldiers was as dark as coal in complexion, tall, a cedar tree with broad shoulders. He was stalwart in build and his uniform was red and black. He was heavily armed, and he resembled a destructive demon capa-ble of consuming a hundred prisoners with one menacing stare. His voice was deep like a lion's; he constantly gnashed his teeth. He yearned to torture and oppress these creatures: How gratified he would be if he could crush one of these gnats!

Standing at the open doorway, the commander surveyed the activity in the cell. He then called the prisoners to go to their walk. Like sheep, they filed out. The officer closed the door and lead the insects out to creep upon the ground. (This was the officer's descriptive phrase as he led them forward.) In this way, they could refresh themselves from the "sweet pleasantness of the pure air"(?!) in the courtyard of the house of death—enclosed on all sides with the walls of the various structures of the Spalerno fortress.

(I had been informed of the following—I personally did not go to walk, even once.) The walking area was approximately eighty meters. In the center of the yard a wooden platform had been built taller than the height of a person. Upon it stood the supervising guard, and it was his responsibility to see that the prisoners observed all the positive and negative regulations of this stroll.

The positive rules for the walk were as follows:

A) To walk along the designated path, which circled the observation tower; B) The prisoners of each cell were to walk together; C) There had to be constant movement, it was forbidden to stand or sit.

The prohibitions for the walk were as follows:

A) It was forbidden to run; the prisoners had to walk slowly; B) The prisoners were not to speak aloud; they would only communicate secretly; C) The prisoners were not to walk with upright posture, thus preventing them from staring into the face of another prisoner; D) It was forbidden to direct one's gaze toward any window of the prison-fortress; E) It was forbidden to pick up any object from the ground; F) It was forbidden to throw anything; G) It was forbidden to wink with the eyes; H) It was forbidden to make any gesture with either one's hand or foot; I) It was forbidden to speak to any of the accompanying guards; J) It was forbidden to give or receive a cigarette.

Suddenly the command was sounded repeatedly: "The walk is over! Stand! Line up! Stand in order!"

At this point all the prisoners of one room were to stand together, leg-to-leg and shoulder-to-shoulder. A second command was given to march forward, and they advanced to the entrance way. Another command was given to form a line, one prisoner behind the other, and they began entering under the guard of soldiers. Each person proceeded to his cell. The cell doors were opened, and the imprisoned proceeded to their cages like submissive, bent-over goats.

9) The announcement was made to lie down and sleep, which caused fear among the prisoners. For if the supervisor were to peer through the peephole and observe any delay, he was authorized to punish the inmates. The nighttime was more dangerous, for he had greater leeway to discipline prisoners. This low-ranking guard could mete out "light" punishment without asking the section head. A lenient punishment was to sleep the night in the dark, humid subterranean dungeon with rancid air amidst vermin and rats. This was considered a light punishment, a subtle hint to ensure conformity with prison discipline, like an admonishing adult waving his finger at the nose of a child.

10) Every day pencil and paper were provided for prisoners to write requests to any official: either the section head, the investigator, the defense attorney, or the prison doctor. The pencil was provided for an hour or two and had then to be returned, because writing was generally forbidden.

11) Once a week, on Wednesday, the prisoner could send home his underwear for laundering; he could also return empty food utensils received from home. These were to be accompanied by an itemized list of what he was forwarding; one word might be added about the state of his health,

whether he was well or ill. On the other side of the paper he could request food or clothing.

12) Once a week, on Friday, food was brought for the prisoners to last for the week. There was a special procedure regarding the transfer of these objects until they arrived in the storage room of the head of each prisoner's section. Aside from the initial examination made when the objects were first brought to the administrative headquarters of Spalerno, there was a second check when they were given to the prisoners in the storage room of this section head.

Any kind of food that was a delicacy or a treat might not be transferred to the prisoners. It was forbidden to give anything in sealed or in whole form. Thus, even bread was to be cut into small sections to prevent the illicit transfer of a note or any form of covert communication. Clothing was also closely scrutinized at the seams for hidden contents.

On Friday all prisoners who had family waited in anticipation of being summoned to the officer of their sections to receive what was sent. This trip to the officer of his section and the pickup of the package uplifted the morale of the prisoner. Though the original written notes of the sender enumerating the gift items in the package were retained by the prison administration, the mere opportunity to see the handwriting of family members revived the prisoner's soul.

Some astute people wrote the package contents on a piece of material and sewed it to the package or sack containing the food and clothing; in this manner the prisoner could keep the actual handwriting for himself.

When the prisoner brought the gift to his cell, he cleared away the most important place upon which to rest his package. Was there any place of greater significance than his bed, which he used almost twenty-four hours a day? Upon it he slept, reclined and sat; upon it he cried, laughed, stretched out—and on his bed he fell asleep, even during the forbidden hours.

With love, affection, and great care he would place the package in the most important place in the cell, which he especially cleared for it. With riveted eyes he would scrutinize each stitch in the gift sack and study the package closely from every possible angle.

With great patience he read the writing attached to the sack, closely examining every single letter. He sought the hidden meanings between the lines, not only if there was an extra or missing letter, but even if one letter was larger and the other smaller, he interpreted this as possibly some important message. Using all kinds of ingenious reasoning the prisoner would formulate various imaginative possibilities. He speculated and analyzed why this letter had a sharp point above or below where it was missing in another letter. He would look at the letter *tzaddik*, for instance, written in two different ways—why was the point sharper in one case than the other? He stared at two *gimels*—why was one rounder than the other? Perhaps this was written by two people, but was it not really written by one person, whose handwriting he recognized? If so, why the variance? It must be a hidden message! But what was the intent?

The prisoner concluded his attentive scrutiny of the writing and began to examine the package closely. Last week the contents were placed in a wrapper from honey; today the wrapping is a flour sack. Was it possible that his family was informing him of a new accusation that he had bought and sold flour (engaging in illegal private enterprise), and that therefore they had sent the parcel in a flour sack?

Thus, the prisoner, with feverish interpretive hyperactivity, generated a million speculations. He closely examined "seventy-seven times" every item sent to him. Then there would be a prolonged silence, which stretched for several hours, each prisoner, lost in his own reveries, wondering about possible accusations and false charges. What condemnations and libels did they plan against him? Then his thoughts focused upon legal self-defense: superstructures of arguments against the charge of illegally dealing in flour, a charge obviously untrue, for neither he nor any of his forebears had ever been flour dealers.

13) Once every two weeks every prisoner could write a postcard to his family. Obviously, it was read by the censor, and therefore it was to be brief, describing the prisoner's health and nothing more.

14) Once every two weeks the prisoner could also receive a letter from his family, but if it was lengthy or otherwise displeasing to the censor, it was withheld.

15) Once every two weeks every prisoner having money in his account in the general administrative office could buy anything he desired in the general cooperative store of Spalerno. He was, however, to write explicitly and specifically what he wanted, stating that it should be paid for from his account. This request was forwarded for approval to the judicial investigator and the head of the administrative department, and if approved, he would obtain the items within two weeks.

These requests were to be submitted on the first and fifteenth of every month and not on any other day. The procedure was that on the first and fifteenth day, printed forms were distributed upon which the prisoners were to write their orders. In the evening a special person came to collect these forms and the prisoner would be informed of the decision within two weeks.

16) Once every two weeks reading material was distributed. Each prisoner was given two or three books, which he could not personally choose. The majority of the books were communist literature.

17) Once every three weeks, the prisoner could get a shave or a haircut. He had to apply a week in advance.

18) Each prisoner was required to go to the bathhouse to bathe once a month. If he so wished, he could do so once every two weeks, but the prisoner was required to bathe once a month minimally.

19) Once a month, the prisoner was obligated to go to the prison doctor's office for an examination. The prisoner had the right to request a visit from the doctor at any time, but it required a written petition to the section head, who then sent it to the general administrative headquarters. When the request was granted, the sick prisoner was accompanied to the doctor or visited by him. Experience indicated that it took three days for the request to be approved.

Once a prisoner had fully mastered the regulations, schedule, the hierarchy of administrators, their responsibility and procedure, he was then a "respected prisoner."

As mentioned, there was no clock in the prison. Therefore, the prisoners told time by the various announcements: time to awaken, bread distribution, warm liquid, food, porridge, hot water, time to sleep. They could approximate these according to the hours of the day. In the summer wake-up time was between 6:30 and 7:30, bread at 7:30, warm water at 8:30, and food was distributed at 1:00 and later. Porridge was distributed from 5:00 onward, and the second hot water distribution was from approximately 6:00 to 7:00. Sleep was at 10:30.

The *Midrash*[2] states: How did Moses know [while on Mt. Sinai] when it was day and when it was night? When he heard the ministering angels say "*Kadosh*" (Holy) he knew it was day; and when he heard them say "*Baruch*" (Blessed) he knew it was night.

Time is both short and long, depending on its content. Sometimes many hours pass by as fleeting moments. In other instances, only three hours are prolonged and experienced as an unusually lengthy period of time.

At this point in Reshimat Hama'aser *the Rebbe writes an account of some of the events of early generations of the* Chassidic *movement, along with thoughts concerning the* Chassidic *path in general. This is followed by recollections of the Rebbe's childhood.*[3]

Notes

1. In one of his talks, the Rebbe's son-in-law and successor explains at length the reason the Rebbe wrote this chapter, its significance, and the lesson that can be learned from it in the service of G-d. (*Sichat 12 Tammuz, Sichot Kodesh 5729*, pp. 262-270)
2. *Yalkut Shimoni, Tisa, Remez 406. Midrash Tehillim* 19:3.
3. These sections are available in *A Prince in Prison*, Sichos in English, 1997.

CHAPTER EIGHT

The First Interrogation

T**he**[1] *first interrogation took place on Thursday night at ten o'clock. The Rebbe was entering the third day of his hunger strike protesting the withholding of his tefillin. Sick, suffering, weary, broken from physical abuse, and even further weakened by his sustained fast, he was brought for interrogation. While this interrogation, as well as those that followed were prolonged and derailed, we present all the facts known to us to date.*

There were four interrogators: two Russians and two Jews, Lulav and Nachmanson. The chief interrogator was a Russian named Dichtriov.

The Rebbe was led into the large hall. The walls were of marble imbedded with large tubes. These were the notorious "walls with ears," for by means of the tubes, the conversation of interrogator and prisoner could be listened to and transcribed by the G.P.U. agents sitting in adjacent rooms.

As the Rebbe entered,[2] he turned to the interrogators and commented: "This is the first time that I have come into a room and not a single person has arisen from his place!"

"Do you know where you are?" his interrogators asked.

"Most assuredly," he answered, "I am in a place that is not obligated to have a *mezuzah*. There are various such places which are not required to have one, as, for example, a stable or a bathroom."[3]

The Rebbe began by saying that he would like to relate a story. The interrogators, their hands resting on the weapons of destruction lying on the table, stared at him with daggers in their eyes and replied, "Answer the questions posed to you, nothing else!"

The Rebbe answered calmly that he was accustomed that even *mitnagdim* would listen to him tell a story…and without hesitating the Rebbe began:

"A *maskil* (proponent of the 'enlightenment') an *apikores* (an atheist), once visited my [great] grandfather, the 'Tzemach Tzedek'"

Nachmanson interrupted: "In all probability a person like myself who does not believe."

"No," answered the Rebbe, "he was a person well-versed in Jewish knowledge, and you are a simple ignoramus….This person," continued the Rebbe, "asked the Tzemach Tzedek: 'why is it that in the *Megillah*, when Mordechai sent word by messenger to Esther of Haman's evil decree, the word *yehudim* (Jews) is spelled to include the letter *yud* twice; whereas in the later verse of the *Megillah*, describing the Jewish deliverance, 'And for the Jews there was light,' the word '*yehudim*' is spelled with one *yud*?'

"The Tzemach Tzedek replied: 'The two *yuds* correspond to the Inclinations, the Virtuous and Evil. Both the Evil and Virtuous Inclinations contain the ten qualities of the soul.[4]

" 'There are two kinds of *yuds*: the *yud* of the Virtuous Inclination and the *yud* of the Evil Inclination. Haman's decree was not directed specifically against G-d-fearing Jews, those of the Virtuous Inclination; he sought also to destroy those who were irreligious, who acted in accord with the Evil Inclination. They, too, were included in his edict.'

"The visitor then asked: 'Why is it that in a later verse, "And the Jews in Shushan gathered," we once again find a spelling of two *yuds*?'

"The Tzemach Tzedek replied: 'This is because the Jews in Shushan, being in the center of all the events, perceived and were profoundly influenced by both the danger and the miracle of *Purim*, so much so that even non-observant Jews returned to the ways of Torah and Judaism.' The Tzemach

Tzedek concluded: 'The same is true of you; when you will suffer greatly, then you, too, will change greatly.'

"Afterwards, the *maskil* was afflicted with fever which lasted three months; affected by his suffering, he repented and returned to Judaism."

The Rebbe concluded his narrative and then added, "When you will also suffer, you, too, will change."

The interrogators, and particularly Lulav, treated the Rebbe in a very coarse and derisive manner. They angrily jeered and mocked him.

"Stop your mockery," said the Rebbe, "and return my possessions to me; you have no right to accuse me."

"Silence!" Lulav cried in wrath. He stretched out his hand and said: "Do you see this arm extended before you? From the time I was fourteen years old it has been engaged in the sacred task of annihilating those, such as yourself, who oppose enlightenment. We will destroy them all. You request *talit* and *tefillin*? We will cast them into the refuse."

The Rebbe pounded on the table and cried out: "Vile creature!"

Their faces then assumed a somber demeanor and the chief interrogator started to cite various accusations, enumerating them in great detail:

"You are accused of abetting reactionary forces in the U.S.S.R.;

"You are accused of counter-revolution;

"The Jews of the U.S.S.R. perceive you as a prominent religious authority and you rule over them;

"You also exert influence upon the Soviet Jewish intelligentsia and, in addition, upon bourgeois America;

"You are the leader of those who rebel against enlightenment;

"We are well aware that you have used your influence to create a network of *chadorim, yeshivot* and other religious institutions throughout the U.S.S.R.;

"You have used your authority to coerce religious Jews to uphold these institutions;

"You have an extensive correspondence with foreign lands and receive thousands of letters from all parts of the world;

"You conduct secret communication through messengers that travel to foreign lands for the strengthening of religion in the U.S.S.R. and thus for waging conflict against the Soviet government."

As he finished, he placed a large bundle of letters upon the table and said: "This package reveals your true face. These letters are filled with strange and suspicious mystical content. What are your counter-revolutionary links with Professor Baratchenko?"

The Rebbe replied patiently: "I will not deny that Jews think of me as an authority, but I am not guilty of any crime. I do not compel or assert my authority over anyone. I have never used my authority in any way against the Soviet Union.

"The charge that I rule over Jews is wholly incorrect. Coercion and force are wholly alien to the ways of *Chassidus.* Leadership, from a *Chassidic* viewpoint, means striving to achieve moral refinement and spiritual perfection, so that others may learn to emulate and proceed in these same paths.

"This cannot be achieved by force or power—only by means of a free will. *Chassidim,* of their free volition, emulate their Rebbe and leader.

"It is my responsibility to concern myself with enabling anyone who so desires to remain faithful to Judaism. All this occurs by free choice and under circumstances of absolute freedom. What crime is there in this?"

During the course of his defense, the Rebbe expounded upon the nature of *Chassidus*; the Russian interrogators asked Lulav to explain.

The cycle of history had come full circle. One hundred and thirty years before, his ancestor the Alter Rebbe had been forced to clarify the concept of *Chassidus* for the officers of Czar Paul. Eighty-seven years before, the Tzemach Tzedek had been compelled to explain *Chassidus* to the minister of Czar Nicholas. And now, their descendant was under constraint to expound the tenets of *Chassidus* for the members of the G.P.U.[5]

The Rebbe continued: "I have never levied taxes on anyone. I have asserted that Jews are obligated to learn Torah. And when Jews adhere to this precept, of necessity they create schools for children and *yeshivot* for those more mature.

"There is no prohibition in Soviet law against *chadorim* and *yeshivot*. Karlinko, the chief State Prosecutor of the Soviet Union, has explicitly declared: 'No official law has ever been promulgated in the Soviet Union against institutions of religious education.' With whom is it incumbent to comply: Karlinko or Lulav?

"None of my efforts and public statements," continued the Rebbe, "are in defiance of Soviet law. If my words concerning the study of Torah evoke a dedicated response, and if our kinsmen in America who send money to aid their relatives add modest sums for Torah study and the educational needs of the children of their relatives, this is not a threat to the Soviet Union. The very reverse is true; in this way, foreign currency flows into the land and strengthens the economy.

"As to the correspondence mentioned, Professor Baratchenko had started a study of Jewish mysticism. He somehow was of the opinion that the *Magen David* symbol expressed profound kabbalistic concepts and that mastery of this knowledge could be a source of great power.

"Four years ago, during *Sukkot* of the year 5685 (1924), he turned to me as an authority on *Kabbalah*, and requested that I reveal the esoteric meaning of the *Magen David*. I tried to convince him that he had succumbed to an illusion, for nothing is to be found in *Chassidus* about great powers inherent in the *Magen David*. Empty-handed, the professor still persisted in sending many letters with the one plea that I reveal the hidden significance of the *Magen David*. This is the full significance of the correspondence with Professor Baratchenko.

"Give heed to me, Lulav," the Rebbe directed in a firm voice, "you desire to accuse me with a new Beilis accusation. Remember how Czar Nicholas engaged professors and scholars in order to direct a blood libel against the Jews and was discredited? You will be frustrated in your intentions. I am very well aware of the unscrupulous methods used by you and your associates when you wish to imprison a simple Jewish teacher: the placing of contraband or illegal whiskey in his possession to enable you to imprison and exile him. Do you also intend to besmirch me with false accusations? To level the filth of falsehood against me? You will not succeed, for the accusations are totally untrue.

"My words and deeds have constantly been open and clear to all. Three years ago, in the year 1924, I wrote a letter to the Jews of America urging them to support the Jewish agricultural settlement in the Soviet Union.

"You imprison me as an enemy of Jews and the state. This is totally false. Though great differences divide us, I support those efforts that are creative, as my letter to America substantiates.

"Do not bring untrue accusations against me. I do not act covertly, but openly and before the eyes of all, and I do not act in defiance of Soviet law."

"True," commented Dichtriov, "we are very well aware of your positive attitude toward agricultural settlement as well as your letters to America, and we regard these actions with esteem."

Ignoring this exchange, Lulav continued his questioning, still in a rude and offensive manner. When the Rebbe once again asked for his *tefillin*, Lulav did not respond, but rather erupted with new abuse, aided by his colleagues. "Remove your *talit katan* immediately! Remove it, remove it! Cast aside all of your foolish observance!"

"If you compel me to remove my *talit katan*," replied the Rebbe, "I will refuse to answer your questions. And if you intend to achieve this by means of fists and guns, I challenge you to do so." This reply stilled any further effort in this matter.

At one point Nachmanson smiled and said: "Lulav, do you know that my parents were childless, and only after my father went to the Rebbe of Lubavitch did they give birth to a son—and that son is Nachmanson who stands before you."

The inquiry concluded late at night; at the end Lulav, who had a tendency to stammer, blurted out in anger: "B-B-B-ut in another twenty-four hours you will be shot!"

Notes

1. From this point the narrative is based on *Yisurim*, pp. 35 ff., and the Rebbe is referred to in the third person.

2.   This story and the one following, were recounted by the Rebbe in 1942, as recorded in *Sefer HaSichot* 5702 pp. 82ff, and elucidated in *Likkutei Sichot,* Vol. 19, P. 126.

3.   See *Berachot* 61a and *Kitzurim V'He'arot L'Tanya,* p. 81ff.

4.   The numerical value of the letter *yud* is ten.

5.   When asked his age the Rebbe replied "over one hundred and fifty years old," referring to the years since the Alter Rebbe's founding of Chabad Chassidism, which was personified by the Rebbe (*Sichat* 12 *Tammuz, Sichot Kodesh* 5718, p. 261).

CHAPTER NINE

Efforts to Free the Rebbe

The Rebbe returned from the questioning racked by agonizing pain. For three full days no food or water had passed the Rebbe's lips. The Rebbe had firmly resolved to maintain a steadfast composure during all interrogations by the G.P.U., never to waver or betray any signs of weakness or anxiety to them. This resolution would not only pertain to religious matters, but also to his general demeanor. He would conduct himself as if these people were insignificant, to the extent that they would be in his eyes, in the words of the Ba'al Shem Tov, "truly naught and non-being."[1]

Finally, on Friday afternoon a Jewish member of the G.P.U. brought him his *tefillin* and sacred books.[2] The Rebbe told him, "I will not eat the prison food—only that which is brought from my home. As for water, I will accept it later from the prison, but only on the condition that it is warmed up in a vessel used only for water."[3]

The G.P.U. official was infuriated: "Do you intend to give kosher supervision for the prison kitchen?"

The Rebbe replied: "I am not a Rabbi who is involved in providing kosher supervision."

He then immediately put on his *tefillin* and began to pray.

A short time passed and the prison guard brought three whole *challah* breads for the *Shabbat meal*—*challot* brought especially for the Rebbe from his house. This was an unusual occurrence. Under normal circumstances, bread or anything else brought for the prisoner was cut into small pieces as a security precaution against smuggling prohibited objects into the prison. The Rebbe received the *challot* whole: this incident expressed a deferential policy toward him. From that time, the cell guard displayed a far more respectful attitude.

The Rebbe's first *Shabbat* meal in prison consisted of a *challah* and some cold water from the faucet. He recited *Kiddush* and made the blessing on bread out loud, chanting them with a particular Chabad melody.

The change of attitude on the part of the guard expressed itself in many ways. One instance: there was no clock in the cell, so the Rebbe had no certain knowledge of the time for the evening prayers, which could begin during the lengthy summer days at approximately 11:00 o'clock at night. The Rebbe requested of the guard that when the time came, he should knock on the door, and thus indicate to him that it was time for the evening prayer. The guard complied with his request.

About four o'clock *Shabbat* afternoon they came to photograph the Rebbe.[4] When they arrived, the Rebbe was praying at length, with his *talit* over his head. Seeing that the Rebbe was absorbed in his prayers they left quietly.

When they arrived a second time, the Rebbe's face was uncovered. The Rebbe didn't understand what they wanted, and was at a point in the prayers where it was prohibited to interrupt, so he motioned with his hand and they left.

When the Rebbe finished praying, his cell-mates explained to him why they had come.

The third time they arrived, the Rebbe explained that it was *Shabbat*, and he could not be photographed.

When they came back after *Shabbat*, the Rebbe sat down with his *yarmulke* on, and spread his *talit katan* with all of the *tzitzit*, so that not only the front two should be seen, but the back two as well. Then they tried to explain that in a Spalerno photograph it is not important to see *tzitzit*.

The Rebbe replied, "If you want to photograph me, you need to photograph me as I look!"

And they took the photograph without requiring the Rebbe to conceal the *tzitzit.*[5]

At the conclusion of the first *Shabbat*, the guard gave the Rebbe two matches so that he could make the *Havdallah* blessing over the flame. Afterward the Rebbe recited the prayer "And may G-d grant you . . ."[6] with profound inner gladness.

When the Rebbe was taken from his cell for fingerprinting, he met there his secretary, Mr. Lieberman, and several other Jews who had been arrested. The Rebbe told them: "Several of you will be sent to Solovaki and several will be freed. Wherever you go, you must relate that you were in Spalerka and that you saw the Lubavitcher Rebbe, who was arrested for establishing *chadorim, yeshivot* and *mikva'ot.* No one should be hindered from these activities, and the work must continue."[7]

During the early days of the Rebbe's imprisonment a different drama had been unfolding outside the prison.

Seven o'clock[8] on the morning of the arrest, a meeting was held at the Rebbe's home. By ten o'clock the meeting moved to a Jewish community center. Representatives from every party attended, except, of course, the communists.[9]

In order not to provoke the G.P.U., it was decided not to turn abroad for help, but to focus all efforts domestically. By noon, the Leningrad Jewish leaders were on the phone with their brethren in Moscow, informing them of the situation and the plan of action.

The Rebbe's son-in-law, Rabbi Shmaryahu Gourarie was dispatched to Moscow.

The Jewish leaders in Moscow concurred that pressure from abroad might worsen the situation—that would be even more proof of the Rebbe's counter-revolutionary activities—the capitalists would be supporting him.

On *Shabbat* morning, a religious Jew from Moscow arrived with the ominous news. The G.P.U. had decided to execute the Rebbe.

Previously, the committee was afraid to turn to the officials in Moscow. It had happened in the past, that when the G.P.U. of one city applied pressure upon that of another city, the latter would immediately shoot the prisoner, so as not to have to succumb to the pressure of another entity. Now, however, there was nothing to lose. Telegrams were dispatched to President Kalinin and Prime Minister Rykov, and the directors of the G.P.U. in Moscow. In order to escape the notice of the G.P.U., the meeting was held in a bank office.

At any moment the G.P.U. could quietly take the Rebbe into a cellar and shoot him.

The news of the Rebbe's arrest had shaken Jewish communities across the world to their foundations. Messengers were sent to Haditz, Niezin, Rostov and Lubavitch, to pray for the Rebbe's safe release at the gravesites of his predecessors.

Important Jewish centers such as Kharkov and Minsk were also notified. Prominent delegations of Jews from the largest Soviet cities came to see Menzhinsky, the director of the G.P.U. He refused to receive them.

The communities in those cities decided to gather petitions vouching for the Rebbe's loyalty to the Soviet authorities. Several hundred thousand Jews across the U.S.S.R. signed petitions begging for the Rebbe's release.

The committee also turned to the President of the Red Cross in the U.S.S.R. Madam Ekaterina Peshkova.

The entire Jewish community, religious and non-observant, received the news with shock and apprehension. Synagogues were filled to capacity. Old men wept while reciting

Psalms. Monday and Thursday of the first week were declared fast days in communities across the U.S.S.R. Russian Jewry observed *Yom Kippur* twice that week. The Rebbe was in the G.P.U.'s net.

Back in the prison, after many requests, the Rebbe was visited by a doctor in the middle of the second week of the Rebbe's imprisonment. Although the Rebbe's health was far from satisfactory, the doctor determined that, although it might be against his will, the Rebbe was able to remain in prison.

There were continued improvements in the treatment received by the Rebbe. On Friday, the tenth day of his imprisonment, the Rebbe was allowed to send a brief note to his family for the first time. "I am well," he wrote, "do not worry. Please send me a Likkutei Torah and a Chumash Devarim."

Forgetting his surroundings, he began *Kaballat Shabbat* (prayer to greet *Shabbat*). In his silk cloak, *gartel* and hat, the Rebbe began to sing *Lecha Dodi* ("Come, my beloved, to greet the bride, *Shabbat*").

Although the Communist government had canceled all outgoing telegram service the previous week due to their national security crisis, word of the Rebbe's arrest spread abroad.

In Germany,[10] the Chief Orthodox Rabbi of Berlin, Dr. Hildesheimer, and Dr. Leo Baeck, Reform Rabbi of Berlin, went to visit Dr. Oscar Kahn, a Socialist Deputy of the *Bundestag*, the German Legislative Body, to enlist his help.

Dr. Kahn went to the German Foreign Minister, Dr. Gustav Strehzman. Immediately, the four of them went off to the German Chancellor, Weissman. Weissman had good relations with the Soviet Ambassador in Berlin, Krestinsky.

Ambassador Krestinsky explained, "I am sure that the Soviet government has no benefit from arresting the Rebbe. It must be the *Yevsektzia*." He promised to do his utmost to clarify the matter with Moscow.

Although the committee had decided not to contact the international community, telegrams began to arrive from across the globe. From England, France, Germany and America, from Israel and the Scandinavian countries.

Chassidim in several U.S. cities notified the synagogues and community organizations of the situation. Many of them immediately sent telegrams to their senators, congressmen, and to the Joint Distribution Committee.

In the United States,[11] Mr. Yekusiel (Sam) Kramer, a prominent attorney, went to Washington. U.S. Senators William Borah (R-Idaho), Royal Coperland (D-NY) and Robert Wagner (D-NY), and Congressman Jacobstein were also involved with the efforts. Senator Borah was the Chairman of the Foreign Relations Committee; the senators were on "The Peace Committee" and were prominent in the Soviet's eyes. The U.S. State Department was also heavily involved.

Most of the *Chassidim* in the U.S. did not believe the rumors, as they heard of it only from the newspapers, and did not rely upon that information.

Considering the historical backdrop of the time, when the entire world was certain of imminent war with Russia, the international efforts to free the Rebbe are all the more impressive, as relations between the U.S.S.R. and the rest of the world were extremely strained.

That first week President Kalinin and Premier Rykov received thousands of telegrams.

In response to their inquiries, the committee received one reply: "The Rebbe was arrested as a serious offender. His situation has not changed."

After several days, many prominent Christians, and even communists, began to speak out on the Rebbe's behalf.

Finally, Madam Peshkova notified the committee; the death sentence had been stayed.

The committee met again. The sentence was now ten years hard labor on the Solovaki Islands. Their work needed to continue.

Another delegation went off to Madam Peshkova: The new sentence was also life-threatening and it was imperative to have it commuted, or at least postponed. And if that was not possible, the government could at least allow the Rebbe to travel first-class at his own expense. The Rebbe was ill.

By June 29th, newspapers the world over were reporting that the Rebbe had been released.[12] The communists had begun to spread this misinformation to ease the international furor.[13]

On Tuesday evening, the 21st of *Sivan* (June 21),[14] the Rebbe was taken for a second interrogation. Lulav was the main interrogator, and the Rebbe was again asked about the nature of *Chassidus* and subjected to the same accusations of counter-revolutionary activity. He warned Lulav that his attempts to implicate religious Jews were likely to result in a Russian anti-semitic backlash against all Jews, himself included. When he returned to his cell he also recorded the details of this interrogation on cigarette papers.

On Wednesday, 29 *Sivan* (June 29)[15] the Rebbe was supposed to depart for the Solovaki Islands of Siberia. The Rebbe's family had been notified of his imminent departure, and they came to the prison to see him off on the 7:00 p.m. train. Word spread quickly, and a huge crowd had gathered outside Spalerka. They didn't know of Madam Peshkova's success.

While the crowd waited outside, the Rebbe was being called for his third interrogation.

New accusations were added. For hours, Lulav and the interrogators tried to get the Rebbe to implicate himself. Finally, Lulav said to the Rebbe, "Your situation is very grave. As an exile-prisoner you will suffer great pain. You can save yourself from this punishment. If you agree to the rabbinical conference, issue a proclamation that you regret your anti-conference position. Give your blessing to the conference, and you will walk out of here momentarily."

"I do not regret anything," the Rebbe answered. "You can threaten me with the worst punishments. You will not achieve your aims. You can send me to Siberia for it, but I will not deviate from my ways."[16]

Thursday, *Rosh Chodesh Tammuz*, (June 30) eleven o'clock in the morning, a guard entered the Rebbe's cell and commanded him to stand. The guards spoke Russian, but it was the Rebbe's decision to respond to them in Yiddish, and he replied that he would not stand.

Prison procedure required that the prisoners stand whenever they received any kind of information. This was to demonstrate that the prisoner was subject to the authority of his captors; it was for this very reason that the Rebbe refused to stand.

It seems that one of the guards was a Jew who understood the Rebbe's Yiddish reply. To the Rebbe's answer, the guards responded in Russian, "If you will not obey, we will beat you." The Rebbe responded with a non-committal "*Nu* ...." The guards beat him harshly and departed.

Later another group of guards entered the cell, with Lulav among them.

"Rebbe," Lulav said, "why this strange conduct with them? Why are you so stubborn? They have come to inform you that your sentence has been lightened; therefore, if you are told to stand, then do so!"

The Rebbe remained totally unresponsive. Lulav asked, "Should they beat you?" Again the Rebbe did not answer.

Once again the guards began to pummel the Rebbe and then left. One of them struck him under the chin, and the Rebbe suffered pain from this blow for years afterwards. A group of guards came to the cell for the third time; among them was a Jew named Kavelov. They instructed the Rebbe to stand, and he again refused. Kavelov began to beat him, but to no avail.

Kavelov, infuriated, cried out in Russian, "We shall teach you!"

The Rebbe replied in Yiddish, "We shall see who will teach whom."

After a while some guards came to the cell and told the Rebbe to proceed to the office. There he was informed that his sentence had been reduced, as Lulav had mentioned. He was to be freed from prison and sent for three years exile to the city of Kostroma.

As the Rebbe approached the table, he observed the documents of his case lying there. He noticed that the first line had been crossed out, nullifying the original death sentence. The next line stated that the Rebbe should be sent away to prison for ten years to Solovaki; next to it was written "*Nyet*—no!" On the last line was written: "Three years Kostroma."[17]

When the Rebbe was told he was being sent to Kostroma for a three-year term, he was asked at the same time which class train accommodations he desired, and he answered, "*Mezhdunarodni*"—"international"—the top class reserved for high government officials and affluent businessmen. He was asked if he was capable of paying the high price, and the Rebbe replied that if the money confiscated from his bureau at the time of his arrest was inadequate, he would instruct the members of his household to pay the remainder.

It was Thursday; the Rebbe asked when the train would arrive in Kostroma, and he was told on *Shabbat*. The Rebbe declared that he would not travel on *Shabbat* under any circumstances, so he remained in Spalerka over Shabbat.[18]

Notes

1.   *Sichah* 12th and 13th of *Tammuz, Likkutei Sichot*, vol. 4 pp. 1061-67.
2.   The Rebbe related in one of his talks:

> When I was there [i.e. imprisoned by the G.P.U.] I did not have any religious books. The first one brought to me was a Book of Samuel. When I opened the book, it happened that it opened to the verse (Samuel II 21:17) "You shall no longer go out with us to battle, so that you extinguish not the lamp of Israel." When I saw that this verse had been providentially designated for me, I rejoiced greatly and took careful note of it." (*Sichat Shabbat Parshat Pinchas* 5687 at the *Seudat Hoda'ah, Sefer Hasichot 5680-5687*, p. 174.)

The identification of the volume as a Book of Samuel seems to be an error in the version of the Rebbe's talk given in this source. The Rebbe's successor reports in one of his talks (*Sichat 12 Tammuz, Sichot Kodesh, 5734* vol. 2, p. 258. Available in *Torat Menachem, Menachem Tzion*, vol. 2, p. 413) that he saw the volume and that it was a Book of Psalms upon which the verse had been inscribed by hand. Both talks are printed from unedited notes made by those present, but this latter version seems much more likely since single-volume Books of Psalms are considerably more common and there are other references to the Rebbe's Book of Psalms in the sources on the arrest. For instance, the Rebbe's successor later identified the books the Rebbe took with him as a book of *mishnayot*, a Book of Psalms, a *Tanya*, and a *Pentateuch* (*Sichat 12 Tammuz 5734*, vol. 2, p. 258).

3. Until his release from Spalerno, the Rebbe continued to fast from morning until evening, and he added to the regular text of the prayers the section said on fast days, to entreat G-d for release from his terrible situation. (See *Sichat 12 Tammuz, Sichot Kodesh* 5734, vol. 2, p. 265; *Yisurim*, p. 27.)

4. The known sources for this event do not seem to conclusively indicate which *Shabbat* it was, but the sense of danger conveyed in some versions suggests that it was the first.

5. *Sichot Kodesh, 12 Tammuz, 5721*, p. 216. See *Torat Menachem 5711* (vol. 3), p. 194.

6. *Siddur Tehillat Hashem*, p. 235.

7. From an as-yet unpublished entry in the *Reshimot*, Journals, of the Rebbe's successor, Rabbi Menachem Mendel Schneerson.

8. *Yisurim*, pp. 42-48.

9. See the prologue for a description of the political situation in U.S.S.R. at the time.

10. *Yisurim*, p. 53. *Yisurim* material continues on p. 145.

11. *Toldot Chabad Be'artzot Habrit*, pp. 32-34.

12. See, for example, *Jewish Telegraphic Agency Bulletin*, June 29th and July 2, 1927.

13. Very little is known of the involvement of the Rebbe's son-in-law and successor, Rabbi Menachem Mendel Schneerson, in achieving the Rebbe's liberation. Unlike the others involved, Rabbi Menachem Mendel himself never spoke of his efforts. This one occurrence though, gives us a hint of the extent of his involvement: At the *Farbrengen* of 12 *Tammuz* 5716 (1956), Rabbi Schneur Zalman Duchman, a *chassid* who was in Leningrad at the time of the imprisonment, stood up and announced, "If not for the Rebbe (Rabbi Menachem Mendel Schneerson) we would not be celebrating the 'Holiday of Liberation' of the 12th of *Tammuz*" and he began to detail the Rebbe's actions. The Rebbe smiled at this "breach of decorum" and gestured for him to stop talking. Later, when *Chassidim* asked him to share his knowledge, he replied "The Rebbe doesn't want me to tell" (*Algemeiner Journal,* July 15, 1977).

14. *Yisurim*, p. 54

15. *Yisurim*, p. 59

16. *Yisurim*, p. 60

17. *Sichat Shabbat Parshat Pinchas 5687* (1927) at the *Seudat Hoda'ah*.

18. *Sichah* 12th and 13th of *Tammuz, Likkutei Sichot,* vol. 4, pp. 1061-67. When the Rebbe re-told the story, he proudly finished, "Thank G-d, I spent that *Shabbat* in Spalerka!" (*Sichat Kodesh,* 12 *Tammuz,* 5729.) See Appendix 9.

CHAPTER TEN

Exile to Kostroma
and Final Liberation

On the afternoon[1] of Sunday, the third of *Tammuz*, (July 3), after nineteen days of imprisonment in Spalerno, the Rebbe was called to the prison office and informed that permission had been granted him to return home, where he could remain for six hours. At eight in the evening he was to take the train for Kostroma on the Volga River, a remote city deep in the interior of Russia, where he would be exiled for a period of three years. The Rebbe was to arrive at the station before eight, for if he missed the train, he would have to spend the night in Spalerno.

In a letter dated *Iyar* 19, 5688 (May 9, 1928) the Rebbe relates:[2]

Prior to my return home, the G.P.U. official warned me:

a) "You can only remain in your home six hours and by eight in the evening you must leave the city;

b) If you remain even slightly longer, you will be returned to prison;

c) At eight o'clock you must travel by train to the city of your exile, Kostroma;

d) If for any reason you miss the train, you must return to the prison, and if you will not come, you will be brought there by force;

e) You must travel directly to Kostroma and not stop at any point along the way. You are scheduled to arrive there tomorrow evening (Monday, the 4th of *Tammuz*);

f) Tuesday morning you must appear before the head of the G.P.U. in the city of Kostroma. You will be in his custody for a period of three years, until June 15th, 1930;

g) You must sign this document stating that you are to appear on July 4th, 1927, before the G.P.U. of the city of Kostroma."

The Rebbe returned home at a time when his family feared they would never see him there again. He entered his office and delivered a short talk to his family expressing gratitude to G-d for having saved his life. *Chassidim* who listened to the talk, which could be heard through the door, related how deeply moved they were, and that a heart of stone could melt at hearing these heartfelt words.[3]

All the rooms of the house quickly became so filled with people that one could barely move. At seven o'clock, the Rebbe started preparing to leave.

The Rebbe took leave of his family within the hour.

Accompanying him on his travel to Kostroma were his future son-in-law, Rabbi Menachem Mendel Schneerson, his daughter, the *Rebbetzin* Chaya Moussia, and also Rabbi Althaus.[4]

A great assemblage of people gathered at the station.

Many persons wanted to buy tickets so they could accompany the Rebbe for at least a short part of the journey, but the G.P.U. had forbidden the selling of tickets for the train. The Rebbe arrived at the station under heavy guard: three members of the *Cheka* Secret Police, Civil Police, soldiers and officers of the Civil Investigation Department.

From the step of the coach, the Rebbe turned to the large gathering and spoke these inspiring words:

> We raise our lips in prayer to G-d:[5] '*Yehi Hashem Elokeinu imanu ka'asher haya im avoteinu. Al ya'azveinu ve'al yitsheinu.*'[6] 'May G-d be with us as He was with our ancestors, to neither forsake nor abandon us.'—and

He will in fact be with us, though our merit is not comparable to that of our ancestors, who endured intense self-sacrifice for the sake of Torah and its *mitzvot*. In the words of one of my revered ancestors in response to a governmental decree regarding Jewish education and the Rabbinate:

We did not depart from the Land of Israel of our own free will, nor shall we return to the Land of Israel by virtue of our own capabilities. G-d, our Father and King, has sent us into exile. He, may He be blessed, shall redeem us and gather in the dispersed from the four corners of the earth, and cause us to be led back firmly and proudly by *Mashiach,* our righteous Redeemer—may this occur speedily, in our times. However, all the nations of the world must know the following: Only our bodies were sent into exile and subjugated to alien rule; our souls were not given over into captivity and foreign rule.

We must proclaim openly and before all, that any matter affecting the Jewish religion, Torah, and its *mitzvot* and customs is not subject to the coercion of others. No one can impose his belief upon us, nor coerce us to conduct ourselves contrary to our beliefs.

It is our solemn and sacred task to cry out and state with the ancient steadfastness of the Jewish people— with courage derived from thousands of years of self-sacrifice: "Touch not My anointed nor attempt to do evil to My prophets."[7]

Thus spoke one utterly willing to endure self-sacrifice. And we lack the minimal measure of courage to tell the entire world of the evil acts of a few hundred rampaging Jewish boys, conspiring against Jewry and the faith of our people.

It is well-known that the law permits us to study
Torah and perform *mitzvot,* and it is only because of
false informers and untrue accusations that we are
imprisoned and sent to hard labor camps.

This is our plea to G-d: 'Forget us not nor abandon
us.' May G-d give us the proper strength not to falter
because of bodily suffering. On the contrary, let us
accept this pain with joy. Every measure of anguish
inflicted upon us for supporting a *cheder* for the learning of Torah, for performance of *mitzvot,* should
increase our fortitude in the work to strengthen
Judaism.

We must remember that imprisonment and hard
labor are only of this physical world and of brief dura-
tion, while Torah, *mitzvot,* and the Jewish people are
eternal.

May all of you be well and strong physically and
spiritually. I pray and hope to G-d that my temporary
punishment will evoke within us might, for the ever-
lasting strengthening of Judaism. And there shall be fulfilled in us that 'G-d shall be with us as He was with
our ancestors to neither forsake nor abandon us.' And
that 'there shall be light for all Jewish people in their
abodes.'

The train moved. After traveling a short while, it stopped,
then moved again, traveling non-stop for the next 24 hours
until it arrived in Kostroma. As soon as word of the Rebbe's
imminent departure to Kostroma was known, the *chassid*
Reb Michoel Dworkin had set out to Kostroma, arrived
earlier than the Rebbe, gathered together children and
established a *cheder,* and also fixed the *mikveh.* A Lubavitcher *chassid* had prepared in advance a lodging for the Rebbe
in the house of the city *shochet.*

The train arrived late at night. According to instructions, the Rebbe was to report to the local authorities immediately upon arrival; however, the Rebbe decided to delay his appearance until the following morning. On Tuesday, the 5th day of *Tammuz*, the Rebbe came to the G.P.U. authorities of Kostroma.

The administrator of the local *Cheka* was very sullen and antagonistic. After filling out the various questionnaires, the official declared: "You are an exile-prisoner. You are a criminal receiving punishment for your crimes against the Soviet government, and you are required to remain in this city. You may not leave the precincts of this city without special authorization. If you desire to change quarters, you must inform the G.P.U. beforehand. And you may be certain that the police will be informed of all your movements and of all that happens in your home. You are also required to make a weekly appearance before the appropriate G.P.U. official."

Kostroma was a large city with few Jews, barely one hundred, simple and unlearned. There was one *shul*, and the Rebbe went there to pray. During the time of his prayers, the synagogue filled with people—many of them Jews who had not crossed a synagogue threshold for many years. They, too, came to see and hear the Rebbe's heartfelt prayers. Kostroma, the remote city of exile, had suddenly acquired a Rebbe!

The Leningrad group dedicated to the goal of rescuing the Rebbe decided to further its efforts to secure his full release. It was decided to appeal to the chief Soviet prosecutor, Karlinko, for clemency toward the Rebbe. They believed that the efforts of Madam Peshkova, together with the intense political pressures from foreign lands, would be of great influence in this matter. It was decided also that Rabbi Shmaryahu Gourary, the son-in-law of the Rebbe, should travel to Moscow and discuss this matter with the rescue group there.

The meeting of the Moscow group came to the conclusion that before meeting Madam Peshkova and appealing to Chief Prosecutor Karlinko, it would be wise to explore their possibilities of success. In response to their inquiries, they were advised to slacken their efforts for the next six months, since the G.P.U. would firmly resist any attempts to achieve full amnesty, having already suffered so great a loss of prestige in this case. It would be perceived as brazen defiance on the part of a religious group to petition for total freedom barely one week after the Rebbe had been sent into exile, and demeaning to the G.P.U. itself.

Despite this advice, they decided to maintain their efforts. Once again they sought the aid of Madam Peshkova, who renewed her own exertions. A Jewish assistant of Madam Peshkova traveled to Leningrad to see Messing, the head of the Leningrad G.P.U., to prevail upon him to soften his stance and not to obstruct the efforts to achieve freedom for the Rebbe.

However, Messing, who had actually been partially responsible for the imprisonment of the Rebbe, refused to listen.

"There is no hope for reducing the sentence," he replied. When asked for a rationale for his position, he replied that it was fear of anti-Semitism: "Many priests and clergyman of the Christian and Moslem faiths have been imprisoned and sent to exile, and none have been released. If liberty is granted to the Rebbe, there will be a clamor and outcry that this entire matter is under the control of the Jews." An ironic aspect of this posture was the fact that Messing was known to be a virulent anti-Semite.

Messing also threatened that, even if Moscow could give the order for complete freedom, he would countermand it.

Should the Rebbe return to Leningrad, he would find some new ruse or pretext to imprison him once again. Madam Peshkova's emissary returned with this negative response.

The Moscow group was undeterred by Messing's obstinate answer and decided to persist in their efforts until they would achieve the complete, unconditional release of the Rebbe. It was, however, self-evident that the Rebbe's return to Leningrad would be perilous, because of Messing's all-pervasive control. Meanwhile, Madam Peshkova made intensive endeavors to exert influence in the highest rungs of Soviet officialdom, finally succeeding.

On Tuesday, the 12th of *Tammuz* (July 12), coinciding with the Rebbe's birthday in 5640 (1880), the Rebbe appeared at the headquarters of the G.P.U., accompanied by Rabbi Althaus, for his obligatory weekly appearance. The local G.P.U. official greeted him genially and informed him of his release: "You are totally freed from the need of any further appearances.

"The order has been received to grant you full freedom, and I regard it as a personal privilege to be the first one to inform you of your complete amnesty." Rabbi Althaus reacted with intense emotion; his face went from deep livid to palest white and back; the Rebbe had to calm him and help him regain his composure.

The Rebbe's daughter Chaya Moussia called the family in Leningrad by telephone to inform them of the liberation, with the added warning to keep the information secret. She also sent a telegram to make sure they understood clearly. They signed the telegram, in the place of the name, *Bli Pirsum*—"without publicity."[9]

The news of the Rebbe's release spread with lightning speed. Even before he returned to the house of the *shochet*, the news was already known. Upon his arrival home, the Rebbe viewed an unusual and moving spectacle—the *chas-*

sid Reb Michoel Dworkin was dancing round the house, a bottle of wine in his hand, and upon his lips a melody with Russian words, singing with great feeling: "*Nyet, nyet nika-vo*"—"Nothing exists aside from G-d!" The small son of the *chassid* danced about in somersault fashion, his feet flailing above and his hands firmly placed against the fence.[10]

On that very day, the 12th of *Tammuz*, a large gathering of Jews assembled in his lodging in Kostroma and he delivered the *ma'amar* (*chassidic* discourse) beginning: "G-d is among those that help me."[11]

The day was a legal holiday and the G.P.U. office could not issue the actual Certificate of Release until the following day.

The order from Moscow was so emphatic that when the Rebbe arrived the next day to receive his release papers, the official asked that he write next to his signature that the delay was not their fault.[8]

After receiving the Certificate of Release, the Rebbe delivered the *ma'amar* "Blessed be the One Who bestows good upon the unworthy, who has bestowed good upon me"[12] (Appendix 1), before the large number of people who again gathered in his dwelling.

On the 14th of *Tammuz* (July 14), at nine in the morning, the Rebbe left the city of Kostroma a free citizen, and on Friday the 16th he arrived in Leningrad accompanied by two emissaries especially chosen by the Jewish community of Kostroma. Because of the aforementioned danger, only a brief stay in Leningrad was planned.

The Rebbe arrived home in Leningrad on the 15th of *Tammuz* (July 15). On the Shabbat following his return to Leningrad, the Rebbe was called up to the Torah (*Parshat Pinchas*), and recited the benediction of *Hagomel*—the blessing to G-d for release from dangerous straits. At the *kiddush*

after the services, the Rebbe said another *ma'amar* beginning with the same verse as the one he delivered in Kostroma, this time elaborating and explaining at greater length
the concepts of the first discourse.

At the Sabbath meal, celebrated also as a *seudat hoda'ah*—
a feast of thanksgiving as required by Jewish law when one
is saved from peril—the Rebbe said another *ma'amar*, "Lift
up your hands in sanctity."[13]

In a letter about these events, the Rebbe wrote,[14] "The
great clamor in the land, the prayers and supplications
through the saying of Psalms day and night in hundreds of
cities, and the proclamation of fast days, all these were heard
in the loftiest of Heavens, and G-d influenced the hearts of
judges to ease their verdict. During the first ten days of my
imprisonment, word of my arrest reached the highest levels
of government here, as well as in the officialdom of foreign
lands. It appears that influence from abroad strongly affected the leaders of this country in their final decision."

Many years later, on the 12th of *Tammuz* 5705 (1945),
the Rebbe declared:[15]

> I was confined for nineteen days. At such a time one
> is subject to the ordeal of controlling one's eyes, sealing
> one's ears, and desisting from speech. In that period of
> my life, I lost all sense of gratification that is derived
> from material things, not only for a while, but perma-
> nently. Then I did not think of myself at all.
>
> What thoughts could I have about myself while
> being constantly confronted with the fragility of life? I
> heard the begging of the prisoners, pleading for life,
> only to see them taken out to be shot ten minutes later.
> My own idea then was that the initial decay of a seed
> is a preliminary necessity for later flourishing and
> growth.[16] I never experienced a sense of solitude; I was
> always mindful of the fact that I possessed revered

ancestors: my father, grandfather, great grandfather, and all the luminous, holy figures whose courage and merit would endure eternally. I reflected on my father's discourse, 'She girds her loins with strength'[17] which I had heard thirty years before.

Notes

1. *Yisurim*, p. 62.
2. *Igrot Kodesh*, vol. 2, pp. 65ff.
3. The Rebbe's talk is printed in *Sefer Hasichot* 5680—5687, p. 168.
4. From a recent interview with the daughter of the man in whose home the Rebbe stayed.
5. *Likkutei Dibburim*, Vol. IV, p. 1384 ff. *Sefer Hasichot* 5680–5687, p. 169.
6. *Melachim* I 8:57.
7. Psalms 105:15.
8. *Sichat 12 Tammuz, Torat Menachem*, vol. 3, p. 193.
9. Deposition of Rebbetzin Chaya Moussia in *Agudas Chassidei Chabad vs. Gourary.*
10. *Sichat Yud-Beit Tammuz*, 5725.
11. Psalms 118:7.
12. *Siddur Tehillat Hashem* p. 186
13. Psalms 134:2. The four discourses mentioned here were printed in Riga, *Kuntres* 14, 5691 [1931]. They were also printed in *Sefer Hama'amarim Kuntreisim*, vol. 1, pp. 352–380. The *sichot* of the *seudat hoda'ah* are printed in *Sefer Hasichot* 5687, pp. 172ff.
14. *Igrot Kodesh*, vol. 2, pp. 64.
15. See *Sefer Hatoldot*, Vol. 3, pp. 222; *Sefer HaSichot* 5705, pp. 114.
16. An apparent reference to the eventual flourishing of Yiddishkeit in the U.S.S.R.
17. Proverbs 31:11.

CHAPTER ELEVEN

Departure From Russia

When the Rebbe returned to his home in Leningrad, it was clear that the Leningrad G.P.U. would not rest in its efforts to retaliate against him. Many people streamed to the house of the Rebbe, but he refused to grant an audience to anyone.

Suddenly, a harsh article against the Rebbe appeared in *Der Emes*, the *Yevsektzia* newspaper, with a demand that he be arrested and imprisoned in the remotest region of Siberia. Lulav, Nachmanson and Messing mounted a sustained campaign against the Rebbe, depicting him as a counter-enlightenment personality who was somehow beyond the law. It became clear that the Rebbe needed to leave Leningrad.[1]

He moved to the village of Malachovka, which was a half-hour's journey from Moscow.

All signs pointed to the necessity of the Rebbe's leaving Russia. Every moment seemed fraught with the peril of re-arrest. Lulav and Nachmanson were obsessed by their antagonism toward him; departure from Russia seemed the only logical alternative. Even now, to accomplish this created a new array of problems. Would the government actually grant permission? Once again Madam Peshkova was asked to intercede, and she gave her assurance that she would do all that was possible to aid the Rebbe.

Dr. Hildesheimer and Dr. Leo Baeck of Berlin once again visited Weissman, the German Vice Chancellor, who in turn spoke to Krestinsky, the Russian ambassador in Berlin. He assured them that he would attempt to influence the government officials in Moscow. It became apparent, however, that this effort was not adequate for the present situation, unless some special justification could be advanced for the Rebbe's leaving Russia.

The religious community in Frankfurt sent a document attesting to the Rebbe's destination as Rabbi for that community. Dr. Oscar Kahn, the Socialist member of the *Bundestag*—the German Legislative body, revealed that he had many close friends in the Russian ministry, and he accepted upon himself the responsibility of bearing the document to Russia and attempting to influence the government officials to permit the Rebbe to leave Russia.

Highly relevant to the situation was Dr. Kahn's unusually great influence in Russian government circles. Many years before, in the period before the October Revolution, Lenin had been arrested abroad, and Dr. Kahn, a lawyer by profession, expended great effort on behalf of Lenin.

Now this very same person was to be the spokesman on behalf of the Rebbe before the highest echelons of the Soviet government.

At the same time, another document designating the Rebbe as Rabbi of Riga, was brought from Latvia by the *chassid* Rabbi Mordechai Dubin, who was also a representative in the Latvian Parliament.

He also had a letter of introduction from the Soviet ambassador to Latvia, who was a Jew. Rabbi Dubin traveled at great personal peril, for he had once been imprisoned during the Great Red Terror in Latvia, but his journey took place at a propitious time.

At that time, England had severed all relations with Soviet Russia, and Russia was now deeply enmeshed in negotiating a friendship-and-commerce treaty with Latvia. Hence, this was a matter of deep concern to the Russian government.

As a representative of the Latvian Parliament, Rabbi Dubin was received with great courtesy and deference, particularly because of his influence on the Agricultural Party of Latvia. It was in this context that Rabbi Dubin operated, and he was received with great honor by the Russian government. At the same time, Dr. Kahn also arrived, and each endeavored in his own way to achieve the departure of the Rebbe from Russia.

Rabbi Dubin first directed himself to the Foreign Office and negotiated with Dubronitsky, Head of the Baltic Division, dealing with Lithuania, Latvia and Estonia. He received a negative reply and was apprised of the fact that the future outlook for the matter was also unfavorable.

Dr. Kahn, who was a friend of Chicherin, Minister of Foreign Affairs, negotiated with him and with Rubinstein, a prominent official in the Foreign Office and also a Jew, but the answer was again negative.

Dr. Kahn worked vigorously, but the obstacles were incredibly formidable. Finally he came to Rabbi Dubin in great despair, saying that he was unable to achieve any further results. Both Kahn and Dubin worked independently of each other, and to the unknowing observer it appeared as if they were actually intensely competing—each of them trying to obtain the Lubavitcher Rebbe as Rabbi of his own community.

Rabbi Dubin renewed his efforts, and once again, utilizing his prestige as a representative to the Latvian Parliament, once again met with Dubronitsky, of the Foreign Office, and pressed his demand for the Rebbe's departure for Riga. Dubronitsky repeated his earlier refusal. This time Rabbi Dubin responded sharply: "You desire that my associates and I aid you in facilitating the negotiation of the trade pact with my country. Yet when we come to you with a simple request, you send us away empty-handed. We strongly desire the Lubavitcher Rebbe as our spiritual leader.

"The entire community is united in this wish, and now, at this very moment, a competing group is negotiating to nominate him as Rabbi in a German community. It may very well be that he will accede to their request and obtain permission to leave Russia. I cannot adequately emphasize the indignation and resentment that you will stir up amongst the Jews of Latvia by such action. They view his assumption of the Riga Rabbinate as a matter of great pride. Frustration in this matter could very well lead to total failure in the trade pact negotiations with Latvia."

Dubronitsky, himself a Jew, was not convinced by this argument and remained unmoved.

In the interim, the Russian ambassador to Latvia returned to Moscow in order to report on the trade pact negotiations. He, too, indicated that success in achieving this pact was to a great extent dependent upon the sentiment of the Jewish population, and it was therefore highly unwise to provoke them by refusing to let the Rebbe leave Russia.

The Latvian ambassador in Moscow aided Rabbi Dubin by arranging a special banquet in the Latvian embassy, specifically for the purpose of providing contact for him with high officials in the Soviet Foreign Office.

Dubronitsky finally agreed to permit the Rebbe to leave Russia, but only on the condition that his mother, wife, daughters and other members of the family remain behind. He also stipulated that the Rebbe's library could not be taken. Thus, by means of these hostages and security, he hoped to deter the Rebbe from anti-Soviet activity.

The Rebbe's obtaining permission to emigrate was in itself a great victory; however, the Rebbe refused to leave unless his family would accompany him.

The efforts for the Rebbe's total release continued. Madam Peshkova and Dr. Kahn were vigorous in their activities on his behalf. It was Rabbi Dubin, however, with his influential role in the negotiation of the pact with Latvia, who brought the greatest pressure to bear. He pleaded, cajoled, and finally emphatically threatened the officials of the Department of Foreign Affairs: "You cannot anticipate our aid in completing the pact with Latvia." The many intense efforts on the Rebbe's behalf finally resulted in a special meeting held at the Soviet Foreign Office on the second day of *Rosh Hashanah* 5688 (1927), with this topic the only item on the agenda. The participants in this meeting were Georgian Minister Georgii Chicherin, Maksim Litvinov, a Commissar of Public Affairs, Fedor Rothstein, Member of the Collegium of the Peoples Commissariat for Foreign Affairs, Dubronitsky and the Soviet ambassador to Latvia. With the exception of Chicherin, all of them were Jews—Dubronitsky and the Ambassador to Latvia were Polish Jews, and Litvinov was a Jew from Bialystok.

The participants decided to permit the Rebbe to leave Russia together with his family. The formal procedure was to be arranged in Leningrad, since the Rebbe was registered as a resident of that city. The Foreign Office in Leningrad was responsible for processing the Rebbe's departure. The head of this section was a Jew named Zelkind, grandson of the famed Rabbi of Dvinsk known as the "*Batlan,*" and his secretary was a Jew named Kerenkin.

Rabbi Dubin traveled to Leningrad to hasten the formal procedures. Upon informing Zelkind of his purpose, he was told that no formal declaration or instructions had been received yet. Rabbi Dubin requested that Zelkind telephone Moscow and inquire if such orders had been dispatched. Zelkind phoned and was apprised that such instructions had been forwarded. It was discovered that a lesser official had received them, and out of error or laxity the information had not been given to him.

Zelkind immediately signed the necessary documents.

Exit visas were issued to the Rebbe, his family, and to six close associates to accompany him.[2] He was also permitted to take his furniture and library. The law, however, required that the Bureau of Publications grant special permission for any books to be transported from Russia. A Jew named Stein who was knowledgeable about both the value and contents of Jewish works was sent for this task. Upon seeing rare printed works and aged hand-written manuscripts, he unconditionally refused to issue permission, asserting that such precious objects must remain in Russia. All efforts to sway him were of no avail, and he left in a state of intense anger.

Rabbi Dubin called the Bureau of Publications, informed them of the entire background of the situation, and asked that another official be sent. They acceded to this request. This time a Russian official was sent and he immediately granted the official permission necessary for their transportation from Russia.

On the day after *Sukkot* 5688 (1927), the Rebbe left Russia, accompanied by his entire family and six *Chassidim*; in addition he brought his priceless library and other possessions. Altogether there were four train cars.

A large assemblage gathered at the train station in honor of the Rebbe's departure.[3] Along the path of the Rebbe's journey, throngs of Jews assembled at every train station to greet him. Many expressed their homage by traveling short distances in respectful accompaniment. On the train, the Rebbe wrote a two-page letter to his *Chassidim* in the U.S.S.R.

When the Rebbe reached Riga, he was asked for his reaction to his many recent experiences, and he answered: "If I were to be offered a million dollars to again experience one moment of my past anguish, I would decline. And if someone would advance me a million dollars to erase a moment of past suffering—I would also refuse."

Notes

1. *Yisurim* p. 66.
2. The Rebbe prepared a list of family members to leave Russia with him. His future son-in-law and successor Rabbi Menachem Mendel Schneerson was included on the list, the officials asked him why he needed to bring along a future son-in-law, "couldn't you find another son-in-law abroad?" they asked. "Such a son-in-law," the Rebbe answered "just can't be found!" (Ben Yochanan, *Di Yiddishe Heim, Kislev,* 5724, p. 1)
3. Rabbi Menachem Mendel Schneerson left for Riga a week later. (Letter of Rabbi Meir Avtzon, cited in *Yemei Melech*, p. 220.) Rabbi Menachem Mendel received permission to leave even though he was "a major counter-revolutionary" with a rich history. His secret police file was full of incriminating evidence detailing years of efforts for Torah and Judaism in the Ukraine helping his father, who led Ukrainian Jewry, and helping his father-in-law, the Rebbe, (*Yemei Melech*, p. 217).

CHAPTER TWELVE

The Struggle Continues

Racked by great suffering for the remainder of his life due to his prison tortures, the Rebbe nevertheless persisted in his activities for the promulgation of Judaism. He initiated a world-wide campaign to bring influence upon the Soviet government to soften its attitude prohibiting religious instruction and practice. Among these efforts was an attempt to influence leading Jewish organizations to intercede and make "discreet representations to the diplomatic representation" of the Soviets in their respective countries. The insensitivity and ignorance evidenced in one response reflects the pain involved in such endeavors. One major group was afraid to involve themselves in any related effort but declared that, since the government permitted each family to educate three children after school hours, then, in thoroughly utopian manner, since there were 600,000 families in Russia, this legal latitude "would thus benefit 1,800,000 children, which is probably far in excess of the total number of Jewish children of school age." One can speculate if the above was a case of quixotic innocence or a transparent evasion of a momentous problem.

A report of that period[1] tells of the sociological and economic harassment brought to bear on those practicing their Jewish religion. *Arbkor* and *Dorfkor*, respectively factory and village correspondents, reported to their local communist newspapers on current happenings. In actuality, they were informers ferreting out religious practices. According to the report, "If a Jewish worker goes to the synagogue on *Yom Kippur* or *Rosh Hashanah*, he is denounced in the newspaper as a counter-revolutionary and an enemy of the people," and this was followed by efforts to have him expelled from his job.

In Moscow an intense campaign was mounted against the observance of Passover. The Rabbis were ridiculed, Jewish children were ordered to appear in school, and all Jewish employees "in government offices, bureaus and factories were told to come to work under penalty of losing their positions." In Kherson "Jewish children were told that if they stayed out on Passover their bread ration cards would be taken away from them!" Tearful parents told of their children being subjected to most vicious forms of anti-Jewish indoctrination and cases were reported where children came home and inquired if their parents were "exploiters" and "counter-revolutionaries."

Small wonder that one activist of that period painfully writes: "Three million Jews inhabit Russia and are anxiously awaiting for their brothers to save them."[2]

After he left the U.S.S.R. the Rebbe founded a number of Chabad-Lubavitch *yeshivot* and other institutions around the globe. But the plight of Soviet Jewry was always a foremost priority. In 1928-1930, the Rebbe visited with Jewish leaders across the world to organize relief for these Jews. In that period he traveled to France, Germany, Israel and the United States.

The 1930's witnessed even greater repression and, in a convolution of history, the *Yevsektzia* and its supporters were ruthlessly purged. This was followed by the incredible struggle and suffering of the Second World War.

The Rebbe left Riga for Warsaw and finally the United States, yet the seeds he planted have borne and continue to produce astonishing fruit, particularly as extended by his successor, the late Lubavitcher Rebbe, and in the wake of the fall of Communism.

The following narrative is but one characteristic illustration of the sustained influence of the Rebbe: On the 12th of *Tammuz*, 5704 (1944), Bucharian Jews gathered in Tashkent to commemorate the liberation of the Rebbe. An informer was in their midst, and the very next day one of the participants was arrested and questioned about the nature of the gathering.

He innocently told them that this was the day when the Lubavitcher Rebbe had been freed and that the festivities were in his honor.

The interrogator inquired: "How do you know about the Rebbe? Who told you? Who influenced you to be followers of the Chabad movement?" Unaware of the significance of his words, the man related that it was a Reb Simcha, specifically sent by the Rebbe, who had been their guide.

Reb Simcha [Gorodetzky] subsequently relates: "I was brought to the prison where I had twice before been detained without being brought to trial. They also arrested another 15 people. A large public trial was held for the 16 persons, myself included. The prosecutor, in reading the indictment, stated that these people had organized an armed rebellion against the government. As he spoke, he withdrew from his pocket a copy of the *Tanya*, the primary work of Chabad *Chassidus*, and a picture of the Rebbe, and cried out, "These are their weapons. These objects were found in the homes of every one of the defendants!"[3]

Notes

1. Paper delivered by Leo M. Glassman at Conference of Jewish Organizations, convened by the American Jewish Congress, Dec. 9, 1929, Hotel Pennsylvania.
2. YIVO Archives.
3. *Shemu'ot V'sipurim* Vol. 2, p. 107, compiled by Rabbi R. Kahn, Kfar Chabad, Israel.

Rabbi Yosef Yitzchak Schneersohn of Lubavitch
Earliest extant photograph

Facsimile of *Reshimat Hamaaser*, transcribed by the Rebbe's son-in-law and successor, Rabbi Menachem M. Schneerson.

The Rebbe with his son-in-law and successor, Rabbi Menachem M. Schneerson. *Adar I* 25, 1935, Pukersdorf, Austria.

The Rebbe in his study in Riga, Latvia.

The Rebbe's father, Rabbi Shalom
DovBer Schneersohn of Lubavitch.

The Rebbe's mother, Rebbetzin
Shterna Sarah Schneersohn.

The Rebbe's residence at Machovaya 22 *(second floor, apartment 10)*.

On December 4, 1924, the Rebbe gave Power of Attorney to his second daughter Rebbetzin Chaya Moussia *(right)*: *I hereby empower citizen Chaya Moussia Yosepuvna (daughter of Yosef) Schneersohn, residing at Machovaya Street 12/22, apartment 10, to receive monies on my behalf or documents that are* addressed to me, in all forms, from the government bank and all of its branches and offices, and from other banks, government or communal, or from other organizations or private persons or by telegraph. This Power of Attorney includes the power to transfer this, fully or in part, to other persons as she sees fit. On June 30, 1927, the day on which it was known that the Rebbe would be exiled to Kostroma, the Power of Attorney was transferred to the Rebbe's youngest daughter, Shaina.

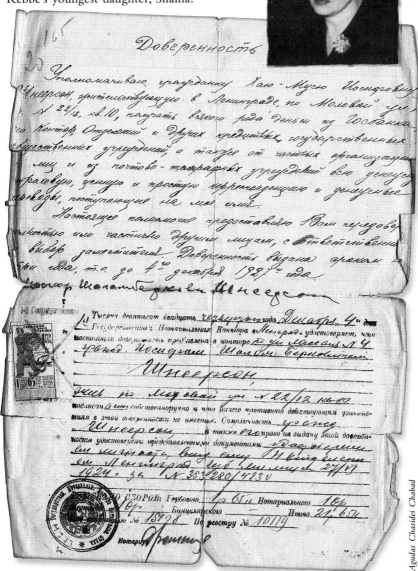

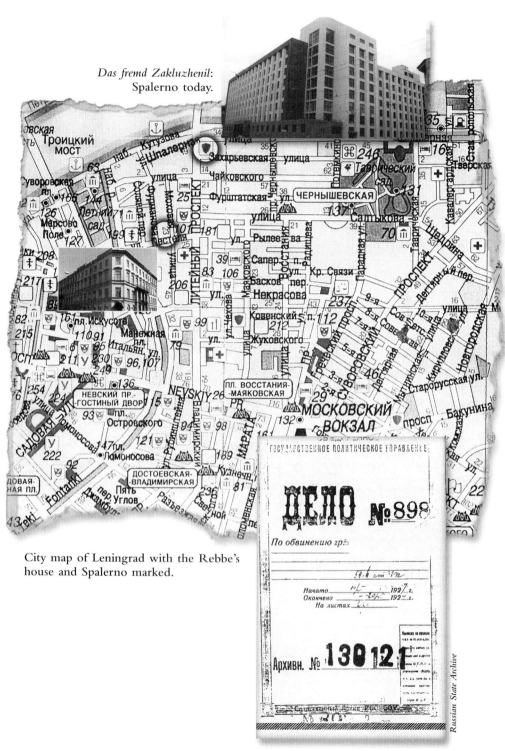

Das fremd Zakluzhenil:
Spalerno today.

City map of Leningrad with the Rebbe's
house and Spalerno marked.

Cover page of the Rebbe's prison
dossier.

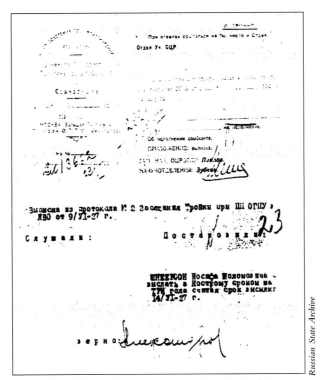

Facsimile of the judgement sentencing the Rebbe to three years exile in Kostroma.

Post-card sent by the Rebbe from his prison cell to his family at Machovaya 22 (see page 143). Even as a prisoner of the Soviet regime, and with his writings certainly to be censored, the Rebbe begins his card with the words "By the Grace of G-d."

The Chassidic Discourse "*Baruch Hagomel*" penned by the Rebbe on *Tammuz* 12—the day of his liberation—June 13, 1927. Translation in Appendix 1.

The Chassidic Discourse "*Gefen Mimitzraim*," penned by the Rebbe while in Kostroma.

ВЫПИСКА из протокола заседания Коллегии ОГПУ/судебного/
от 11 Июля 1927 г.

Слушали:

63. Пересмотр дела ПП ОГПУ в ЛВО
ШНЕЕРСОН Иосифа Шоломовича
прет-пост.Колл.ОГПУ от 27/С
27 г. к высылке в Костромскую
г. сроком на ТРИ года

Постановили: 16

Прежнее постановление ОТМЕ
НИТЬ ШНЕЕРСОН Иосифу Шоломовичу
разрешить свободное проживание
по СССР.

д. 898-27

Секретарь Коллегии ОГПУ/подпись/

в е р н о:

Certificate of release granted to the Rebbe.

The certificate of freedom, issued by the Kostroma
Political Bureau on July 13, 1927, permitting the
Rebbe to "dwell in the entire U.S.S.R."

In the summer of 1921, after the communists shut down the
yeshiva *Tomchei Tmimim* in Rostov, the Rebbe was forbidden to
leave the city limits without special permission. This document
certifies the end of that restriction.

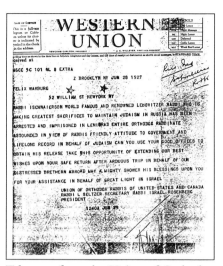

Telegram from the Union of Orthodox Rabbis of the USA to Felix M. Warburg, Chairman of the JDC (American Jewish Joint Distribution Committee).

Cable from JDC's Dr. Joseph Rosen to the Kremlin.

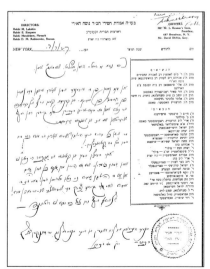

A letter from Agudas Chasidei Chabad of the USA and Canada to Felix M. Warburg appealing for his aid in the Rebbe's release.

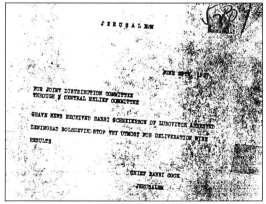

Cable from Palestine Chief Rabbi A. Kook to the JDC.

WESTERN UNION

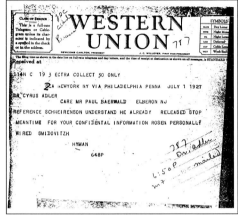

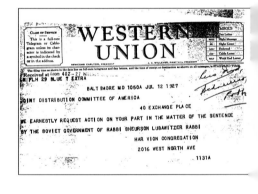

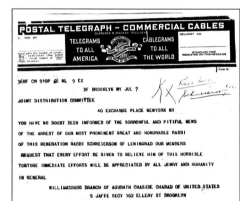

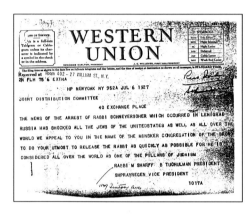

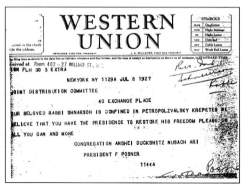

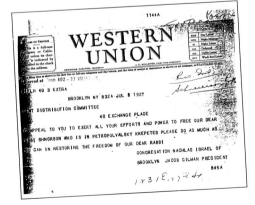

Cables to the JDC requesting that they intercede on the Rebbe's behalf.

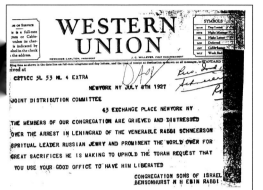

C271CC 5L 53 NL 4 EXTRA

NEWYORK NY JULY 8TH 1927

JOINT DISTRIBUTION COMMITTEE

43 EXCHANGE PLACE NEWYORK NY

THE MEMBERS OF OUR CONGREGATION ARE GRIEVED AND DISTRESSED
OVER THE ARREST IN LENINGRAD OF THE VENERABLE RABBI SCHNEERSON
SPRITUAL LEADER RUSSIAN JEWRY AND PROMINENT THE WORLD OVER FOR
GREAT SACRIFICES HE IS MAKING TO UPHOLD THE TORAH REQUEST THAT
YOU USE YOUR GOOD OFFICE TO HAVE HIM LIBERATED

CONGREGATION SONS OF ISRAEL
BENSONHURST N H EBIN RABBI

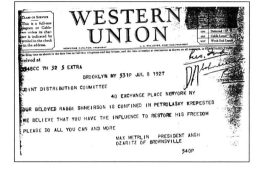

848CC 7H 32 5 EXTRA

BROOKLYN NY 531P JUL 8 1927

JOINT DISTRIBUTION COMMITTEE

40 EXCHANGE PLACE NEWYORK NY

OUR BELOVED RABBI SHNEIRSON IS CONFINED IN PETROLASKY KREPESTES
WE BELIEVE THAT YOU HAVE THE INFLUENCE TO RESTORE HIS FREEDOM
PLEASE DO ALL YOU CAN AND MORE

MAX METRLIN PRESIDENT ANSH
OZARITZ OF BROWNSVILLE

540P

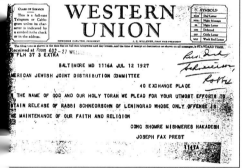

FLH 37 3 EXTRA

BALTIMORE MD 1116A JUL 12 1927

MERICAN JEWISH JOINT DISTRIBUTION COMMITTEE

40 EXCHANGE PLACE

IN THE NAME OF GOD AND OUR HOLY TORAH WE PLEAD FOR YOUR UTMOST EFFORTS TO
OTAIN RELEASE OF RABBI SCHNEERSOHN OF LENINGRAD WHOSE ONLY OFFENSE IS
HE MAINTENANCE OF OUR FAITH AND RELIGION

CONG SHOMRE MISHMERES HAKADESH

JOSEPH FAX PREST

1147A

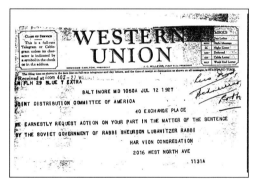

FLH 29 BLUE 7 EXTRA

BALTIMORE MD 1050A JUL 12 1927

JOINT DISTRIBUTION COMMITTEE OF AMERICA

40 EXCHANGE PLACE

WE EARNESTLY REQUEST ACTION ON YOUR PART IN THE MATTER OF THE SENTENCE
BY THE SOVIET GOVERNMENT OF RABBI SHEURSON LUBAWITZER RABBI

HAR VION CONGREGATION

2016 WEST NORTH AVE

1131A

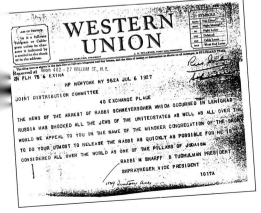

2N FLH 75 6 EXTRA

HP NEWYORK NY 952A JUL 6 1927

JOINT DISTRIBUTION COMMITTEE

40 EXCHANGE PLACE

THE NEWS OF THE ARREST OF RABBI SCHNEYERSOHER WHICH OCCURRED IN LENINGRAD
RUSSIA HAS SHOCKED ALL THE JEWS OF THE UNITEDSTATES AS WELL AS ALL OVER THE
WORLD WE APPEAL TO YOU IN THE NAME OF THE MINSKER CONGREGATION OF THE BRONX
TO DO YOUR UTMOST TO RELEASE THE RABBI AS QUICKLY AS POSSIBLE FOR HE IS
CONSIDERED ALL OVER THE WORLD AS ONE OF THE PILLARS OF JUDAISM

RABBI M SHARFF B TUCHULMAN PRESIDENT

SHPRAYREGEN VICE PRESIDENT

1017A

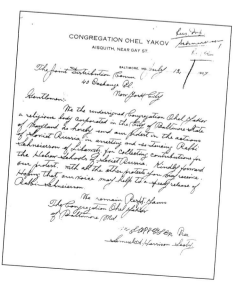

CONGREGATION OHEL YAKOV
AISQUITH, NEAR GAY ST.

BALTIMORE, MD. July 12 1927

The Joint Distribution Comm
40 Exchange Pl
New York City

Gentlemen:

We the undersigned Congregation Ohel Yakov
a religious body corporated in the City of Baltimore State
of Maryland do hereby send our protest in the actions
of Soviet Russia in arresting and sentencing Rabbi
Schneierson of Libavity for collecting contributions for
the Hebrew Schools of Soviet Russia. Kindly forward
our protest with all the other protests you may receive.
Hoping that our voice may help to a speedy release of
Rabbi Schneierson

We remain Respt. yours
The Congregation Ohel Yakov
of Baltimore Md.

S. APPELSEN Pres.
Samuel A. Harrison Secty.

June 24, 1928

Hon. Prof.

CYRUS ADLER, Chairman

on Cultural Affairs at the

J.D.C. New York.

My dear Prof.

some time ago, I informed You about the necessities of our brethern in Sowiet Russia, conserning their religious life, as schooles
Synagogues, ritual bathes etc. Surely had been also received at the
J.D.C. the detailed report of the Rabbi Shneersohn, now in Riga, the
repport about the same matter and also concerning his Project about
the support to the Jewish workers, to help them to be organized into
the "KUSTAR":

Jn the next time we will forward to You a detailed report signed
by the " CHOFETZ CHAIM" and by me. We hope You will protect the plea
of Rabbi Shneerson and take care to this very necessary matter.

Last time I received very tremendous informations about the
position of the whole cultural and religious life in sowiet Russia.
As a matter of fact, the Government himself acknowledget permition
to some affairs, but the"Yevseki" are interdicting and prohibiting
everything. The Russian Government passed the Bill to allow teachers
to teach with two or three children religion, but the "Yewseki" in
the cities and towns are arresting the same teachers and transmited
them into Sibiria for hard labour. The same fataling is coming to
the parents whom the "Yewseki" find teaching with their own children praying and Bible. There is no power in a pen to describe the
dreadful history of the tremendous actions, taken by the "Yevseki"
against the Jewish religion and tradition. This extrem pain leads u
us to the time of middle age, when our parents, brothers and sisters
had been tortured by the "torkwomades" and their people.

The "Yewseki" closed all (the ritual baths-MIKWOES- inspite of
their higienical position, the Synagogues for daily and SABBAT-
prayings are rebuilding through the "Yewseki" in theabers and night-
Clubs and with their coersive power the Rabbis must sign compulsory
letters to the world, that everything is in best order.

It is the higest time to undertake an action to paralyze this
inquisition upon our brethern in Sowiet Russia. The J.D .C. which
is conected with the Russian Government and with the Jewish Commites
There , has the power to case the Government in this matter to ordain

-2-

and appoint the "Yewseki" in every town and city to allow the
Jewish to observe their religion for teaching with the Jewish
children praying and religion, to open the ritual baths everywhere and to return all the rebuilled into theaters Synagogues.

In the hand of the J.D.C. is now the lot of our brethern
in sowiet Russia and we hope, that to Your order the "Yewseki"
will pay attention to better their getting to the religious
necessities of our poor unhapy brethern in Russia and we are
awaiting the good results of Your intervention. May G-D help
You.

Very sincerely Yours

Rabbi CH.O. Grodzienski

Wilno, the 24.6. 28.

JDC

A letter from Rabbi Chaim Ozer Grodzienski, who together with Rabbi Yisroel Meir
Kagan (the "Chofetz Chaim") called on the JDC to support the Rebbe's continued
work on behalf of Soviet Jewry.

Riga,d.23.Oktober,1928

Herrn

Professor C.Adler

Philadelphia.

Sehr geehrter Herr Professor,

Wir haben,wie Sie sich wohl erin-
nern dürften,Ihnen bereits ein Budget für die Mikwoos über-
sandt und wollen Ihnen nun heute ein Ergänzungsbudget,das wir
vom rabbinischen Komitee Russlands neuerdings erhalten haben,
zugehen lassen.

Die Mikwoosfrage ist bis jetzt lei-
der noch nicht gelöst und wir haben vorläufig noch keine Hilfe hierfür erhalten,da jedoch diese Frage eine sehr brennende
ist und das rabbinische Komitee uns das Budget mit dringlichen
Bitten um Hilfe eingesandt hat,so wollen wir hoffen,dass Sie,
geehrter Herr Professor,Ihr Möglichstes tun werden,um die
Mikwoosfrage zu einem guten Resultat zu führen.

Mit vorzüglicher Hochachtung

A letter from the Rebbe to Cyrus Adler, dated October 1928, in which the Rebbe
appeals for funds for *mikvaot* in the Soviet Union.

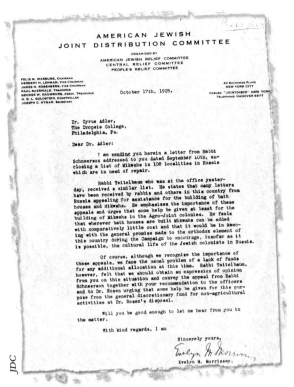

Letter from the JDC to Cyrus Adler regarding the Rebbe's plea for financial assistance with the building of *mikvaot*.

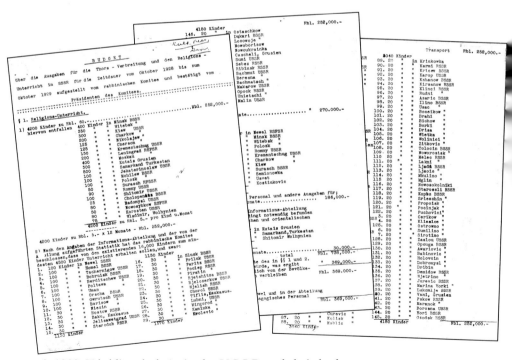

A 1929 *Va'ad* list, *chadarim* in the U.S.S.R. and their budgets.

RABBI SCHNAYERSON WELCOMED IN CITY

Leader From Riga Says Soviet Oppression of Jews Has Been Exaggerated.

Rabbi Joseph Isaac Schnayerson, chief rabbi of the dynasty of Lebowitzer rabbis, one of the most influential world leaders of Jewry arrived yesterday on the French liner France to confer with American co-religionists on current Jewish problems. He was met at quarantine by a delegation of prominent Jews and escorted in a police boat to the Battery, where more than 500 awaited him.

Before coming here from his headquarters in Riga, Latvia, Rabbi Schnayerson visited Palestine on the day before the rioting began there. He would not discuss this situation, but talked of the status of Jews in Russia, where he was imprisoned last year as a result of educational activities among his people. "The dark picture usually painted concerning the oppression of Jews in Soviet Russia is exaggerated, he said.

When the police boat Patrol landed at Pier No. fifty cantors' chanted religious songs until Rabbi Schnayerson came to the pier and was greeted by Police Commissioner Whalen.

A few moments later a statement was issued by his secretary in which the rabbi expressed his appreciation to the Mayor, the Police Commissioner and all public officials. The statement added that he would confer here with Jewish leaders and rabbis and leaders of Chasidic groups "to strengthen religion and Torah."

Among those who met him were Henry I. Chanin, builder; State Senator Philip M. Kleinfeld and many rabbis of the city. Later in the day Rabbi Schnayerson was taken to 4315 Fourth Avenue, Borough Park, Brooklyn, where a synagogue and home have been prepared for him.

SOVIET PARDONS RABBIS.

Sentences Are Annulled Because of Their Advanced Ages.

MOSCOW, June 6 (Jewish Telegraph Agency).—The sentences of six months' imprisonment at hard labor, imposed upon Rabbi Schneerson and Rabbi Perlov of Gomel for performing rabbinical functions which the Court held to be properly the function of the State, have been annulled.

The annulment was ordered owing to the advanced ages of the rabbis.

Fascisti Jailed for Attack on Priest.

PERUGIA, Italy, June 6.—Count Fabiani, a member of the Fascisti, has been sentenced to ten months' imprisonment for having forced the parish priest of Gubbio to drink castor oil because the ——— led an ———

New York Times 6/7/23
Note that the Rebbe's sentence in this case was annulled due to his "advanced age." This is four years prior to the 1927 imprisonment.

SOVIET WON'T NAME 3 RABBIS STILL HELD

Minsk Press Prints Individual Charges Against Fourteen Originally Arrested.

CALLED FOES OF REGIME

Preaching, 'Trading With God' and Opposing Revolution Alleged— Three Anti-Semites to Die.

MOSCOW, Feb. 25 (Jewish Telegraphic Agency).—Soviet authorities refuse to reveal the names of the three Jewish rabbis still under arrest. The Communist press in Minsk today printed the names of the fourteen originally arrested and the charges against each one, but the name of Chief Rabbi Gluskin was not included.

While the general charges are in accord with those published yesterday in The London Times, the individual charges are as follows:

Benjamin Sakowizki, "a preacher with a crooked Talmudical mind, was sentenced to be shot in 1919 because of stock speculations, but he escaped. When business was bad he began trading with God, holding sermons and preaching 'save our children from the fire that is destroying the Jewish people.'"

Jacob Nizes, head of a rabbinical seminary, accused of having headed a number of illegal seminaries.

Simon Kabakov, called a bourgeois ringleader.

Krengel, former jeweler and silversmith, said to have utilized confiscated metal for making spoons and forks.

David Shachor, "an important former trader, was the organizer of clerical unions and rabbinical seminaries."

David Salomon, "president of a society of rabbinical students which is an outspoken counter-revolutionary organization, whose object is to fight the Soviet, and at whose meetings anti-Soviet speeches were held and sometimes a sermon ending with 'uva lezion goel,' a dangerous Zionist slogan."

Asher Kirsntein is a rabbi said to be "a speculator who established loan societies that supported nepmen from ruin; is a reactionary clerical and a counter-revolutionary enemy, an enemy to the workers and an active supporter of the illegal rabbinical clique."

Moses Gabrielov, "Rabbi Gluskin's right-hand man, became chairman of the Jewish community after the White Poles arrived and hanged a revolutionary. He helped the latter with his death-bed confession."

Gabrielov, "also a prominent member of the Agudath Israel and leader in the religious community."

Iwianski, an ex-merchant, is accused of being "an industrialist in whose house during the search correspondence was found with foreign ——— counter-revolutionary organ-

Braude, "an ex-millionaire banker who is terribly furious at the Bolsheviki, who took everything from him."

Rabbi Pevsner, of whom it is said "all illegal meetings met in his bathhouse. The good Jew cried and sighed at the meetings, saying the Bolsheviki are hurting his soul and his spirit. He was the nerve centre of the rabbinical anti-revolutionary organization maintaining and receiving instructions from the Fascist Zádik Lebbavitcher Rebbe, who sent instructions as to how to conduct the counter-revolutionary campaign in the Soviet Union and how to create illegal rabbinical seminaries. Such instructions were found in Pevsner's house, signed by the Lebbavetzcr Rebbe. The Fascist Zadik from Riga supplies all anti-Soviet organizations with information regarding the Soviet and his Minsk confederate transmitted the necessary material."

Rabbinovitch, accused of being "well-known itinerant preacher and a cunning person, who camouflages his poisonous counter-revolutionary sermons with examples and stories. With his Jesuit speeches he incites villages and towns against the Bolshevik."

Gordon, charged with being "a leader in the students' organization who preached that the Jewish position is no better than in Egypt or in Spain under the Inquisition, and argued that it was necessary to fight unbelievers. He also travels in the province and delivered inciting harangues."

Moseh Chaim Levine, accused of being "a preacher who created a rabbinical seminary in Preobank, suburb of Minsk, where a copy of a letter addressed abroad was found in which he said, 'I repeatedly requested your help. You must know that the Jewish population is suffering hunger, need and trouble. Why have you deserted us? Save us.'"

Alexander Gaupt, Nikolai Zlate merzhev and Ivan Potchupov, three prominent agronomists in the Odessa region, have been sentenced to death for driving Elena Goldman, young Jewish agronomist, to death by suicide by their persisting anti-Semitic acts. Twenty others involved received lesser sentences. The trial lasted four days.

[The Lubavitcher Rebbe (Rabbi Joseph Schneursohn), who has repeatedly been mentioned as one of those with whom the Minsk rabbi were in communication and whose letters and instructions mailed from Riga as to the formation of secret rabbinical seminaries were found in the possession of those arrested, now in Chicago. He is the leader of the "Habat" sect of chasidism (Pietists). In 1927 his arrest by the Soviet Government and subsequent release following world-wide protest and the stand he took when the Soviet Government attempted to bring pressure to bear on him by exiling him gave him an international reputation.]

Some New York Times clippings about the Rebbe.

JEWISH DAILY BULLETIN

ONLY ENGLISH DAILY RECORD OF JEWISH NEWS.

Vol. IV. Price, 4 Cents. New York. Tuesday, July 12, 1927. No. 811.

...leader that "hith... ...loyal opponents. I hope that henceforth you will be loyal collaborators."

LUBAWITSCHER REBBE RELEASED AS COMMUNITIES GUARANTEE HIS LOYALTY
(Jewish Telegraphic Agency)

Moscow, July 15.—The Soviet government granted the request of leaders of the Jewish population in the Union and abroad to release from arrest and exile Rabbi Schneurson, the celebrated leader of the Chassidic Chabbad school, known as the Lubawitscher Rebbe.

It was announced today that the "case" will be dropped against Rabbi Schneurson, who was exiled for having collected funds to maintain Yeshivas, Jewish religious schools, in Russia. Rabbi Schneurson will return to Leningrad this week from Kortroma, where he was exiled.

It is understood that the Jewish communities of Moscow, Leningrad, Kiev, and Minsk have given guarantee to the Soviet authorities of the famous rabbi's "complete loyalty".

Copyrighted

CHASSIDIC FOLLOWERS REJOICE OVER RABBI'S RELEASE FROM PRISON
(Jewish Telegraphic Agency)

Riga, July 1.—The despatches concerning the release of Rabbi Schneurson, the leader of the Chassidic Chabad school, were received here with tremendous interest by the numerous followers of the rabbi.

When the first despatch of the rabbi's arrest was received, his followers, the Lubawitscher Chassidim, called for a day of fast and assemblage in the synagogues.

The office of the Jewish Telegraphic Agency was continually besieged by the Rabbi's followers, asking for further news. When yesterday's despatch announcing his release from prison was received, the Lubawitcher Chassidim celebrated the event.

Riga, July 1.—A conflicting report concerning the Lubawitcher Rebbe was received here, according to which he is still held under arrest.

Orthodox leaders here stated they will ask their co-religionists abroad to hold protest meetings, asking for the Rabbi's release.

SOVIET EXILES CHASSIDIC RABBI, SCHNEURSON
(Jewish Telegraphic Agency)

Riga, July 11.—Exile of Rabbi Schneurson, known as the Lubawitscher Rebbe, the leader of the Chabbad Chassidic school, was decided upon by the Soviet authorities, a despatch received here states.

The Rabbi was held on the charge that he was guilty of collecting funds for the maintenance of Yeshivas and religious schools in the Soviet Union. The despatch states that Rabbi Schneurson will be exiled to Kostroma.

Riga, July 11.—Pleas for financial assistance for Zionist exiles in Russia was received by the Jewish members of the Latvian parliament. In their letters, the Zionist exiles state that they have received permission to emi-

(Continued on Page 4)

SCHNEURSON, FAMOUS CHASSIDIC LEADER, IS RELEASED BY SOVIET
(Jewish Telegraphic Agency)

Riga, June 30.—Rabbi Schneurson, known as the Lubawitscher rebbe, the leader of the Chabbad Chassidic school, was released from imprisonment, according to despatches received here from Leningrad.

The Chassidic leader was arrested on the charge that he collected funds for the maintenance of a Yeshiva. The despatch states that following his release he was placed under the supervision of the Ogpu, the political police of the Soviet government.

Rathenau's grave.

M. M. USSISCHKIN,
(Jewish Telegraphic Agency)

...July 11.—Bobkoc, direc...
...strial Trust in the Dis...
...was sentenced to ...
...ment at hard labor fo...
...activities.
...sentence was imposed
...district court after
...nd guilty of insulting

LUBOWITSCHER REBBE PLACED UNDER ARREST
(Jewish Telegraphic Agency)

Leningrad, June 27.—The famous Lubowitscher Rebbe, Schneursohn, a Chassidic rabbi, has been arrested on the accusation that he collected money for the maintenance of his Yeshiva. The Yeshiva of the Lubowitscher Rebbe enjoyed great prestige in the Jewish world, being one of the most famous Yeshivas.

Rabbi Schneursohn holds a position of high regard and esteem. His arrest has caused great excitement among the Jewish population.

A selection of some of the numerous newspaper articles in the U.S. regarding the Rebbe's imprisonment, exile and release. Many more appeared in European Jewish and non-Jewish dailies.

ne Chamber also demands the exclusion. The resolution is
Mexico, South America and the West Indies.
being forwarded to President Coolidge and to Congress.

RABBI SCHNEUERSOHN OF LUBAVITCH ARRESTED IN LENINGRAD: CHARGED WITH COLLECTING FUNDS FOR YESHIBAHS.

Riga, June 24th. (Jewish Telegraphic Agency).
Rabbi Schneuersohn, the famous Rabbi of Lubavitch, has
been arrested in Leningrad, states a report just received here.
The Rabbi is charged with having been collecting funds for Yeshibahs.
The message adds that there is much anger among the Jewish
population over the arrest of the Rabbi.

Studio.

LUBAVITCHER REBBE RELEASED: REMAINS UNDER OGPU SURVEILLANCE.

Riga, June 29th. (Jewish Telegraphic Agency).
Rabbi Schneuersohn, the famous Rabbi of Lubavitch, who was
arrested a few days ago in Leningrad on a charge of collecting funds
for Yeshibahs, has been released, states a message just received here
from Leningrad. The Rabbi is, however, being kept under surveillance
by the Ogpu.

GOVERNMENTS WILL TAKE SEVERE MEASURES TO PUT A STOP TO

FAMOUS RUSSIAN RABBI EXILED BY SOVIETS: WILL BE KEPT ISOLATED FROM JEWISH ENVIRONMENT.

Riga, July 10. -- Jewish Telegraphic Agency. --

The Soviet authorities have decided to exile Rabbi
Schneuersohn of Lubavitch, the leader of the Hassidic Habad
sect to Kostroma in Central Russia and to keep him there isolated from Jewish environment. The Rabbi was recently arrested
in Leningrad on a charge of collecting funds for the maintenance
of Jewish theological schools.

London, W.C.1.   END.

Vol. VIII. No. 160.   5 pages.   12th. July,

LUBAVITCHER REBBE TO BE EXILED AND KEPT ISOLATED FROM JEWISH ENVIRONMENT.

Riga, July 10th. (Jewish Telegraphic Agency).
The Soviet authorities have decided to exile Rabbi Schneuersohn of Lubavitch, the leader of the Hassidic Habad Sect to Kostroma in Central Russia and to keep him there isolated from Jewish
environment. The Rabbi was recently arrested in Leningrad on a
charge of collecting funds for the maintenance of Yeshibas.

EXILED ZIONISTS IN RUSSIA RECEIVE PERMISSION TO EMIGRATE TO PALESTINE

esti
the   Riga, July 10th. (Jewish Telegraphic Agency).
for   The Jewish Deputies here have recently received letters
carry out firs... Zionists in Russia who have been exiled to Siberia,
the ceremonies in connection with... permission to go to Palestine.

SOVIET AUTHORITIES QUASH CASE AGAINST LUBAVITCHER REBBE: WILL RETURN FROM BANISHMENT.

Moscow, July 14th. (Jewish Telegraphic Agency).
The case against Rabbi Schneuersohn, the famous Rabbi of
Lubavitch and head of the Habad Hassidic Sect, has been quashed.
Rabbi Schneuersohn, who has been exiled to Kostroma, (as reported
in the J.T.A. Bulletin of the 11th. inst.) is returning to Leningrad
this week.
The Jewish communities in Moscow, Leningrad, Kiev and
Minsk have guaranteed his complete loyalty to the present regime in
Russia.

THE NEW ROUMANIAN PARLIAMENT: CONSISTS ONLY OF LIBERALS, PEASANTS AND MINORITIES.

Dispatches from the Jewish Telegraphic Agency.

Forward פֿאָרווערטס Forward

Vol. XXX. No. 10,833.—Daily · New York, Tuesday, July 12, 1927 · 12 Pages · PRICE THREE CENTS

ליובאוויטשער רבי זאָל ניט פֿאָרשיקט.

רינא, יולי 11. (א״פ).

דער בעשלוס אז דער ליובאוויטשער רבי זאָל פֿאָרשיקט ווערען קיין קאָסטראָמא אויף שווערער ארבעים, איז נאָר געלאָזען. דורכגעפיהרט נישט געוואָרען, וויל דער סאָוויעטישער רעגירונג.

ליובאוויטשער רבי אין פּעטראָפּאוולאָװסקער פעסטונג

בעגרייכטמען וועגען דעם ארעסט פֿון דעם ליובאוויטשער רבי זיינען געשריבען אונז מים די אנדערע. אנפֿאנגס זיינען געווען בעדייכטמען...

From the Yiddish press—the *Forward*.

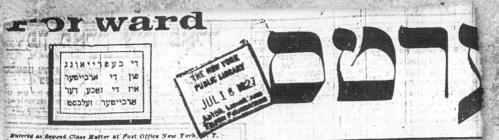

ᴀᴏʀward צײַט

די בעפֿרײַונג
פֿון די ארבײַטער
און די זאַכן דער
ארבײַטער וועלטכעס

Entered as Second Class Matter at Post Office New York, N.Y.

Vol. XXX. No: 10,836.—Daily   New York, Friday, July 15, 1927

אידישער געגענד אי
ירושלים שטארק געטמ
פֿען פֿון ערדציטערניש

קיין אידען צווישען די אומגעקומענע זײַנען נישטא, אבע
אַ סך הײַער זײַנען רואיערט געוואָרען און געבליי
האַלטען נאָ דאָיצט אין אײַן צוזאַמענברעכען. — האַ
רייסענדע סצענעס צווישען אראבער, וועלכע פֿן
באַרדינגען זײַערע קרבנות

ליבאָוויטשער רבי ארעסטירט פֿון סאָ־־
וועט פֿאַר זאַמלען געלד פֿאַר ישיבות

ליבאַוויטשער רבי בא
פֿרײַט פֿון אַרעסט אין
רוסלאַנד

מאַסקווע, יולי 15 (איטא). — די
סאָוועטישע רעגירונג האָם הײַנט אינ אויס־
געלייזען די רבין די קיין גענען דעם ליבאַ־
וויטשער רבין צו שניאורסאָן, וועלכער אינ
פֿאַראַרטשיילט געוואָרען אויף סיביר פֿאַר
זאַמלען געלד פֿאַר ישיבות.

לױט אַ פֿאַרערגנונג פֿון דער הײַנטיגער
ניורונג, וואָס ווערט רבי הײַנטיגער ווארט
געבראַכט ווערט צורינג קיין לעניגראאר
פֿון דער שטאַט קאַסטראַמע, וואוהין ע
מען האָם אים אזא פֿאַרשיקט.

די פֿיר גרעסטע אידישע קהלות פֿון
סאָוועט פֿארבאַנד האָבען נאַראַקלאַגט
צו דער רעגירונג אין דער ליבאַוויטשער
רבי וועם סלאַוונעט מאָכט. די פֿאַוואַ נ
נאַקסיע אין גענוגען נעוואַרעג דורך די
קהלות פֿון מאַסקווע, לעניגראאר קיעוו.

אינגרונים
וואַלקענם
טומאַן

נאַלען, וואַס מ׳שיטט
ען ניט פֿליהען וועה
ליוו 42 מיל א שטונ
אנג צוזיונגען זיי ארא
ען, אז זיי זײַנען
ניע ברעג

בען מעהר ווי 42 סא
ים ־ נעכטעם פֿליהאַנ

ליבאַוויטשער רבי
ארעסטירט פֿון סא־
וועט פֿאַר זאַמלען געלד פֿאַר ישיבו

לעניגראאר, 30 טען יוני, (איטא) — דער
ליבאַוויטשער רבי, שניאורסאָן, אינ רער
הײַנם דא ארעסטירט נעוואָרען אײַף ד
קלאַנע אז ער האָם נעזאַמעלט נעלד פֿאַ
ישיבות.

דער ארעסט פֿון די ליבאַוויטשער רבי
האָם ארױסגערופֿען גרױס אױפֿרעגונג
צווישען דער אידישער באַפֿעלקערונג.

דער ליבאַוויטשער רבי, אינ אײַנער
פֿון די וויכטיגסטע פֿיהרער פֿון אַרמא
ראָבסישען אידענטהום אין רוסלאַנד צ
הײַנטיגען אירגעמהום סאַ ער אינ גערוהט דער אײַנ

גרוים שמחה צווישען
ליבאַוויטשער חסידים

פֿריר, יולי 1. (איטא) — גרױס
האָם נעכטען נעהערשט אין
לינגם חסידים צווישען אין
האַרן חסידים טױן עס, אינ אַכעד אַנגעקומען
נאָם ארױסגעלאָזם דעם ליבאַוויטשער
רבי'ן פֿון טורמע.

וועגם די נײַעם וועגען דעם אז דער
רבי'ם זײַן ארעסטירט נעווארען אינ עד
שיען, אינ די וואַרשאַווער אידישע
איזמיגען, אינ דער וואַרשאַוואר אַפֿיס
מוי׳ נעשטעמפעלם נעלאַזבאַמעם שגעד
צו ירה נעשטעמם נעטומען אױך ד
רונק רי
צוואַ נאַרישען נעזאַמען אינ אמת.

די ליבאַוויטשער חסידישע נעלאַנעם
אין וואַרשע האַם עלילאַנטער א תענית
אינ נעוואַרע איצ דער קאַ
צו אַ נ נם זאַל נעטעה אין דער קרב
וועגען דער בעפֿרײַונג. וועגען רי נײַעם
נעקטומען, האָם נעהערשם אונגעשריב
ליכע שמחה צווישען די חסידים.

ליבאַוויטשער רבי
בעפֿרײַט פֿון סאָוועט

רינא, טען יוני, (איטא) — דער
ליבאַוויטשער רבי צו שניאורסאָן, וואַס אינ
מיט אײַניגע טעג ארעסטירט
פֿאַר אײַנגעשטעלם 50 טענ
זײַן ישיבה, אינ נעכטען בעפֿרײַם נעד
וואַרען, וועם אַהער נעפֿאַרידרוזען פֿון סא־
וועט רוסלאַנד.

אינדיאנא ליידעם פון א ש...
צו סלום סלטן ירושה

THE JEWI

"THE AMERICA...

אגעבלאט

...SARASOHN and LEON KAMAIKY, Proprietors
SARASOHN & SON, Publishers

THREE CENTS. — DAILY — New York, Monday, July 11, 1927 ★ ★ ★

סאוויעטען רעגירונג פערשיקט דע...
ליובאוויטשער רבי אויף קאטארג...

דער רבי אין ארעסטירט געזארען פאר איינהאלטען חדרים און ישיבות. — די הרשע סאוו...
...ווען פערשיקט אדם דער פאר אין די סלם נעמענדען פון קאטארגא. — ...
...טשער רבי דאם אויסגעבראטען מירער אין פערטעטט אסטא...

ליובאוויטשער רבי ווערט געהאלטען אן פעטראפאוולאווסקי פעסטונג

דושולאי פראקלאמירט אלם פארדיכט חודש

ליובאוויטשער רבי נאד ניט פערשיקט

גרויס שמחה צווישען ליובאוויטשער חסידים

The Jewish Daily Newspaper—*Tagblatt*.

Monda... 16, 1927   THE JEWISH

הרב שניאורזאן דער גרויסער מארטירער
פון אונזער צייט

פון י. ל. דאליראפסקי

סכסוך

THE JEWISH DAILY
"THE AMERICAN NEWSPAPER PRINTED IN YIDDISH"
ESTABLISHED 1885

טאגעבלאט

ארגאן פאר כל ישראל

LEON KAMAIKY, Proprietor
...SON, Publishers

...LY — New York, Tuesday, July 12, 1927   ★   VOL. XLIII, No 160

"יינגסט חורבן און טויט איז אונזער"

פארדעמגעשטער אין סא
האט געשאלטן הורבא

ליבאווישער רבי
נאך ניט פטורס...

דער פארלאנג האט חיינט ארויסגע
לאם א מעלדונג אז ער גרייט זיך דרו
סען אויף גרייט און איבערגעזאנג פון
שיינען.

ליבאוויטשער רבי בעפרייט; אידישע קהלות
נאראנטירען אז ער וועט זיין לאיאל צו רעגירונב

פון דער שטארם סטארטסטא. וואוכין
מען האט איהם פערשיסם.

מאסקווע, יולי 15. (איטא) —
סאוועטישע רעגירונג האט היינם ארוים
געלייזט די קיים געגען דעם ליבאווי
טשער רבין שניאורסאן, וואס איז פער
אורטהיילם געווארען אויף פיבור מאר
זאמלונג געלד פאר ישיבות.

לוים א פערארדענונג פון די רבי רע
נירונג וועט מען רעד רבי היינטינע וואר
נעבראכט וועדען צוריק קיין לענינגראד
נינענראד, קיעוו און סינספ.

אידישער קינסטלער צום אכטען מאל פרעזי

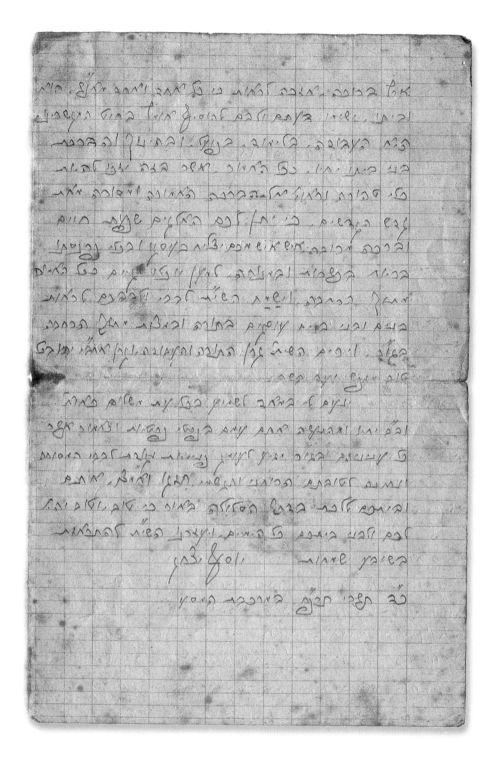

While on the train that would take him out of Soviet Russia for good, the Rebbe penned this heartfelt letter to his *chassidim*.

ב"ה.

אל ידידי [illegible]

ה' עליהם יחיו.

כאשר הגיעה אלי השמועה, לבי עד מאוד נרגש בנועם

[illegible] עוד [illegible] התרגשות [illegible] של

[illegible] יחיו, [illegible] בחייה, ובעזרת השי"ת כי יהיו לברכה

במקום תורה ועבודה, ובהם [illegible] עתה [illegible] במה ברכה

[illegible]

כי טוב, ואין טוב אלא תורה חיים, המאירה בעבודה שבלב

[illegible] העבודה [illegible]

[illegible] והגבורה [illegible]

והברכה [illegible] בהברכה [illegible]

ובנותיהם, [illegible] חיים [illegible] התורה ובמעשה

האמונה בתום לבב.

ידידי [illegible], הנה [illegible]

בניהם ובנותיהם ובני בניהם, הנה ברכותם [illegible],

[illegible] והברכתם [illegible]

[illegible] לבבי. [illegible]

אשר ראיתי [illegible] לא [illegible]

ומאור [illegible] העולם [illegible]

DECLARATION OF NON-IMMIGRANT ALIEN

ABOUT TO DEPART FOR THE UNITED STATES

AMERICAN CONSULAR SERVICE

AMERICAN CONSULATE, _____RIGA LATVIA_____ _____May 17, 1929_____
(Place) (Date)

I, ___Joseph Salomon SCHNEERSON___, a {citizen / subject} of ___Soviet Russia___
(Face) (Country)

bearer of {Passport / Laissez-passer} No. __116280__, dated ___October 1, 1927___
(Other document) 214797

issued by ___Soviet authorities Leningrad Russia___
(Nationality and title of issuing authority)

am about to go to the United States accompanied by ___none___
(Names of persons included in declarant's passport, photographs of whom are attached thereto)

I was born __Oct. 8. 1871__ __Lubovichi__, ___Smolensk___ ___Russia___
(Date) (City) (Province) (Country)

My occupation for the last two years was ___Rabbi___

and at present is __Rabbi__

I desire to proceed to the United States for the purpose of ___religious investigation___

to remain for __six__ months, and my address in the United States will be ___

My references are ___Joint Distribution Committee New York N.Y.___
(In the United States)

M. Dubin, M. P. ___Krishian Barona iela 52, Riga Latvia___
(Local)

I consider myself as a non-immigrant under the provisions of the Immigration Act of 1924 on the following grounds:

___that I am proceeding to the United States purely for___

___purpose of temporary visit___

and offer for inspection the following documents in support of my claim: __letter from__

___M. Dubin, M. P. to American Consul Riga Latvia dated Jan. 30.___

___1929___

The Rebbe's immigration papers.

I have informed myself of the provisions of the Act of February 5, 1917, particularly of the exclusion provisions of Section 3 of that Act, and of the Immigration Act of 1924, and am aware that the latter provides:

"The admission to the United States of an alien excepted from the class of immigrants * * * * shall be for such time and under such conditions as may be by regulations prescribed, including, when deemed necessary, the giving of bond with sufficient security to insure that, at the expiration of such time or upon failure to maintain the status under which admitted, he will depart from the United States."

I realize that if I am not one of a class exempted from the provisions of any of the immigration laws of the United States regarding the exclusion of aliens, or if my classification as a non-immigrant alien is not approved upon arrival in the United States, I may be deported or detained by the immigration authorities in the United States, and I am prepared to assume the risk of deportation and of compulsory return.

I solemnly swear that the foregoing statements are true to the best of my knowledge and belief.

Joseph Schaezroth
(Signature of declarant)

Subscribed and sworn to before me this _17th_ day of _May_, 192 9

L. M. Harrison

__Vice Consul__ of the United States of America

Fee No. _708_
($1.00)
Passport Visa No. _68_
($0.00) No. _709_

Consul's findings on exempt status:

status as non immigrant approved
by Consul A. W. Kliefoth

Passport Visa granted _May 17_, 192 9
and the following notation placed on passport—
Visa granted as Non-immigrant under Section 3
(_2_) of the Act of 1924—

(Non-immigrant class)

Passport Visa refused _____, 192

9/17 19 29 under Reasons: _____
Section 3, Immigration Act
of 1924, for _____

W. A. Thomas
Immigration Inspector

Visa granted as
Non - Immigrant under
Section 3 (2) of the Act of 1924
Temporary visitor
L. M. Harrison
Vice Consul.

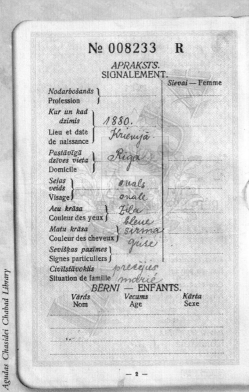
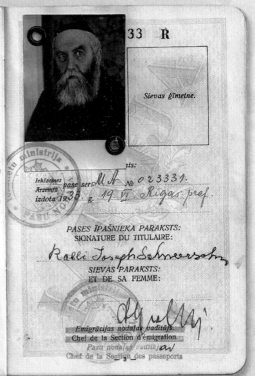

№ 008233   R

APRAKSTS.
SIGNALEMENT.

	Sievai — Femme
Nodarbošanās Profession	
Kur un kad dzimis Lieu et date de naissance	1880. Krievijā.
Pastāvīgā dzīves vieta Domicile	Rīgā.
Sejas veids Visage	ovals ovale
Acu krāsa Couleur des yeux	zila bleue
Matu krāsa Couleur des cheveux	sirma grise
Sevišķas pazīmes Signes particuliers	
Civīlstāvoklis Situation de famille	precējes marié

BĒRNI — ENFANTS.

Vārds Nom	Vecums Age	Kārta Sexe

— 2 —

Sievas ģīmetne.

Iekšzemes pase ser. M.A. № 023331.
Ārzemēs pase ser.
izdota 1933. g. 19. VI. Rīgas pref.

PASES ĪPAŠNIEKA PARAKSTS:
SIGNATURE DU TITULAIRE:

Rabbi Joseph Schneersohn

SIEVAS PARAKSTS:
ET DE SA FEMME:

Emigrācijas nodaļas vadītājs.
Chef de la Section d'émigration.
Pasu nodaļas vadītājs.
Chef de la Section des passeports

№ 008233   R

Apceļojamās valstis:
Pays pour lesquels ce passeport est valable:

Amerika
Amérique

Šīs pases termiņš notek
Ce passeport expire le

1941. 3. februārī
3. février 1941

ja netiek pagarināts,
à moins de renouvellement.

Par pases neapmainīšanu vai nepagarināšanu laikā
pases īpašnieku sods.

Izdota Délivré à	Rīgā
Kad Date	1940. 5. februārī le 5. février 1940.

— 4 —

Pase pārbaudīta
5 FEB 1940

№ 008233   R

... nāts līdz 19

La validité du présent passeport est prolongée
jusqu'au 19
№ ....
Nodeva .... nomaksāta.

Pase pārbaudīta 19. Tā derīga vienreizējai
izceļošanai 14 dienas pēc izsniegšanas.
Ja šinī termiņā neizceļo vai ja no ceļo-
juma ... — pase 7 dienu laikā
... iestādei.

19 g. februārī

Pasu nodaļas vadītājs

2 9 FEB 1940

The Rebbe's Latvian passport.

The Rebbe in his stateroom aboard the S.S. Drottingholm upon his arrival in New York in 1940.

The Rebbe (location unknown).

The Rebbe.

The Rebbe's oldest son-in-law,
R. Shmaryahu Gourarie.

R. Mordechai Dubin.

R. Eliyahu Chaim Althaus.

R. Michoel Dworkin.

R. Elchanan Dov Marasow.

Rabbi Yosef Yitzchak Schneersohn
1880-1950

Ma'amar: Baruch HaGomel

The following chassidic discourse (Kostroma 13th of Tammuz, 5687 / July 13, 1927) is one of three delivered by the Rebbe in Kostroma (see page 158) after his liberation from Soviet prison. Like the others, this discourse places the events of the Rebbe's imprisonment and liberation in their ultimate spiritual context, especially as it relates to the spiritual service of the individual Jew.[1]

I.

Our Rabbis tell us that if a person has lived through a perilous experience, he should recite the blessing of *HaGomel*—"Blessed be the One Who bestows good upon the unworthy, Who has bestowed good upon me." Why does the text for this blessing vary from that recited upon the occurrence of a miracle, which is: "Blessed be He Who has performed a miracle for me"? Why doesn't the *gomel berachah* state: "Who has *performed* good for me"? What is the uniqueness of this "bestowal"?

It is well known that the descent of the soul into the body at birth—though this is an awesome descent—is actually a requisite for the soul's subsequent ascent. The Jew's *Nefesh Ha'elokit*—G-dly soul—descends and garbs itself in a physical body, which also has a *Nefesh Ha'behamit*—animal soul—which it must transform to the service of G-d. At the time of the *galut*—exile—the work of the G-dly soul is rendered even more difficult because it is confronted by fearsome obstacles and hindrances to the learning of Torah and the fulfillment of *mitzvot*. The intense effort needed to surmount these obstacles results in a subsequently greater ascent for the soul. Additional barriers which burden the soul and impede it from the achievement of its lofty goals are the anxiety and preoccupation involved in earning a livelihood, which greatly distract the Jew from his primary religious quest.

Encountering this challenge, the Jew exerts intense, disciplined effort. He sets aside fixed times for the study of Torah and for the service of the heart—prayer; he fulfills G-d's commandments with pure faith and submission to the Heavenly Yoke, undeterred by obstacles. He stands with the firm resolve to learn and to teach. By these very means the soul achieves an ascent which surpasses its earlier level before its present descent to worldly existence and vestment within a human body.

Our Sages of blessed memory state: "Before its descent, the soul is made to swear, 'You shall be a righteous person and not be a wicked person!'"[2] It is known that the word "shavuah"—"oath"—is linked by chassidic interpretation to the word "sova"—"satiation." Thus, the soul prior to its descent to mortal existence not only swears that it will be righteous, but is endowed and "sated" with unique capabilities to overcome the physicality of the body, subjugate the animal soul, and vanquish the forces that conceal its light.

II.

Our Sages of blessed memory identify our major enemy in the battle to be righteous:[3] "The evil spirit of man attempts to prevail upon him every day, desiring to slay him, as the verse states: 'The evil one strives to overcome the righteous man and attempts to slay him.'[4] Were it not for G-d's help, the righteous man would be unable to fight his adversary, as it is said: 'G-d will not abandon him in his hands.'"[5]

The nature of the animal soul is to be drawn to physical and material matters, hence the term "animal," for just as the primary concern of an animal is eating, drinking, and other physical matters, similarly the animal soul within man is drawn to physical gratification. It pursues that which the eye perceives; it desires all forms of gratifying indulgence, such as sensual pleasure and the pursuit of vain honor. "And the *alukah* has two daughters, 'Give, give'"[6] The "*alukah*" is normally translated as "bloodleech." One Talmudic explanation of this Biblical verse is that the *alukah* is *Geihinom* and it cries out demanding punishment for the "two daughters" that cause moral depravity in man, namely political tyranny and lack of faith.[7] The basic nature of the evil inclination is to covet all that it can see of the material world. It has great vanity and believes that its great superiority deserves the honor and accord of others. It selfishly withholds kindness to fellow beings, for it is incapable of sharing. Moreover, it desires what belongs to others, unceasingly pursuing its heart's lust and delights—like an animal. The mind's sole preoccupation becomes devising means to gratify the soul's lust.

III.

Our Sages of blessed memory state that the evil inclination is like "a fly sitting upon the two openings of the heart." Just as the gnat consumes and does not produce, so the animal soul desires everything for itself. Our Sages say: "The eye sees and the heart desires," and the Jerusalem Talmud comments: "The eye and the heart are the intermediaries for sin."[8] Our Sages say further, "The evil inclination can only prevail upon what the eye sees."[9] The eye's perception awakens within the man thoughts and desires which influence him to seek gratification. The primary cause for moral failure is self-love and egotism: Man is incapable of self-restraint and self-discipline because of his vanity. Insatiably he transgresses every moral and religious boundary. The absence of "The fear of G-d from before his eyes" is not his sole defect; he is capable of acting like a creature of prey, grasping and stealing from others and using various stratagems to satisfy the lust of his heart. Experience has repeatedly demonstrated that the thoughts, speech, and deeds of those controlled by their evil inclination focus totally on self-gratification. Everything that they think, say, and do is directed towards pleasure, as a result of the evil inclination's attempts to cause man to veer from moral abyss to moral abyss.

IV.

Our Sages offer the following advice to aid in the struggle against evil: "I have created the evil inclination, and I have created Torah as an antidote. If you are preoccupied with Torah, then you will not be given over into his hand. If you have encountered this vile creature (meaning a person's evil inclination—Rashi's commentary) draw him to the House of Study. If it is like a stone, it shall be pulverized, and if it is like iron, it shall be shattered."[10] For there are many types of evil, individuals whose hearts are stone and others whose hearts are like iron. In either case, it means that evil has gained such a wide influence that man's heart is like iron or stone; as unresponsive as inert matter to the influence of reason. So calloused is such a person that he no longer possesses spiritual sensitivity; he is unable to experience the awe normally aroused by G-dly spiritual influence.

He is, may G-d have mercy, like one completely transformed into stone, with neither interest nor joy in the fulfillment of Torah and *mitzvot*. The remedy for this condition is the intense study of Torah, constant attendance in the *Beit Midrash*—the House of Study. One must be *osek*—preoccupied with—Torah; *eisek*—preoccupation—means more than just studying for one's self; it means there must be involvement, as there is in any actual vocation, to effect the widest promulgation of Torah study in the Jewish community. It is written "From the mouths of babes and sucklings you have established *oz*, strength,"[11] and our Rabbis of blessed memory tell us that "*oz* has no meaning other than Torah."[12] Torah study has the power to vanquish the Jews' enemies! Similarly, going to the House of Study to pray *betzibur* (with the quorum prescribed by Jewish law), participating in classes given before and after the regular services, engaging in study groups at all other available times; all these cause the evil inclination to be "ground to dust."

We can often see that persons assiduously involved in Torah study despite great personal difficulties, are exalted to a high spiritual level which far surpasses the one they would seem capable of normally achieving. Even one not himself capable of learning who supports the learning of others is uplifted and exalted. Indeed, our Sages call him "a master of good deeds." There are various sources which attest to the great merit of those who are preoccupied with Torah: "When a person is preoccupied with Torah, then physical suffering departs from him."[13] "And he is successful in his material enterprises."[14]

V.

At the time of the giving of the Torah, all the Jews who were physically present at that time and all those souls destined to vest themselves in physical form in the future till the time of the coming of Mashiach, all of us as one collective entity, accepted the obligation for ourselves, our children, and children's children to fulfill the Torah and its mitzvot.

It is written, "And the Jews fulfilled and received,"[15] which our Sages, of blessed memory, explain to mean that the Jews fulfilled to an even greater extent that which they had already received at Sinai in the past.[16]

When there are great hindrances and barriers to the learning of Torah and the fulfillment of *mitzvot*, a Jew must intensify his efforts to better serve G-d. This response of deepening commitment can be repeatedly seen throughout Jewish history—at the time of Mordechai and Esther, for example, when Haman sought to inflict harm against the Jews, to totally destroy the Jewish people and to uproot Judaism; or when the Syrian-Greeks declared to the Jewish people: "Write upon the horn of an ox that you have no share in the G-d of Israel." It was specifically at comparable times of crisis that the Jews evoked new, hitherto concealed inner wellsprings of courage and strength to "fulfill" with even greater intensity that which they had already "received" at Sinai.

The prophet declares "I, G-d, have not changed."[17] The prophet cries out in astonishment to the Jewish people: "You are very well aware that G-d has not 'changed,' has not forgotten His assurances never to abandon His nation Israel, 'one lamb among seventy wolves, but protected.'" Therefore the prophet inquires, "Why, sons of Jacob, have you not achieved *kelitem*"—derived from *klot hanefesh*—outpouring of the soul: i.e., "Why do you not learn and observe Torah with *klot hanefesh*—intense yearning and dedication?" If Divine Providence is perceived by all, then the inevitable response of the Jewish people should be wholehearted commitment to, and preoccupation with Torah and spiritual service.

If a person has not realized his true potential, then he is challenged and aroused from Above. This is the meaning of the blessing we make when surviving danger: "He who has bestowed good upon me," for our Sages declared, "Good is none other than Torah," i.e. He has bestowed upon me Torah—the antidote to evil.

G-d confronts the Jewish people through the veil of history. In each era they are beset by new adversaries that threaten their very existence. This, in turn, awakens new spiritual qualities hitherto dormant within their souls. These qualities are awakened and actualized, resulting in an intensified commitment to the fulfillment of Torah and *mitzvot*.

Thus G-d, by means of these confrontations, "bestows good" upon us, creating a sequence of events that brings about a more intense dedication to Torah: "Good is none other than Torah."

Notes

1.   *Sefer Hama'amarim Kuntreisim,* vol. 1, pp. 365-368
2.   *Niddah* 30b.
3.   *Kiddushin* 30b.
4.   Psalms 37:32.
5.   Psalms 37:33.
6.   Proverbs 30:15.
7.   *Avodah Zarah* 17a.
8.   *Berachot* Chapter 1, Law 5.
9.   *Sotah* 6a.
10. *Kiddushin* 30b.
11. Psalms 8:3.
12. *Shir Hashirim Rabbah* 1:4.
13. *Berachot* 5a.
14. *Avodah Zarah* 19b.
15. Esther 9:27.
16. See *Shabbat* 88a and Rashi there.
17. Malachi 3:6.

The First Anniversary:
A Letter by the Rebbe

The following letter by the Rebbe, Rabbi Yosef Yitzchak, marks the occasion of the first anniversary of the first day of his imprisonment:[1]

By the grace of G-d, Sunday, *Sivan* 15, 5688 (June 3, 1928)

To our friends, Chabad adherents, and to all those to whom Torah is dear, those occupied with the study of Torah and its practice, wherever they may be. May G-d bless you all.

Shalom u'vrachah!—Greetings and Blessings!

Today [marks a year] to the first day of my imprisonment in the Spalerno prison in the Sixth Division, room 160; Wednesday, corresponding to the Torah reading of "And now may G-d's power be magnified,"[2] on the fifteenth day of *Sivan* 5687. There I was subject to physical torture till the Torah reading "How goodly are your tents, Jacob, your dwelling place, Israel,"[3] the third day of *Tammuz*. On that day I was compelled to go into exile to the city of banishment, Kostroma and to be there for the term of three years.

It is clearly known to all that the imprisonment and the exile occurred to me through the accusation of informants, our brothers, implacable enemies, who seek revenge against those observing the laws of Moses and Israel. Their actions are against the law of the state and government.

These individuals could not endure the blossoming of "The rose of Jacob," through the promulgation of Torah study throughout our entire land. For this reason they fabricated false accusations to oppress me and thus, Heaven forbid, to cause an end to the "House of Jacob." "G-d's mercies are boundless,"[4] and the merit of our ancestors has not ended, nor shall it end, to all those going in their footsteps, for all future generations. And [last year] on the twelfth day of *Tammuz*, corresponding to the Torah reading "I herewith give you my covenant of peace,"[5] I was freed. G-d did not liberate me alone on the twelfth day of *Tammuz*, but everyone to whom our holy Torah is dear, including those merely bearing the name Jew. For every Jew (without taking into account his individual level of Torah and *mitzvah* observance) is wholeheartedly faithful to G-d and His Torah.

The twelfth day of *Tammuz*, is a festival of liberation for those preoccupied with the promulgation of Torah. For on this day it was made known in a revealed manner for all to see, that the great endeavor for which I strived, the promulgation of Torah and the strengthening of religion, is permissible according to the law of the land, which grants freedom for those religiously observant as much as for all other citizens of the land.

This day, in the merit of the many loyal to Torah, whose light banished the darkness of the informers and the false accusations, it is appropriate to designate as a day for public gatherings to motivate and activate the participants for the strengthening of Torah and *mitzvot* as is necessary and appropriate.

May G-d bless our brothers living in the land of Russia; May G-d strengthen their hearts and the hearts of their children to be faithful Jews and may the evil tormentors cease from oppressing them.

As we approach the holiday of liberation of all those actively involved in the promulgation of Torah; I herewith bless all of our brothers to whom Torah is dear, those studying Torah and those giving public Torah classes, may G-d bless them. May He open up His goodly treasures and bestow His bounty upon them, amidst all our brethren, the Jewish people—may G-d grant them all life—bountiful life and boundless blessings. May G-d strengthen their hearts to increase in the promulgation of Torah and strengthening of Judaism. May we all merit to see children and grandchildren occupied with the study of Torah and its commandments, in affluence and bountiful material sustenance.

At the beginning of 5687(1926)[6] I requested from our *chassidic* brethren to establish the custom of reciting Psalms, as divided according to the days of the month, in all of the synagogues, immediately after the morning prayers. *Kaddish* was then to be recited as is the custom after public psalm recitation.

This request stands at present with its full force so as to bring "merit upon the many" [the entire Jewish community]. It is appropriate to do in all synagogues at large [regardless of their affiliation] because this is not a matter related specifically to the *Chassidic* movement; and they shall thereby merit blessings from the source of blessings in all matters of goodness, from spiritual and physical.

Enclosed herewith is the discourse on the *Mishnah* teaching, "Ten who sit and learn Torah, the Divine Presence rests among them."[8] May our eyes see the flourishing of Torah, of Israel and our *chassidic* brethren, and may we merit "the light, for it is good." I remain your dedicated devotee, supplicating for your peace and success, and the success of the members of your household, their children and their children's children. May G-d grant them all life in all spiritual and material matters.

With blessings,

Yosef Yitzchak

Notes

1.   *Igrot Kodesh* Vol. 2, pp. 80–82.
2.   Numbers 14:17.
3.   Numbers 24:5.
4.   Lamentations 3:22.
5.   Numbers 25:12.
6.   Bold typeface in the original.
7.   *Avot* 3:6.
8.   *Sanhedrin* 84a.

The Seven Arrests

The following letter by the Rebbe, Rabbi Yosef Yitzchak,[1] summarizes all of the Rebbe's imprisonments and reflects on the significance of the one in 5687 (1927).

By the grace of G-d, Wednesday, 12 *Iyar*, 5694 (1934)

This is in reply to your inquiry concerning the days of my imprisonment and the days of my exile in the "city of refuge" Kostroma—it is all written in my diaries; however, for various reasons it is impossible to reveal this material, except for a few passages and general reminiscences that contain nothing prejudicial to anyone's interests.

The imprisonment of 5687 (1927) was my seventh, for I was imprisoned five times in the days of the old [Czarist] regime, and twice in the days of the new [Communist] regime.

The first imprisonment was in Lubavitch when I was 11 years old.[2] This was the time—5652 (1892)—my teacher Reb Nissan instructed me to begin writing down my memories in a book, so I also recorded this incident in the diary of 5652.

The second imprisonment was in Lubavitch in *Iyar* 5662 (1902) due to slander spread by school teachers, members of the *haskalah* movement, in Lubavitch.

The third imprisonment was in Lubavitch in *Tevet* 5666 (1906) due to the participation of members of the Labor Zionist party in an uprising against the police in Lubavitch.

The fourth imprisonment was in Petersburg in *Tevet* 5670 (1910) due to the slander of the Jewish scholar K.

The fifth imprisonment was in Petersburg in *Shevat* 5676 (1916) due to my efforts in obtaining materials about the regulations and laws exempting religious officials from military service.

The sixth imprisonment was in *Tammuz* 5680 (1920) in Rostov-on-Don, due to slander by the head of the *Yevsektzia* there.

These were all actually imprisonments of merely a few hours; the seventh imprisonment was the equivalent of all of them together.

It is the way of the world that the metaphor is always less momentous than its subject: if imprisonment of the body in a building of wood and stone is affliction, then how much greater is the suffering of the Divine Soul imprisoned in the body and animal soul—one must contemplate this deeply.

I will not deny that [memories of] the seventh imprisonment at times give me a special pleasure, as is evident from the fact that although it is about seven years after the event, I still occasionally take time to be alone and picture for myself things heard and spoken, the visions and dreams that I heard and saw and dreamed in those days.

There are set periods in life—infancy, childhood, youth, early adulthood, maturity, old age, dotage—and there are differences in abilities, whether one is average or outstanding—and also character, whether shy and gloomy or joyful and exuberant. In addition to all this, however, Divine Providence sometimes arranges special periods that change a person's character, developing his abilities and giving him a lofty perspective from which he can behold the ultimate purpose of human life on this earth.

A person's spiritual progress and the development of his abilities are affected most strongly by a period rich in suffering for the sake of energetic activism of any kind, and especially the suffering of one fighting oppressors for the survival and strengthening of his religion.

This period, though it is inextricably associated with bodily and spiritual suffering, is nevertheless rich in powerful impressions, and these days are shining ones in a lifetime.

Every incident in this period is significant and notable, especially the imprisonment: considering the great spiritual benefit that came in its wake, it is appropriate not just to mark the days and the nights, but also the hours and minutes, for every moment of suffering, mortification, and affliction produced an excellent benefit and a boundless strengthening of character—even a weak person is transformed into the mightiest of the mighty.

The imprisonment began at 2:15 at night, Tuesday night before Wednesday 15th of *Sivan* 5687 (1927) and continued until 1:30 in the afternoon on Sunday, the 3rd of *Tammuz*, in the city of Leningrad (Petersburg).

Eighteen days, eleven hours, and fifteen minutes.

On that day, after I was detained in my house about 6 hours, until 7:30 in the evening, I set out on a journey to Kostroma, and I came there the next day, on Monday, the 4th of *Tammuz*, and I was kept in exile until Wednesday 13th of *Tammuz,* 12:30 in the afternoon.

Five days and seventeen hours.

And I hereby fulfill your request, and I am sending you selections from the diaries about the imprisonments in their various times.

Notes

1. Originally printed in *Hatamim* Journal, issue 7, p. 60.
2. See Appendix 4.

The First Imprisonment

The following memoir of the Rebbe describes the first of his seven imprisonments. Eleven years old at the time, the Rebbe had already actualized the philosophy inherited from his predecessors of willing self-sacrifice for the sake of a fellow Jew.[1]

I had accumulated a sum of over thirty rubles as reward for the study of *mishnayot* by heart. Following my father's suggestion, I divided it into smaller sums, ranging from three to five rubles, which would constitute a charitable loan fund for the merchants in the market place and the tradesmen who traveled about in the village, dealing in bundles of flax, hides or leather, chickens, eggs and onions, and the like.

At the direction of my teacher, Rabbi Nissan, I kept written accounts of all the transactions, and the day before and after the market day I would be occupied with distributing and receiving repayment of sums that had been borrowed from the loan fund.

Among those who frequently borrowed and repaid was Reb Dovid the Butcher. Reb Dovid was about fifty years old, and there were eight people in his family. He was very poor and supported them solely by the work of his own two hands. Nothing was too difficult for him to do—whether in summer under the burning sun, or in winter with its heavy snow storms, or during the time of the heavy rains; as long as he could make a profit of a few pennies through his efforts, he would work energetically, unmindful of the difficult conditions. He was never heard to complain about his life circumstances or his poverty.

Reb Dovid was a simple person. Though he had attended *cheder* in his early childhood, he had forgotten much of what he had learned. His knowledge was limited to the daily prayers and those of the holidays and High Holy Days. He also knew the Psalms, the *Haggadah*, and the *mishnayot* of Ethics of Our Fathers. Beyond this, he knew nothing, but he was a sincere and honest person, and every day, aside from the times when he journeyed about to the villages, he was among the first ten to arrive in the synagogue for the recitation of Psalms and for the sunrise *minyan*.

I would always try to anticipate those times on Friday afternoon, immediately before *Shabbat* or in the late afternoon prior to a Jewish holiday, when Reb Dovid would return from the bathhouse to his home. I liked to see his reddened face, the edge of his white garments flapping as he walked along hastily, and his four children all running after him. Shortly afterwards, he could be seen serenely walking to the large *Beit Midrash* where he usually prayed.

At that time, my parents were away on a journey, and I stayed in the home of my grandmother, the *Rebbetzin* Rivkah, famed for her sincere piety. I pursued my studies in the home of Reb Yeshayah Kostier, who lived on Shileva Street.

The Constabulary in Lubavitch consisted of two officials—a *pristov, uradnik,* and three subordinates, known as "*diestnyekes.*" On the market day, their number would be increased by the arrival of another five *diestnyekes* to aid in maintaining order.

On the market day in the month of *Menachem-Av*, 5651 (1891), I was walking with my friend Shimon, the son of Reb Shmuel the Scribe, from *cheder* to our afternoon meal. The marketplace was so busy, filled with so many farmers, wagons and horses, that there was an overflow to Shileva Street, upon which we walked, as well as onto the other streets adjacent to the marketplace.

On our way we met Reb Dovid the Butcher, carrying a calf upon his shoulders and bearing in his arms a small lamb. A basket of chickens was also tied to him. When he met us, his dark face lit up and his teeth gleamed in a radiant smile, as he said: "With G-d's help, I hope to make a good profit." As he spoke, one of the minor police officials approached with quick strides and struck Reb Dovid with such force that blood flowed from his nose. I immediately shouted at the officer, "You wretched drunkard!" and pushed him forcefully.

The officer lunged toward me with the angry accusation that I had torn off a copper medal of commendation sewn to his chest and that I had obstructed him from fulfilling his task. He commanded one of his deputies to bring me to the local police station, and before I could attempt to reply, a half-drunk peasant took a firm grip on my garment by my throat.

There was a great tumult in the marketplace, and it was with great effort, because of the large crowd, the many wagons, and the variety of livestock, that we were pushed through this assemblage. Because of the clamor of tradesmen vying with each other to sell their wares, loud arguments between sellers and buyers about prices, and the sounds of many animals, no one paid attention to me or to the captors forcibly leading me.

We passed through the marketplace, Hachluka Street, and finally reached the police courtyard. The officer opened the door of the police station, handed me over to the custody of another officer, and informed him of the charges against me. The police station officer's face contorted in anger; he looked at me contemptuously and abruptly slapped me on the cheek. He took hold of my ear, and thus leading me to the cell, opened the door, thrust me in and closed the door after me.

I was gripped by fear, and also felt the pangs of hunger. But these were fleeting thoughts, for suddenly I realized that I was in a situation which had occurred so many times to my revered ancestors. I was in prison because of a desire to fulfill G-d's will in the world. I had to respond to the crisis with courage and faith. I had to concern myself with the study of Torah. I had already mastered by heart two of the six orders of the *Mishnah, Moed* and *Zera'im,* and I immediately began to review them by heart.

Suddenly, I was frightened by a sound of protracted groaning; my imagination further intensified my fear. I attempted to focus my thoughts intensely and wholly on the *mishnah* that I was reviewing and moved away from the corner where the fearful groaning and whimpering was to be heard.

To this very day, I recall the problem of Jewish law which arose in my mind at that time. The cell was in total darkness. I had no idea of the hour; I hastened to recite the afternoon prayer of *Minchah.* I recited *Ketoret, Ashrei,* and just as I was about to begin the silent prayer of *Shemoneh Esrei,* I suddenly was confronted by the problem: What is the proper manner of reciting the prayer? Should I recite the additional prayer of *Aneinu,* normally said on a fast day or in a time of peril and add the confessions of *Al Cheit*— repentance also, or should I omit these additional prayers?

As I reflected, it suddenly occurred to me that neither of these prayers should be said; and even more, that the supplicatory prayers, *Tachanun,* should also be omitted. On this day, Almighty G-d, may He be blessed, had bestowed upon me the great *mitzvah* of being imprisoned for defending the honor of a fellow Jew. Indeed, for me this was a day of spiritual joy. Deeply moved by a feeling of profound inner gladness, I said the *Shemoneh Esrei* with added devotional thoughts in accordance with my understanding and knowledge at that time.

After *Minchah*, I resumed the recitation of *Mishnah*, repeating the order of *Zera'im*, and once again I heard the moaning and whimpering and the sound of an extended scuffle in the darkness. I was deeply fearful; suddenly I remembered that a box of matches, which my friend Shimon had purchased for his brother Leib, was still in my pocket. In the great confusion at the time of my arrest, the matches had remained with me. I struck a match, and saw a calf lying bound in a corner of the room with a muzzle on its mouth. My earlier fears vanished; this was the source of the groaning and scuffling that had so frightened me. I finished the recitation of the order of *Zera'im* and began the order of *Moed*. In the midst of my study, I suddenly heard the sound of footsteps approaching my cell. Abruptly the door opened, and I saw a police station officer.

"Forgive me," he said, "I did not know that you were the nephew of the RaZA." All of the townspeople called my uncle Rabbi Zalman Aharon by his acronym; even the non-Jews referred to him in this way. "The commanding officer has just arrived and ordered that you be freed. I beg of you, have mercy upon me and do not tell how I struck you and dragged you by your ear. I did not act out of hatred, but merely due to the force of habit. After all, your nose did not bleed and you lost no teeth. So it is really of no importance."

When I entered the commandant's room Reb Dovid the butcher, who had been beaten, and the police officer who had tormented him were already there, as well as the witnesses, Reb Yoel the Coal Seller and Reb Shaul the Wagon Driver. The commandant's assistant argued that the calf borne by Reb Dovid the Butcher was stolen from Reb Meyer, another Jewish butcher, who in turn had purchased it from the brother of the assistant to the commandant. It was for this reason that he had struck Reb Dovid and then, turning to me, he exclaimed: "And this young boy then acted disrespectfully toward me and tore off my medal." The witnesses, however, testified that the calf carried by Reb Dovid had actually been purchased by him.

In the midst of these proceedings, Reb Mordechai Zilberbord, a servant of my uncle RaZA, entered and handed a slip of paper to the commandant. He read it intently and then said to Reb Zilberbord that I could leave with him, for I was innocent and undeserving of any punishment.

As I left the police headquarters, I discovered all my friends waiting for me, and I chose to go with them, rather than with the coach sent for me from my family; and I told them all that had occurred.

Upon hearing my strange account of the calf in the prison, Reb Zilberbord hastily went to Reb Meyer the Butcher, who in turn rushed off to the prison to find the commandant still deliberating the case of the officer and Reb Dovid the Butcher. Reb Meyer excitedly interrupted and stated that he had heard that there was a bound and muzzled calf in one of the cells.

The commandant, enraged at having to come to the station and leave a card game with close friends, arose in great anger, and, accompanied by his aides, Reb Meyer, Reb Dovid and the witnesses, went to investigate the matter. They entered the cell and stood astonished, for Reb Meyer was indeed correct—before them they saw the calf purchased by Reb Meyer from the brutal guard.

After an extended investigation, it was discovered that both the guard and his brother had stolen the calf from Reb Meyer. The policeman, after being held in prison for a week, was brought to trial, and it was discovered that he had been guilty of other criminal acts. As a result, he was relieved of his post.

My friends told me that it took them five hours to discover the commandant in the company of the nobleman Azmidov, in the house of Dr. Yarmakov, all engaged in a game of cards.

My father was away at that time. When my father returned from his journey, my uncle related the entire incident to him and praised me highly for my firm stand, and for being responsible for the freeing of Reb Dovid, the discovery of the guard's guilt, and the return of the calf to Reb Meyer.

My father at that time said to me: "You have acted in a praiseworthy manner. And if you endured suffering for a few hours for a fellow Jew—then what of it? You have also discovered the importance of knowing *Mishnah* by heart. If not for this knowledge, what difference is there between yourself and Reb Meyer's calf that was with you in the cell? But by virtue of your repeating *Mishnah* and the recitation of prayer while imprisoned, you were enabled to spend time in Torah and prayer, which is what truly differentiates man and makes him superior to the animals."

The words of my father then are still hewn upon my mind and heart: "You must respect every Jew who conducts himself with honesty, without distinction as to his being a greater or lesser Torah scholar. And it is necessary to defend the honor of a Jew, even if it entails danger. You must also prepare spiritual provision for yourself by knowing sections of Torah by heart, so that in any situation you will not be disturbed from the study of Torah, even for a short while." My father then gave me a gift of ten rubles so that I could have even greater opportunity to help others charitably.

Notes

1. Originally printed in *Hatamim* Journal, issue 7, p. 65, under the heading "Letter from the Rebbe to one of his sons-in-law."

Spiritual Courage:

A Talk by the Lubavitcher Rebbe
Rabbi Menachem M. Schneerson

The following is a brief sample of the many talks and discourses of the Rebbe's son-in-law and successor, on the events and significance of the imprisonment and liberation of his father-in-law, Rabbi Yosef Yitzchak Schneersohn. The Rebbe's talks for the 12th and 13th of Tammuz provide an illuminating supplement to Rabbi Yosef Yitzchak's own writings, in the present example relating another incident in which the Rebbe willingly sacrifices himself for a fellow Jew prior to becoming Rebbe.[1]

During the time of the Czarist regime in Russia, an individual named Stolypin[2] headed the government for a number of years. He was notorious for his hatred of Jews and the harsh decrees he promulgated against them. The fifth Lubavitcher Rebbe, Rabbi Shalom DovBer Schneersohn, learned of an imminent edict planned by Stolypin and dispatched his son and later successor, Rabbi Yosef Yitzchak, in an effort to nullify the decree.

Rabbi Yosef Yitzchak (hereafter referred to as "The Rebbe") travelled to the capital city, Petersburg, to discuss the matter with communal figures. After many futile efforts, it was decided to attempt to sway Stolypin through a man named Pobedonostsev,[3] whom Stolypin esteemed highly and who had exerted great influence upon him. Though this official was an anti-Semite, he was very pious, and therefore accorded reverence to clergymen of all faiths, including rabbis.

After many efforts, an audience was arranged for a Friday evening. Since Pobedonostsev lived in a remote suburb of Petersburg, the Rebbe had to leave Petersburg early and spend the entire *Shabbat* in that area.

The capital and its suburbs were forbidden to Jews at that time. Despite notable exceptions in the city itself, such as affluent merchants, physicians, and others of a similar social rank who could circumvent the regulations against Jewish inhabitants, in the suburban area there lived not a single Jew.

Not having access to a single home where he could stay, and knowing it was impossible to walk the streets for any length of time because of the severe cold as well as the physical dangers involved, the Rebbe was compelled to seek refuge in a tavern. He waited there for a few hours till the time of his appointment. After successfully fulfilling his mission, he returned to the tavern and spent the entire *Shabbat* there.

It is not difficult to imagine the Rebbe's emotions, trying to remain inconspicuous in the company of drunken peasants in a tavern, particularly on the sacred day of *Shabbat*. There was, in addition, the ever-present danger of being among people notorious for their hatred of Jews. The Rebbe was willing to endure this perilous and difficult situation on the mere *possibility* of revoking an evil decree against the Jewish people.

It is very possible to advance reasons to question this behavior. If, on the one hand, the Heavenly court had rendered a decision that the decree should take effect, then his efforts with the official would be of no avail. If, on the other hand, the Heavenly tribunal had decided that the decree would be nullified, then no endeavor was necessary. It is indeed true that one must strive and use normal actions in order to achieve one's goal, but these actions are merely the external means by which a man receives Divine blessings. As

the Torah declares, "And G-d will bless you in all that you
will *do*."[4] The Torah commands that man must "do" in the
earthly world in order to enable the Divine blessings to per-
meate his efforts. This does not, however, apply in the case
when one's life is actually endangered, as when it is necessary
to spend a *Shabbat* among drunkards, assume a false identity,
and remain unobtrusively in their midst until able to return
home.

The above reasoning is valid according to Jewish Law, and
as a result, one may render such a decision to others. However, when the Rebbe was confronted by the possibility that
Jews would endure anguish and oppression, it affected him
profoundly, to the very core of his soul, where there is no
place for speculation and logic. He acted wholly based on the
possibility that *perhaps* he would be successful in nullifying
the decree.

When the Rebbe recounted this incident, it was not to
indulge in nostalgic reminiscences: It was done with the specific intention of indicating paths for those who follow in his
ways and adhere to his teachings.

When one is informed of the pain and anguish of a fellow Jew, whether physical distress or most surely spiritual suffering—that a Jew is enmeshed in vain and futile worldly
endeavors and is remote from G-d and His Torah—love for
a fellow Jew should affect the very essence of one's soul. And
it is obvious that this empathy will impel a Jew to do all that
he can, without hesitation or reflection, even on the basis of
the *possibility* that he can help another Jew.

Notes

1. *Sichot Kodesh*, 24th *Tevet*, 5711, section 12.
2. Pyotr Arkadyevitch Stolypin, President of the Council of Ministers

following the Russian Revolution of 1905.

3. Konstantin Petrovich Pobedonostsev, Russian civil servant and political philosopher. Tutor to the Czars Alexander III and Nicholas II. Nicknamed the "Grand Inquisitor."

4. Deuteronomy 15:18.

Moscow, 1927:
From the Rebbe's Diary of 5687

The following diary, covering the events of the Rebbe's trip to Moscow several months prior to his arrest, is a particularly rich source of information concerning the events leading up to the Rebbe's arrest. It displays much of the uniquely personal character of Reshimat Hama'aser, *the Notes of the Arrest, and provides glimpses of the Rebbe's outstanding qualities as a spiritual leader: his courage, determination, and above all, his concern for the physical and spiritual welfare of all Jews, regardless of community affiliation. Since it is, in fact, a diary, the reader will note wide variations in the style and the subject matter, but perhaps for this very reason, the drama of the* Yevsektzia's *pursuit of the Rebbe and the Rebbe's indefatigable determination to continue to strengthen Judaism are especially relevant.*[1]

Motza'ei Shabbat Tetzave, 10 Adar I 5687 (February 12, 1927) 7:30 p.m.

In about an hour and a half, at 9:15, I am to take the express train to Moscow. The purpose of the trip is to make all necessary preparations for the thirteenth meeting.[2]

My purpose and schedule are known only to my wife, to Rabbi Elchonon Dov Morosow, who will keep it secret, and to my secretary, Mr. Lieberman.

On Friday morning Rabbi Morosow informed me that visitors had arrived, in addition to those who came Thursday and whom I received for audiences that evening and night. Since he knew that I was going to travel to Moscow after

Shabbat, he suggested that I receive them for an audience on
Friday afternoon, and I assented.

Among the guests were about ten people who study
Chassidus in depth and who engage in the "service of the
heart,"[3] and although two or three of the younger ones are
involved in reviewing the *ma'amarim, Chassidic* discourses,
generally I must review the *ma'amar* with them once or
twice until they master it.

Usually, I recited the *ma'amar* after *Minchah* on *Shabbat.*
On Sunday morning it is reviewed in my presence, and I
correct the reviewer's mistakes. It occurred to me this time
to recite the *ma'amar* on Friday night before *Kaballat Shabbat,* to review it on *Shabbat* morning, and to say it a third time
at the normal time for reviewing it. Then they would defi-
nitely have it mastered. I told Rabbi Morosow, and he notified the guests and the reviewers. I was surprised that the
Gaon, the "*Illuy,*" as he referred to himself, Avraham from
Slutzk, was present for all three recitations. I thought he had
already left on Thursday.

"This *Shabbat,*" Rabbi Morosow said, "was a true Lubavitcher *Shabbat.*" After the recitation of the *ma'amar* everybody
(approximately thirty people) went to Reb Eliyahu Chaim
Althaus's house, reviewed the *ma'amar,* made *Kiddush,* and ate
the *Shabbat* meal. The guests went to rest, and the reviewers
studied the *ma'amar* until daybreak, went to the *mikveh,*
arrived for reviewing the *ma'amar* with me, reviewed it again
on their own, prayed slowly, ate briefly, and rushed to attend
the regular public review. It was very helpful, Rabbi
Morosow said, that I chose to review the *ma'amar* a third
time, so that the guests also knew it. It would be good, he
added, if I would organize it this way every *Shabbat.*

"The visitors," Rabbi Morosow said, "are satisfied and in
a happy mood. They are preparing for a *chassidic* gathering,
and the *ma'amar* recited this *Shabbat, Ve'atah Tetzaveh,* should
be in writing as soon as possible."

Moscow
11 *Adar I*, 5687 (February 13, 1927)
10:30 a.m.

I have just arrived at the Stara Varvarsk Hotel. The hotel staff received me warmly since I have not stayed here for four months. On my last trip to Moscow I was forced to lodge at the Bolshoi Sibirsky Hotel for reasons explained in my diary. I am staying on the second floor, room 16.

My friend N. G.,[4] the treasurer of the General Fund, was waiting for me. Since I was very tired I arranged to meet with him at the place we both know, at seven o'clock. I asked him to notify my house that "the elderly Yosef Chaim is well."[5]

2:00 p.m.

I have just awakened, and I am continuing to write from where I left off yesterday.

Unfortunately I didn't have enough time to speak last night before leaving with the elderly Rabbi Tzemach Dovid from Luchin, who arrived Friday afternoon. He has a childhood memory of seeing the Rebbe, the Tzemach Tzedek, as he left Petersburg. His father, Rabbi Tuvia Aharon, one of the *chassidim* of the Alter Rebbe, took him along to the town where the Rebbe stopped and rested for a day on his return from Petersburg, *Elul* 5603 (1843).[6] A large crowd from the neighborhood and the surrounding areas gathered there, and his father picked him up on his shoulders so that he merited to see the holy face of the Rebbe, my grandfather. After 5613 (1853), when he married the daughter of the well-known *chassid* Reb Yaakov Zev the *Mashpia,* he would go to Lubavitch every two years.

My diaries from 5685 (1925) record other recollections that he related to me, how he merited in his first audience with the Tzemach Tzedek, in the year 5613, among other things, that the Rebbe told him: "*Chai chai yoducha*"—The living, the living, shall thank You.[7] "Two times *chai* equals 36."[8] What the Rebbe intended with these holy words he didn't know. And as much as he labored and worked with himself he was not able to understand. So he left it at that, saying that G-d knew that he truly wanted to understand what the Rebbe meant, and certainly He would arrange the circumstances so that he would at the proper time. He related:

Seventy years passed from that time—5613—when I heard the Rebbe's holy words at my first audience, "*Chai, chai yoducha*—Two times *chai* equals 36," and I came to Lubavitch in the summer of 5683 (1923) to merit to "prostrate" myself upon the grave[9] and to visit the holy chamber [the enclosure around the grave] of the Rebbe[10] and his son the Rebbe.[11] When I was standing next to the holy grave and pouring out my prayer before the exalted G-d, I suddenly remembered the first audience and the saying "*Chai, chai yoducha.*" It seemed to me that I saw the Rebbe alive as I saw him then— in 5613—in holy white garments like those of the High Priest standing in front of me, and he said: "Tzemach Dovid, this is your thirty-sixth time in Lubavitch: "*Chai, chai, yoducha*—two times *chai* equals 36."

Immediately I fell onto the holy ground and cried bitterly from the depths of my heart: "*Rabotai*, have pity on me!"—that at the end of my days I should correct everything for which my soul descended to earth. I spent a full week in Lubavitch, and every day from morning until night I was in the holy chamber and in the synagogue next to it.

This was the story that this Reb Tzemach Dovid told me yesterday, just as he had previously done in 5685. He added that he was growing weaker and he was preparing to travel to Rostov-on-Don to receive a parting blessing from my holy father resting there, and from there to Lubavitch to receive the blessings of the Rebbes resting there. Then he would return home to prepare himself to go, in the way of all people, for he was already 93 years old.

Upon my request he agreed to stay over in Leningrad until I would return from my travels. I want to spend several days with him in Leningrad—"Lubavitch," as the *chassidim* and students now call it. He has related to me many things that he witnessed himself—as is written in my diary of 5685. He has a remarkable memory, and he is very orderly. Much can be learned from him.

As always, I went on the express train. It was six to eight minutes from my house to the Nikoliev Train Station, and I walked from the vehicle to the "sleeper car" in three or four minutes. Then there were only two or three minutes until the train pulled out. I find it unpleasant to remain in the station or on the platform for longer than that due to the surveillance of people with "seven eyes," who pace the length of the platform and intensely observe every passer-by.

Every time I travel, one of my daughters escorts me to the station, this time my daughter Shaina. When we came to the train we had four minutes remaining. It seemed that everybody was already in their places, except for a few scattered individuals who preferred to be the last ones to board. Near my car stood a man with a brutish face, tall and heavy, with big black eyes that inspired fear.

My daughter entered the compartment with me, and we chatted for about three minutes. She told me that the man standing near the train looked sinister and that he looked at us as if collecting information as we walked by. She requested that when I arrived in Moscow, "somebody should notify whomever" that the elderly Mr. X was healed, and she would know the meaning.

Following the summer of 5686 (1926), I was informed by
Mr. Goren that the *Yevsektzia* was demanding that my family and I be expelled from Leningrad, and that several times
the G.P.U. sent agents to ask about us. He answered that I was
a good neighbor, and the woman Mrs. Mardochovitch (the
mother of Mr. Sharov who lives across from me) also told me
that her son—he is the deputy of Messing specifically to
watch over individuals suspected of having anti-government
opinions—said that the *Yevsektzia* is demanding that he evict
me. They are watching my steps and stalking me to see if they
will find a pretense for slander. I have been careful lately not
to be on the street for even an extra moment, and certainly
this applies to the station. I do not fear anything serious, but
merely something that will cause an uproar since the *Yevsektzia's* goal is at least to frighten me. As soon as the train
moved, my mind rested easier.

The sleeping car looks new this time. My compartment is
large enough, and it has a good table with a lamp, and a chair.
The best feature is that the train does not vibrate. If that
remains the case when it picks up speed, then I will write the
ma'amar Ve'atah Tetzaveh which I recited this past *Shabbat*. I
will finish it in the free hours I will have in Moscow, G-d
willing, and when I return they will be able to copy it and
to send it to the guests who heard it.

A short while later I found that I could write, and I began
the *ma'amar*. I busied myself in this way for over two hours.

I was still sitting and writing when there was a knock at
the door. I did not answer since I presumed it was one of the
train attendants who would visit the travelers and ask them
if they wanted hot water to drink, etc. Half an hour passed,
and there was another knock. I answered "come in," and the
attendant entered. I saw the person who was earlier standing
near the train pacing the length of the hallway. As he passed
the door of my compartment, he paused for a moment and

looked at me and everything in the compartment—a quick glance, but a penetrating one.

The Attendant: "I am sorry to disturb your rest. The person who has been travelling in the nearby compartment since we pulled out demanded that I show him your ticket (on a sleep-car ticket they write the name of the traveler), and I refused. However, when the conductor came to check the passengers' tickets, the man showed him his documents and the conductor showed him all of the passengers' tickets, including yours.

"The man checked all of the tickets, wrote something in his book, and returned to his compartment. About a half hour later or more, he called me and instructed me to tell you that a certain traveler wished to visit you. I answered that you were surely sleeping, but when we passed the last station, he saw through the window that you were sitting and writing, and he insisted that I knock on your door. I knocked, and Your Honor did not answer. A while later he called me again and instructed me to knock loudly and to tell you he wished to speak with you."

I answered that he should tell the man, "I am not accustomed to making acquaintances during my travels. A late hour such as this is not suitable for visits, and I am preparing to sleep." I then asked the attendant to wake me at six in the morning.

My thinking took a sad turn, and various occurrences of anti-religious persecution entered my thoughts: closing synagogues, destruction and condemnation of *mikva'ot*, arrests of rabbis, *shochatim* and children's teachers, and libels against ordinary observant Jews. In the past six years, experience has proven that in the cities where the officials are gentiles they don't mind the synagogues or the *mikva'ot*. It is only where the officials are Jewish that they carry out schemes which are even against the laws of the government. How long will this continue?

As whenever an event troubles me, I remembered the ominous words of my father, the Rebbe, about the new regime, and about the three leaders of the regime—this was about three weeks before his passing:

> Dark clouds are descending upon Russia. Twenty two years definitely. The [Alter] Rebbe said that a regime that persecutes the Jewish religion and forbids the study of Torah must meet its destruction eventually. So it was in the last years of Nikolai, who for years persecuted religion and Torah. He was sent a war, and it broke him and his advisers. In the end, G-d will also destroy the band of young Jews who persecute religion, but until then we will suffer greatly from their wickedness and libels. The fate of the three leaders will be that L. will die insane. T. will be banished and liquidated. S. will follow the spirit of the moment. If necessary, he will put on epaulets.[12]

I was gripped by trembling upon originally hearing these holy words. We will suffer twenty-two years from the black clouds—oh Heaven, what has come upon Judaism, Torah, and religious Jewry throughout the last seven years! Now my entire body shuddered upon recalling the situation which, G-d forbid, the next fifteen years might bring, and I cried in bitterness.

I mentally pictured the scene of that day, Friday, *Adar* 8, 5680 (1920) in the morning, as my saintly father, the Rebbe, uttered those holy, ominous words—and also the following: "Yosef Yitzchak, for disseminating Torah with fear of heaven and strengthening Judaism you must have not only potential but actual self-sacrifice."

I slept, and I saw my father the Rebbe in a vision, as though he was sitting in his room, at a table between two

windows on the western wall, in festival attire. The cande-
labra was in the middle of the room lit up with candles, and
on the table were two candles and an open *Pri Eitz Chaim*.
When I entered, he placed a red silk handkerchief on the
open book —it was open to *Sh'aar HaPurim* chapter 6, *Sod
Mordechai V'esther* by R. Chaim Vital, of blessed memory.[13]
His holy face was very serious, and he told me: "Why are you
crying? 'When the month of *Adar* begins, we increase in
joy.'[14] If your work is very hard upon you, remember my
instruction to sacrifice yourself for disseminating Torah study
with fear of heaven, and for strengthening Judaism, actually,
not only in potential."

I woke up, and I looked at the clock. It was 3 o'clock, and
I slept again. My sleep was sweet, and I rested well.

The attendant woke me up at 6 o'clock. I washed, got
dressed, prepared for prayers, and prayed. I drank a cup of hot
water, and at 8 o'clock I sat down to write the *ma'amar* since
there was another hour until we would arrive in Moscow.

The attendant notified me that the train would be more
than half an hour late—at one of the stations we stopped for
an hour due to a major search of five cars in which 12 people were arrested—and instead of 9 o'clock, we would arrive
in Moscow no earlier than 9:30. For about an hour and a
quarter I wrote the *ma'amar*, and the attendant came again,
sent by my neighbor, who was requesting permission to
enter and make my acquaintance. Though I was greatly
averse to the idea, I could not refuse him, and I said I would
organize and stow my belongings. Then I would announce
that he might enter.

The man entered and said, "My name is Mark
Saminovitch Bashkov." He was the chairman of the
Sovnorkom in the city of Tsheliabinsky, and a member of the
general U.G.P.O.[15] What surprised me was that he entered
with his hat on.

Me: My name is Yosef Yitzchak Schneersohn.

He: Your title?

Me: *Yid.*

He: All Jews are "*Yidden,*" what kind of a title is that?

Me: So it is, every Jew is a Jew, and that alone is their true title. It is never lost or replaced by others. If someone bearing an ordinary title commits a crime, he loses it. But even the sinner does not lose the title "Jew," as it says, "a Jew, although he has sinned, is still a Jew,"[16] since his essential spark of Jewishness is eternal. But there are various levels in this: there are some who merely love their nation, honor Jewish wisdom, honor the Jewish Torah, cherish G-d's commandments, and cherish Jewish customs; and there is also one who is prepared to literally sacrifice himself for the fulfillment of a single Jewish custom, and surely for a positive commandment or to prevent the violation of a negative commandment. All of this is a direct effect of the essential spark of Jewishness, but the person's education and various life experiences are crucial in revealing it.

The attendant announced that in several moments the train would arrive at the Moscow station.

He: I was born in Arsha in the Mohilev region. I would very much like to make your acquaintance more closely.

He said that for two or three days he would be very busy, and on the third day he would be freed from his work. If I would still be in Moscow he wished to visit me, and if I was travelling home to Leningrad he would come there specifically to meet with me, for he honored his parents' memory and his elderly father. They and their entire families were Lubavitcher *chassidim,* and the Lubavitcher Rebbes' names did not cease from their mouths, as was also true of his grandparents. His paternal grandfather's parents and his maternal grandfather were already travelling to Lubavitch one hundred years ago. "Tell me," he finished, "in what hotel are you staying in Moscow?"

Me: Stara Varvarskaya.

He: Thank you. Be well, and much success.

11 *Adar I* 5687, (February 13, 1927) Moscow. 2:00 p.m.

The train arrived 35 minutes late. I was still impressed by the meeting with the chairman of the Tsheliabinsky *Sovnorkom*[17]—especially because he was a member of U.G.P.O., which is feared by all citizens of the country, whatever their rank. Moreover, the executive officer of U.G.P.O. is Menzshinsky, who is known as a very serious person who demands truth, and he himself is from a *chassidic* family in Arsha. The Lubavitcher Rebbes' names also did not cease from their mouths or their forefathers, for they also went to Lubavitch 100 years ago.

My meeting with Bashkov was not mere chance—even a single straw blowing in the marketplace, as our Rebbe the Baal Shem Tov says, is by Divine Providence. G-d himself takes the wind from his "storehouse" to move the straw from side to side or from place to place. All of this is a link in the chain of G-d's blessed will, and how much more so in an event like this.

My wisdom is inadequate to understand the lesson of this Divine Providence, but the incident in general strengthens my assertion that it is only the *Yevsektzia* youth who disrupt religion and destroy religious institutions. It is all their doing.

I was walking slowly, deep in my thoughts. The porter carried my belongings. When I left the station, the rapid wagons—"*lichatchi*"—which I usually took were already gone. One of the wagon drivers asked "hotel?" and I got on.

I paid the porter and told the driver to take me to the Stara Varvarskaya Hotel.

"*Gut*," the driver[18] replied in Yiddish.

For a moment I thought I had just imagined he had answered in Yiddish, but several moments later, as we were driving through a short alley, he turned to me and greeted me in Yiddish.

"It's been many years since I've seen you," he said. His father would travel to Lubavitch, and he would engage in Torah study every day with the other married men between *Minchah* and *Ma'ariv* and after *Ma'ariv* with Reb Velvel Gitel's. Reb Velvel was one of the children's teachers whom I knew. Now he is old and weak and lives with his son Reb Shraga Melamed in Horodok in the Vitebsk region. Reb Zev[19] is on my list of recipients of "Elderly Support," and Rabbi Shraga Melamed is listed as a teacher supported by "The Fund."

"I did not wish to study Torah," he continued. "Until the draft I dealt in business and became lax in donning *tefillin*. When I traveled I sometimes ate non-kosher food, and when it benefitted me I violated *Shabbat*. When the war broke out and they drafted the youth, I was one of the first they mobilized. My father told me to go to the Lubavitcher Rebbe[20] to receive his blessing, and so I did. I came to Lubavitch in *Elul* of 5674 (1914), about one month after the war was declared."

When he went in for an audience, my father told him, "Be scrupulous not to eat non-kosher food and put on *tefillin* every weekday. You should also resolve not to violate *Shabbat*, for when one violates *Shabbat* during the war it is not considered a violation except when done deliberately. If you will fulfill these three things, G-d will watch over you so that no bullet shall find you, and He will bring you home in good health."

A full year, related Yaakov Lifshitz, he was in the front lines. Bullets and death flew from all sides and he was never injured. Then he was given two month's furlough. Before he returned to the war he traveled to Lubavitch. When he arrived at the Rudnia train station,[21] he saw my father the Rebbe about to get on the train to Smolensk. He got back on and traveled with him. My father blessed him a second time. When the war ended and the new regime took over, he chose a livelihood that would allow him to observe *Shabbat*. He prays every day, he and his wife observe *Shabbat* and they are giving their children a Jewish upbringing. He continued, "I live in a good house. Because of my work I am considered important. I have three rooms and I can give you one of them. My wife will cook for you. Why stay in a hotel where every person is examined with 'seven eyes'?"

I thanked him for his suggestion and told him how I enjoyed his story. Surely if he would continue to fulfill my father's instructions his blessings would continue. But I asked him to speed up. A half-hour had already passed because he had driven slowly, and time is precious.

When we arrived at the hotel he refused to accept payment, and my arguments were to no avail.

When I stepped down I wanted to tell him something, but he said, "Be well," and was off.

I inspected the central account's books and I read their reports. Everyone was asking for additional funds. They all were hoping to expand their activities. As I see it, the budget for this coming half-year—*Adar II* through *Tishrei*—will be about 40,000. The Fund's deficit for the first half—*Rosh Hashanah* through *Adar I*—was about 5,000.

The budget for manual vocations must be doubled at least. I am worried, for Rabbi M. and Mr. A. H. are very jealous of me since these efforts have been outstandingly successful. Undoubtedly, they will demand the transfer of the direction of this project from the central office, which is under my direction, to the regional offices. Surely G-d will help me and show me how to proceed.

12 *Adar I* (February 14)
8:30 a.m.
Bolshoi Moscovsky Hotel, Room 16

It is indeed true that "a man's gifts will make room for him."[22] Since I have been traveling for community matters in summer of 5655 (1895)—and steadily in 5658 (1898)—I have developed rules: 1) to try to travel in my own compartment, 2) to lodge in a business hotel, and 3) to tip the attendants of the hotel and the office workers, especially in Moscow and Petersburg where the Jews' dwelling rights used to be limited.

Even nowadays, when the confines of the old regime upon the Jews are removed and a Jew may live anywhere in the country, I am among those who "throw their bread upon the water,"[23] as I will detail later.

The truth is that the government has changed: a new regime has replaced the old one. But for us, the Jews, nothing is altered. The only difference is that in the old regime they hit us with the right hand—the Czarist Black Hundreds[24]—and in the new regime it is the left hand; the *Yevsektzia*. Sometimes the leftists are stronger than the rightists, and their blows are more painful. Last night at 9:00 when I returned from the *chassidic* gathering, I wrote the *ma'amar* until 1:00 a.m., I then stopped writing to prepare for bed.

I recited the *Shema*, undressed, washed, and lay down. There was a knock on the door, but I ignored it. I thought that surely somebody had mistaken my room for my neighbor's—for I had heard people there. I turned out the light and expected to sleep.

After several minutes the telephone rang. I picked it up and heard the voice of the hotel clerk Kuznetzov. He apologized and asked me to open the door since he had something important to tell me.

I opened the door, and he told me that a quarter hour earlier a man had come to the hotel office asking if Rabbi Schneersohn had already arrived, and he explained that he was a member of the *Yevsektzia*. Their colleagues in Leningrad informed them that Rabbi Schneersohn had traveled to Moscow yesterday. He was surely busily engaged with his fellow rabbis, in activities connected to strengthening religion. They had directed them to watch my every step. "All day we looked for him," he said, "and we could not find him. Together we decided to intimidate him, to come with the police and take him to stay in one of the stations where we have friends, overnight. Over the course of the night we will learn why he came and what he is doing here."

"I answered," the clerk continued, "that the guest Schneersohn had not yet arrived. I was told that Schneersohn had said when he left that he would be back no earlier than 2:00 a.m.. The youth wrote down my telephone number and told us to notify him when Rabbi Schneersohn arrived.

"Now," the clerk continued, "you must leave the hotel. I will go with you to the Bolshoi Moscovsky Hotel. One of the office staff there who works the night shift is my friend. I have already discussed it with him: you'll spend the night there."

A quarter-hour later I left the hotel through the kitchen as the clerk instructed—he was afraid they were watching for me. A quarter-hour later we arrived at the Bolshoi Moscovsky. All the rooms were occupied, so they gave me the guard's room until one of the rooms would be vacated. At about 2:30 I lay down to rest. I got up at about 7:00, prayed, and had a hot drink. The clerk promised to give me room 33, which would be available at 12:00 for six *tchervantzes* per day. I paid for two days and then I gave the clerk a handsome tip and thanked him for his kindness.

The man from the Bolshoi's office knew of the situation, for his friend from the Bolshoi Sibirsky had told him that I was eluding the *Yevsektzia*. He told me to leave the hotel through a different way without going through the lobby. He asked me what time I expected to arrive. If it was after 11:00, then he would be at his watch—he worked the night shift—and he would open a door for me so no one would see.

It seems that the words of our treasurer, Mr. G., are correct. He said that the head of the G.P.U., Menzshinsky, was against the *Yevsektzia*, and he rejected Litvakov's suggestions to target religion. This is also the case with the Special Committee to Uproot Religion, which is a youth group assigned to searching for observant Jews, chasing them, libeling them, and destroying them—heaven forfend. Menzshinsky gives them no power as far as G.P.U. is concerned. It is rumored that twice Litvakov complained about Menzshinsky to the general committee and he left broken hearted. But at one of the meetings, a month ago, at which Messing—the head of the G.P.U. in Leningrad—took part together with his first deputy, Rapaport, Litvakov convinced Messing to strengthen the *Yevsektzia* in general and the Special Committee in particular, to give them the power of the G.P.U. Rapaport opposed it, but the second deputy, Rubin, agreed. Menzshinsky, however, strongly opposed it, and the committee decided that each of the directors of the G.P.U. could do as he saw fit without receiving permission from the main G.P.U. office. Menzshinsky gave an order to the Moscow G.P.U. office to fire any member of the *Yevsektzia* that was among the G.P.U. staff. Messing, on the other hand, gave the

Yevsektzia considerable power, and organized a special *Yevsektzia* committee within the Leningrad G.P.U.

11:30 p.m.

When I arrived I met the hotel clerk, who gave me the key to room 33 on the second floor.

In the morning, when I arrived back at the Stara Varvarsk Hotel and entered the office to take my key, one of the clerks looked at me and asked, "Where were you last night, and what time did you leave the hotel?" I suspected that this clerk was new since I did not recognize him and he used the slang currently popular among the young people. I suspected that he was a Jew. Although he restrained his anger, his cheeks burned and his eyes betrayed fury. The two clerks whom I knew for many years sat bent over and wrote. I noticed they were enraged at the youth who spoke to me.

Although I was very afraid, I acted unfazed and I smiled faintly. Before I had a chance to answer, the youth began to speak.

The Clerk: When I arrived this morning I learned that the police came twice to ask about the guest in room 67 on the second floor. The key was in the office, and I took it and saw that the bed was unmade as though someone had gotten up in middle of the night. No one was there. I asked the attendants, and they told me the guest in room 67 left at 8:00 p.m.. So where were you all night?

Me: It is almost 25 years that I have been travelling to various cities from time to time and staying in numerous hotels. This is the first time that I was asked in the hotel office—and not only that, interrogated—concerning my whereabouts by day or night. I see no reason to answer. I turned to go.

"*Gait nit avek!*"—"Don't go"—the clerk said to me in Yiddish, "Your *gemara kepl*[25] won't help you. We—the Jewish members—know who you are. You will not escape us; we will still get you."

Me: Who I am, all of Russia knows, and who my parents are, all of Russia and the entire world know, but nobody knows who you are.

The Clerk (furiously): If I call the police to have you arrested, they will respond immediately.

Me (patiently): I have yet to hear that the police should arrest a person for no reason.

The Clerk: We, the young Jews—the *Yevsektzia*—will demand it from the police, and the secret police will also be involved.

When I came to my room, I organized my belongings. I took my *talit* and *tefillin* in the small case and left through the kitchen. I took the key with me.

12 *Adar I* (February 14)
11:30 p.m.
Bolshoi Moscovsky Hotel, Room 16

The meeting began at 12:15 p.m. and lasted until 4:30. We checked the financial records and discussed the proposals. We also debated the vocational work that we had organized. Rabbis G.[26], K.[27] and M.[28] prevailed over Rabbi M. and Mr. A. H. that the direction and support of the vocational work should be under the central office, as it had been until then. For a long time we debated whether we should all go to the Doctor[29] or if I should go alone. We also debated the amount of support we should request. It was decided that I should go alone and that I should request the amount I found appropriate, depending on the situation at the time of the visit.

We prayed *Minchah* together and arranged to meet at 4:00 p.m. the next day at the home of Rabbi S.Y.[30] at the engagement meal. The treasurer Mr G. and I went to the Doctor. We came at the appointed time, 6:00, the Doctor came out to receive us, and I saw that he was in good spirits. I understood that it was surely due to some successful community work, for that inevitably puts him in a good mood. He loves productive community work in any area.

The Doctor brought us into his "paved chamber"[31] and said happily, "Yesterday in the bank and today in my office, I heard about you and your tremendous work in several areas of the country, both in religious matters and concerning material support.

"As I sat yesterday in the Jewish Bank, Mr. A. L. Fuchs and Mr. Orenson[32] told me of the successful results of your work for the vocational project, in addition to your helping dozens of families purchase machines for weaving and sewing, and also for making copper buttons and shoelaces, etc.—the campaign has stirred the interest of hundreds of families in vocational work.

"Yesterday and today I was also visited by people from the Kiev, Poltava, Zhitomir, Minsk, and Vitebsk regions, and I heard from all of them that various young men had visited their towns—secretly they were told that these were Rebbe Schneersohn's emissaries—to inspire them to undertake hand-vocation work. Some of them were promised support to purchase equipment, which had a significant impact.

"This work impresses me, and I am prepared to help you with all of my abilities since I see it as a source of livelihood for thousands of families."

At that moment I saw that G-d had given me a proper view. My assessment, as I told the treasurer Mr. G., was correct.

After we left the meeting,[33] Mr. G. and I went to my friend, the *chassid* Reb Boruch Shalom Kahn in Zharadye to eat lunch.

Mr. G. told me of the committee's discussion after I left them alone to decide my two questions. "All of us as one spoke of the diligence of your work, and the unbiased way it was carried out, without distinguishing between the *chassidic* and Ashkenazic communities—not to mention that all of those involved with the efforts, which involve mortal danger, are students of the Tomchei Temimim Yeshivah. Rabbi Y. K. stressed that if not for your great effort in the country and abroad, we would not have received even 10 percent of what we do now. So we decided that you should go alone and decide yourself what to propose to the Doctor."

"I am firmly resolved," I told Mr. G., "to ask the Doctor to double his support for the vocational budget. I still do not know how to discuss it, but surely G-d will help, as it says: 'The preparation of the heart is man's,—one must prepare one's heart to focus on G-d. Then one can be sure that '…from G-d is the answer of the tongue.'"[34]

As we traveled to the Doctor, we discussed the proposal to double the budget, but we did not know how to present it. However, since the Doctor himself began to praise the vocational project, I saw the hint of Divine Providence giving me an opening, and I said:

"This is true, the vocational project work that I began three years ago did not net huge results for the first two years, except from the cigarette factories and weaving in Rostov and in Tchernigov and Mohilev. But this year the project was completely successful, and many more people want to participate. I have come to suggest that the Doctor bring machinery and equipment from abroad. A certain amount will be donated, and a specific amount will be paid off gradually."

The Doctor: Bringing equipment from abroad is immensely difficult.

But he was prepared to help buy equipment within the country, and he was interested in hearing an organized proposal.

Me: The Jewish committee for manual vocation proposes that within several months various pieces of equipment should be distributed worth more than 60,000. It can be purchased domestically.

The Doctor: When do you need the amount you mentioned?

Me: Presently 50 percent will suffice. In a month or five weeks another 20 percent will be needed, and the rest in 8-10 weeks.

The doctor pondered and then scribbled with a pencil on a piece of paper. My heart was to the heavens. I prayed to G-d that heaven's mercies would be evoked in the merit of my holy fathers and that He give the Doctor the proper decision: to cover the budget.

The Doctor: Yes, I am giving you the above budget at those times: 50 percent now, 20 percent in one month, and 30 percent in two months.

He turned to Mr. G. and told him to come the next evening to receive the first payment. He also told his assistant and his agent about the two payments, for he was planning to travel abroad in two weeks.

Me: Now I wish to propose something regarding support for the religious and Torah institutions, *yeshivot*, *chadorim*, rabbis and *shochatim*.

The Doctor: Yes, I have heard of your work in the Crimea settlements, that you appointed rabbis, *shochatim* and children's teachers. Last week Professor Haffkine[35]—whom you know well from last year—returned from his travels to visit the settlements. In every place he visited he also interested himself in the religious institutions, and he was amazed at how they were organized. He was told that they were all Rabbi Schneersohn's work and he expressed a desire to meet with you. But now he is visiting the cities of Caucasia to investigate cholera, with which he has been involved for 40 years, and he will remain there for around two months. It would be good for you to meet with him when he returns to Moscow; it could benefit the communal work.

Yesterday one of my relatives visited me. He is a young man, my sister's son, who belongs to an anti-religious organization, and he attended a meeting of the special Committee to Uproot Religion; he told me that the leader of the *Yevsektzia*, Litvakov, delivered an address describing his opposition to religious activism. He singled out Rabbi Schneersohn in particular for his far-flung influence throughout the whole of Russia—his support of Torah schools for children, advanced Talmudic schools, his aid to Rabbis and *shochatim*. He said that he has printed prayerbooks, that he supports *mikva'ot*, and that he pays for the construction of new ones. He sends young men to encourage and inspire other Jews, and he has a highly significant influence on the adult Jewish population. The activities of his followers display forethought and intense effort.

"Listen to what happened to me," continued Litvakov, reading from a written text:

When I came to the city of Kulash in the region of Tiflis, the city council met and I addressed them. After my speech, the chairman expressed thanks for my words and praise for the Central Committee in Moscow, which had sent me to encourage them. He continued: "I must also express our gratitude on behalf of the local Jewish comrades to the Central Committee in Moscow for sending an emissary to build a *mikveh* for our women. The *mikveh* has been standing next to the bath house for over ten months. I am deeply honored to invite our illustrious guest from the Central Committee to accompany us to personally view the *mikveh* with his own eyes. He can then describe this project to the Central Committee and transmit our profound thanks to them."

I immediately understood that this was the result of Rabbi Schneersohn's efforts, because of other events I had experienced during my travels in that area. I was compelled to maintain a genial composure, although I was intensely angry inside. The chairman innocently continued that Comrade Shavelov had visited with them for a week and then with great effort had influenced them to close the synagogue and transform it into a club, and had blocked up the *mikveh* despite the strong objections of the local women. Two weeks later a young emissary arrived who spoke Russian fluently. He was accompanied by an associate who spoke the Georgian dialect. They presented themselves as emissaries from the Central Committee who had come to restore the *mikveh*. To quote the chairman, 'They offered us two hundred *tchervantzes*[36] to aid in the effort. We did not accept the offer, and in a few days, reconstructed the *mikveh* under our own initiative and dispatched Rabbi Slavin, a student from Rabbi Schneersohn's *yeshivah*, to oversee that it was built in accordance with Jewish law. This caused boundless joy in our community.'

I accompanied them to the *mikveh*; perceiving the prevailing spirit of pride and exhilaration in the *mikveh*, I was cautious about expressing my personal feelings. I also realized that my words would be of no avail.

When I came to the farewell dinner in honor of my visit, a document was handed to me. It was signed by one hundred and twenty nine members, and had, as well, the official endorsement of the local council. It was a request for the removal of the club and the restoration of the synagogue so that they could pray there. The emissaries had informed them that, according to the law, fifty signatures would be adequate to effect this change.

Litvakov then read to his colleagues the text for the plea for the revival of the synagogue in Kulash. Litvakov continued, "I came to Ony. There too, after Shavelov had closed the synagogue and stopped up the *mikveh*, young men arrived speaking in the name of the Central Committee. They provided funding of three hundred *tchervantze* to re-open and renovate the *mikveh* and requested that Rabbi Perlov, a student of Rabbi Schneersohn's *yeshivah*, come and oversee that it was in accordance with the strict requirements of Jewish law. On their own initiative they transferred the local club from the synagogue, which they then restored to its former status."

"It is a shame and a disgrace," read Litvakov from his printed speech, "to the leadership of the League of Anti-religious Jewish youth that they do not have the ability to silence and tie the hands of one man who ruins all our work."

"Truly," Chairman Litvakov turned to all the assembled, "the words of Comrade Dmitri"—the author of the speech—"are true: can it be that we do not have the ability to stop Schneersohn's mouth and tie his hands? Let us all resolve together to put away Schneersohn for ever, and then after a short time, his whole organization will fall apart.

"Comrades from Leningrad," continued Litvakov, "I tell you that yesterday night Schneersohn travelled to Moscow and I advise that a committee of three be chosen of the anti-religious youth league who will take responsibility for eliminating Schneersohn and destroying his organization.'

"All the assembled agreed unanimously."

Me: Now, given the decision of the *Yevsektzia* directors and members to break the organization and remove me, we must strengthen and intensify the organization more so. Large sums will be needed.

The Doctor: Isn't it only two weeks since I gave 20,000?

Me: Yes. The 20,000 were payment for covering the budget of the first half year, from *Tishrei* until *Adar I*. Now we must organize the budget for the second half year, *Adar II-Elul*. A certain part I take upon myself, and whatever will be short, must be covered.

The Doctor: How much?

Me: Not more than forty thousand.

The Doctor: And not less . . .

Me: . . .than forty thousand.

The Doctor: Good. In two installments. I believe you must be careful, for the members of the *Yevsektzia* are extremely bold and are capable of anything.

The Doctor went to his office with Mr. G. to arrange the financial matters and I remained alone. When they returned, I received a parting blessing, and the Doctor came to see me off. When we came outside it was 8:00 p.m.. Knowing that I could only enter my room in the Bolshoi Moscovsky after 11:00, we went to visit Mr. Ostrovsky and Mr. Shneurov.

When I was visiting Shneurov, it occurred to me to visit Mr. Orenson and to describe the current situation, to seek his advice on how to proceed. I learned by telephone that he was at home, and I told him that I was on the way to see him.

Mr G. wished to come along with me. I said that it was not advisable, and I asked him not to call me by telephone. I said further that, G-d willing, tomorrow at 12:00 p.m. we would meet at Reb Boruch Shalom Kahn's.

Mr. Orenson received me warmly and listened especially intently to everything I told him. He told me that in Moscow the *Yevsektzia* had no power at all. The regular police, and surely the G.P.U., he said, consider all of the *Yevsektzia's* actions foreign. The statement of Lizshinsky was already known: "The *Yevsektzia* is a patch on the eye of the government." "They," Orenson said, "can frighten and nothing more. If anybody comes, even with a police officer, do not be afraid. On the contrary: be strong. Demand that the police officer show you his certificate and ask in the police station if there is such an officer (Mr. Orenson gave me the telephone number—unlisted—of the special division in the police station), and then demand his authorization to tire you with his questions."

Mr. Orenson told me of the secret meeting the community leaders had held in the Jewish Bank with the participation of Mr. R. and said that they spoke about the diligence of the work being done in the whole expanse of the country. Mr. Fuchs and Mr. Mendele described my success in the manual vocations and asserted that the Jewish Bank, too, should focus on it.

This time Mr. Orenson displayed more warmth towards me than previously. When I got up to leave, he told me of an acquaintance of many years, who "sits in the secret offices." Today he visited Orenson in his home, and when I spoke to him—from Shneurov's home—he was sitting there. He told Orenson of his lineage and his work. Orenson was very surprised to learn that he was a descendant of the Lubinsky family of Susnitza—Tchernigov Region—who were "related to Schneersohn" and he wished to meet me face-to-face. Mr Orenson promised him that the next time I visit him in Moscow, he will arrange an opportunity to meet at his home.

As I was walking from Mr. Orenson's, I came upon Rabbi Mendel Elkind at the Varvarsky Gate. He told me he was coming from the Stara Varvarsk Hotel because he wanted to see me, to suggest I go to his estate to rest for a day or two. I thanked him for his excellent suggestion, saying that this time I was unable to fulfill it, for my work was very pressing.

When I arrived at the Stara Varvarsk Hotel and entered my room, the clerk entered and told me "they came four times to inquire about you. It was a group of young men, and one time they were even accompanied by a police officer. My police friends tell me that this officer is not even from this area and they do not recognize him. Kratov—he's the one that tried to intimidate me this morning and who fought with me—left an urgent order that when the guest Schneersohn from Room 67 would arrive, he should immediately be notified at a telephone number which he wrote down.

"I thought," Kuznetzov continued, "that I must tell you everything I heard and that the entire day Kratov was cursing angrily, saying that he would take revenge from 'Schneersohn the stubborn bourgeois.'"

While still in his parents' home in Amtzislov—Mohliev region—Kratov had heard about the Schneersohn family of Lubavitch and in the dark days of the fifth year—5665, 1905 on the Gentile calendar—when he was 15 years old, he needed to leave his town of birth and travel to his uncle, his father's brother, who was a teacher in one of the *chadorim* of Rebbe Schneersohn of Lubavitch. He said, "The four months I stayed by my uncle the teacher, the principal—that's what they called Rebbe Schneersohn's son who ran the *yeshivah*[37] and the *chadorim*—did not allow me rest. He ordered them to watch me with 'seven eyes.' Now I will exact revenge from him."

"I must tell you," Kuznetzov continued, "that in the last three months since Kratov was hired by the hotel, because of his despotism and cruelty the entire office staff and the hotel attendants are afraid of him. Besides his other bad traits, he is a terrible slanderer."

I told Kuznetzov that in another quarter of an hour I would decide whether to lodge here or I would go. "If I stay here," I told him, "then you should fulfill Kratov's orders."

K. left and I sat down to think. There were things to be said for both possible courses of action. I am not afraid at all. But regardless, there will be trouble and they might libel me and take me to the station to investigate. They could find ways to hold me for a day or two, and that would have bad consequences. I decided to leave the hotel, and I took my case and my walking stick to go.

As I left, I saw K. walking towards me, his eyes wide, his face white as lime, and his voice trembling. "They just asked by telephone whether citizen Schneersohn is in his room. The lad—the assistant telephonist—answered that he is in room 37. You can't leave through the entrance. What shall we do?"

Me: Calm yourselves, I am not afraid, and I will go through the normal entrance. As we were walking, the lad (the assistant telephonist) ran towards us and told the clerk that he was being called to the telephone. The lad turned around and the clerk rushed after him. I walked slowly because of my melancholy thoughts. As I walked by the hotel office, the clerk whispered to me that the clerk from the Bolshoi Moscovsky said that he was waiting for me at the kitchen entrance. I told him to pass along my thanks, but not to wait for me, for I would come through the normal entrance.

As I entered the entrance hall, I saw Rabbi Boruch Shalom standing there. I asked why he had come at this late hour. He answered, "I came to tell you that the students Bentzion[38] and Avrohom Yosef have arrived." I told him to tell them that tomorrow at 10:00 we would meet at his house.

Reb Boruch Shalom went on his way, and I went to the Bolshoi Moscovsky. I entered through the normal entrance hall, and the clerk greeted me in a friendly manner.

13 *Adar I* (February 15)
2:00 a.m.

My sleep was very sweet because of the vision I saw tonight. At the time I knew it was a dream, and I forced myself to remember what I saw and the talks concerning holy matters, the verses, the *agadot* from the sayings of our Sages, and the three stories. Thank G-d, I was able to remember it all, each item at its place. When I arose at six o'clock, after the morning blessings, I recorded the main points of all of it. G-d willing, when I arrive home, I will write it at length as I heard it. I am in a very good mood.

I washed and prayed, and at 8:30 I called the hotel clerk to pay him for the room.

The Clerk: Your Honor can use the room until 7:00.

I paid him and thanked him for his interest, telling him I would in fact keep the room until 7:00. I then went to the Stara Varvarsk Hotel and drank a cup of hot water.

At ten o'clock I met with individuals very dear to me, who literally sacrifice themselves for Divine service, Bentzion and Avrohom Yosef, and for about three hours they presented their reports of all details of the work. The treasurer Mr. G. visited all of the members of the committee individually, for he had to give each one the money, according to the budget, for the work for the second half of the year, *Adar II-Tishrei*. Meanwhile he also notified them that the meeting would be at 3:00 and not at 5:00, and that during these two hours they would hear reports from the heads of the Executive and Review Committees and that I would arrive at 5:00.

I ate lunch and returned to my room in the Stara Varvarsk Hotel. I then worked on the *ma'amar*, which I had only half finished.

When 4:30 arrived I needed to stop. I recited *Minchah* and left my room to go to the meeting. In the hallway I saw the assistant telephonist running toward me, and he said that I was being called to the telephone in the hotel office.

Me: Who is calling?

The Lad: I do not know.

When I entered the office, Officer Kratov said to me, "Speak into the phone on the wall, and I will listen on the phone on my desk: I want to hear who is speaking with you and what you are discussing."

I turned to the telephonist and said: "Tell the caller to state his telephone number and a name to ask for, and tell him that in another quarter hour I will call him back, because I will not speak from the hotel telephone."

Officer Kratov was shocked and could not utter a word. The telephonist did his job and repeated loudly: "U.G.P.O., Room 47."

Kratov: I order you to speak. If you don't, you will regret it—
    it won't get you anywhere.

I took the telephonist's note with the telephone number, and I turned to leave.

Kratov shouted out: Citizen Schneersohn, know that I warned you before witnesses.

I remembered the meeting with Mr. Bashkov. Surely he would speak with me about setting an appointment. When I left the hotel, I entered the first store I saw. I asked them if I could use their telephone, and read off the telephone number and room number. I said my name, and they told me to wait a moment, for Comrade Bashkov wished to speak with me, and I waited several moments.

Bashkov: Is it possible to meet with you at 6:00 p.m.?

Me: Had I known earlier, I would have arranged my schedule differently. Now that I've already arranged my schedule, I will try to return to the Stara Varvarsk, room 67 at 7:00.

Bashkov: Good. I will come at 7:30.

I rushed to the meeting and arrived 25 minutes late. I asked the members' pardon, and Rabbi Z. briefly told me the content of the debates, and that all of the members were satisfied by the reports of the young men (the members of the Executive and Review committees.)

Rabbi M: I did not think that Mr. G. would visit me today with the "splendid gift"—meaning part of the budget in cash.

They considered several other matters, and I told my friends that I needed to be back in the hotel at 7:00. We agreed to meet at 11:00 p.m. in the home of A. R. Mr. G. wished to come along with me, but I told him we would meet at 11:00 as discussed.

I left covertly, and I went to Novi Rodi, which is in Kremlin Square, and bought fruit. I went to the hotel and ordered

them to bring hot water with tea and honey, and then I waited to receive the son and grandson of *chassidim*: Mark
Saminovitch Bashkov—chairman of the Tcheliabinsky
Sovnorkom and member of U.G.P.O.—to chat about his
memories. Moments after 7:30, Mark Saminovitch entered,
hat in hand.

I asked him to sit and he inquired as to my health and said
that if I had time for him, he would be free till 9:30. He
would then have to leave for a meeting scheduled at ten, and
the next day he would be travelling to Tcheliabinsk.

Me: I have arranged my schedule so that I will have adequate
   time.

It was very significant to me to hear his family recollections of years past, which were intertwined with my own
family history and religious traditions that were then being
uprooted from their source without logic or reason.

Bashkov: My father was a *cheder* teacher named Shimon
   Bashkas. His mother arranged weddings for professionals
   and prominent people in Arsha, so her name was known
   even outside of Arsha, and his father the *melamed* was
   named after her. His mother's brother Menachem Shmuel
   Ragalin (who was in the business of making raisin wine)
   was one of the prominent professionals in Arsha.

His grandfather on his father's side and his mother's
father—Menachem Shmuel's father—were among the
prominent *chassidim* of, in Bashkov's words, "the old Rebbe
of Lubavitch." Bashkov continued, "I don't remember his
name, but I remember that Nikolai I summoned him to
Petersburg and asked him to set up secular schools for the
Jewish children. The Rebbe refused and was placed under
arrest."

Me: That was the Tzemach Tzedek, my father's grandfather.

Bashkov: I heard many stories about this Rebbe and also his
   son who had visited Alexander III, attempting to inter-

vene to still the pogroms and the intense anti-semitic agitation in the Kiev area.

Me: That was my paternal grandfather, Rabbi Shmuel of
Lubavitch.

Bashkov: I was a good student, and until the age of fourteen
I learned diligently. I then decided to travel to a *yeshivah*
in Minsk. I was there for three years and became non-
observant. When I returned home, I could not adjust to
the family's lifestyle. I fled from home and joined the
socialists in Warsaw, and from there I went to England and
learned various vocations.

Afterwards I returned to my homeland and worked in
various factories where I was a political activist, recruiting
people to socialism.

He then related at length about his imprisonment, his
flight from Russia, his return to Russia during the Revolution, and of his present significant work, matters that did
not interest me.

With particular concern he spoke about his parents. He
had not seen them for twenty years, since he was already a
member of the *Cheka* secret police in Moscow. He traveled
specifically to Arsha to visit his parents and learned that his
mother had passed away two years ago. In her memory he
decided to change his name to Bashkov. He could not recognize his father—aged, bent over, emaciated and gaunt-
faced. Upon entering the room in the dwelling of Zalman
Yaakov Lipkin, an eminent member of the Arsha community and a distinguished *chassid*, he found his father lying in
bed and groaning. His father saw him, but he did not recognize him, calling out in anger, "Have you come to arrest me
again? Give me some time to recover from my illness," and
he wept.

Bashkov: It took a long time for me to calm him and
make him aware that I was his Meir. My father gazed at me

with a cold stare, not saying anything. Despite my lengthy
plea that he come to Moscow and that he would lack for
nothing there, he answered, "In the past, it was necessary to
be a teacher of children. And now, for teaching, one is cast
into prison and beaten. To be a teacher now it is necessary to
endanger one's life and learn with children in secret.

He tried to give currency of forty *tchervantzes* to his
father, but he would not accept it, saying that he had sufficient funds.

I wondered to myself how he would react if he learned
that his father Shimon and his uncle Reb Aryeh Shlomo
were secret Torah teachers in Arsha and his uncle Menachem Shmuel, a secret Torah teacher in Yekatrinaslav, all
in the employ of our organization.

He spoke at length about his travels as a member of the
G.P.U. to visit various cities until he was designated to a high
position.

Suddenly the door opened, the official Kratov and three
youths entered with him, one of them in a police uniform.
All of them, aside from Kratov, had guns in their hands. Kratov, in a rage, called out: "Citizen Schneersohn, you are under
arrest. Do not move from your place. If you do, they will
shoot you and you will be to blame for your own death. Tell
us where your luggage is so that we can search it. "Garshka,"
he said to one of his deputies, "close the door."

Bashkov sat staring; though his face reddened he did not
utter a word. Already accustomed to searches and to the
investigators' constantly saying things designed to induce
fear, I sat placidly and answered, "The small suitcase is there,
and the large one is next to my bed behind the partition
between the living room and the bedroom."

Kratov commanded his assistants to search, sat on one of
the chairs, and related how he had beaten Jewish rabbis and

teachers, knocking out their teeth and destroying their eyes. In his birthplace, the city of Amitzlav in the region of Mohilev, there were two rabbis. One was 75 or 80 years old and the other one about 50. He had harnessed both of them to a wagon of refuse from the stable of Kuzma the shoemaker, ordering them to pull it. The older Rabbi stumbled, fell to the ground, breaking his hand and foot, and died on that very day. The other Rabbi pulled the wagon and threw up, falling to the ground. Kratov said, "I honored him with a kick, and he rolled over with an outcry of great pain. After two days he also died."

His comrades scattered my clothing about, searched in the pockets of the garments and shuffled the pages of my books. They placed the writings on the table, and Kratov commanded me to stand. He searched the pockets of my clothing, placing everything on the table, and said, "We atheists and communist youth will destroy the fanatic Jews, the rabbis and teachers and those like them; we will totally eradicate them, leaving no trace. You, too, Citizen Schneersohn, will share their lot. There are two possibilities; either to the wall, that is to be shot by the firing squad, or to the exile region of Solovaki where you will rot!"

After concluding the search of my pockets, he turned to Bashkov saying: "And now, Comrade, stand and we will also search you. Perhaps—or certainly—you are an emissary of Citizen Schneersohn to build mikva'ot or to organize children's Torah classes to support the counter-revolutionaries, the rabbis, teachers, and their colleagues from the "Black Hundreds."

Bashkov (coldly and deliberately): Comrades, it appears that Citizen Schneersohn is not knowledgeable in the law of the land, but you are most assuredly apprised of the legal requirements, (he cited the chapter and the section of the law): Anyone who makes visits to conduct searches, whether from the police, the G.P.U. or U.G.P.O., must show his identification with his picture attesting to his identity. Moreover, he needs to show a more specific document—a Warrant—for his activity conducting searches in the dwelling of such-and-such a person, and if he finds something relevant to his search he can arrest whomever he wants; he has that permission. This document needs to be sealed with the stamp of the agency that assigned the search to him. And therefore, show me your documents, and I will know who you are.

Kratov exploded in rage and began to shout: "I am a member of the *Yevsektzia* appointed by ...(he named one of the agencies, but I don't remember which one). I am responsible for the surveillance of this hotel, overseeing its officials, orderlies, guests and all those visiting. A nobody comes from the street, a glutton, look"—he pointed with his finger to the table of fruit— "a bourgeois glutton." He ridiculed Bashkov: "And this dog also demands to see my documents! Stand and let me search your pockets. If not, I will deal you a blow that will disfigure your face. Pig, son of a dog! Comrades, let us commence our task. It looks like we have caught a fat fish in our net." He placed his hand on Bashkov's shoulder, commenting, "We will find a place for you also in the dungeons of the clinic on Lubyanka Street."

Bashkov: I demand obedience to the law.

Kratov and his associates laughed derisively and approached Bashkov. Abruptly, Bashkov rose in anger, removed his hat from his head and said a single word in a loud voice, the meaning of which I did not know, taking his identification from his pocket.

Kratov's face turned white. They all recoiled and stood like blocks of wood, petrified as if thunderstruck.

Bashkov (to Kratov): Come here and show me your identification.

Kratov (in a trembling voice): It is in the desk of the hotel office.

Bashkov: Go and bring it.

He then commanded the others to approach in order and display their identification. He made a notation in his book and then inquired for the search warrant. They answered that they did not have one, but that Kratov surely did. He informed them that they could leave and that tomorrow they were to appear in the G.P.U. office to see the investigator, Comrade Yarmulov.

Kratov presented his identification.

Bashkov: Where is the search warrant?

Kratov: I have no such document. I acted on my own judgement due to my responsibility over the hotel guests. I suspected Citizen Schneersohn of being a counter-revolutionary, and so I was allowed to conduct a search.

Bashkov: Fine, tomorrow morning come to the G.P.U. office to Investigator Yarmulov. He will explain to you the laws regarding investigations and searches. He will also teach you the proper way to address people.

Kratov stood to plead for mercy.

Bashkov: I must conclude my conversation with Comrade Schneersohn. Do not detain me, for I must leave in a few minutes.

Bashkov apologized for the incident and said that it was caused by the wild youth, impetuous and displaying inadequate self-discipline. He assured me that they would never dare to do this again.

Me: This will not improve the situation; it is common knowledge that the harassment is from the *Yevsektzia*, overwhelmingly consisting of hot-headed youths, impulsive in their actions.

Bashkov requested of me that should this recur, I should contact him at his residence at the address he had given to me. He left. I closed the door of my room and recited the evening prayers. I reflected on Divine Providence, perceiving with my own eyes actual Divine intervention.

Twice I heard knocking at the door, but did not answer. I surmised that Kratov or his friends would ask me to plead on their behalf, and I did not want to see them. The telephone rang a number of times, but I did not respond. Finally, the fourth time I answered, asking who was calling.

Kratov: I knocked at your door and you did not answer. I wanted to speak with you for a few minutes.

Me: I am very busy now. I have to leave shortly, and I will return at a late hour.

Kratov: Only for a few minutes.

Me: Excuse me.

I replaced the phone and left for my meeting.

In the corridor I met Kratov. He pleaded with me to intervene on his behalf. He assured me that henceforth he would act in a way beneficial to me. He would inform me of all that transpired in the *Yevsektzia* office so that I could protect myself, and he had a network of friends who would intervene on my behalf. In these critical times I needed people such as he and his colleagues, he said, and he assured me that if I would speak on his behalf, then he and his friends would save me from many dangerous situations.

Me: I cannot involve myself in this.

Kratov: You will be ensnared in fearful problems caused by the *Yevsektzia*.

Me: One cannot flee from fearful problems, and if G-d so desires, He will provide paths of rescue and protection under any circumstances. I will not do anything against the truth, against honesty, or against my convictions.

Kratov: You are glad about my sufferings.

Me: I am not glad, but I am not saddened or anxious.

Affected by this event that Divine Providence had prepared for me, I left for Kremlin Square. When I saw that only about ten minutes remained until my meeting, I took a taxi to the designated place.

The *Chassidic* Gatherings

Admonition and encouragement to the members of the *Tiferet Bachurim* to strengthen and maintain the schedule of Torah regiment. Each one should influence friends and acquaintances and create an environment of Torah study and piety in the spirit of self-sacrifice — and also to stand defiant against the *Yevsektzia* and the anti-religious forces.

I related the words spoken by my father in 5659 (1899), about the Alter Rebbe who, when he was once taking leave of his teacher the Maggid of Mezeritch, was escorted by the Maggid's son Avraham[39] (also known as "the Angel" for his ascetic conduct) to a waiting wagon. As the Alter Rebbe ascended the wagon, "the Angel" said to the driver, "Whip the horses until they cease to be horses."

Upon hearing these words, "Whip the horses until they won't be horses anymore," the Alter Rebbe took his bag and returned to his lodging, saying that "the Angel" had awakened him to a new path of spiritual service in which he needed instruction. He said, "One should whip the horses until they know they are horses. However, 'whip them until they are horses no longer' — that is a completely new path."

On the above, R. Yitzchok Gorowitz[40] commented: "The horse knows that he is a horse and he is not ashamed to be one," and he wept. This was followed by a heated discussion, lasting about an hour, between R. Yitzchak and Rabbi

Yaakov Landau. After the argument — as to whether the service of the heart is primary (Rabbi Yitzchok's opinion) or if
the service of the mind is primary (Rabbi Yaakov's opinion)
— subsided, and after the assembled were roused by singing
melodies, I explained the story, which referred to two modes
of spiritual service, as follows:

*At this point the Rebbe delivers a chassidic discourse on
Ezekiel's prophecy of the heavenly throne-merkava, and provides
an explanation based upon chassidic concepts of man's spiritual psy-
chology.*

It is written: "And on the likeness of a throne the likeness
of a man upon it from above."[41] Through fulfillment of the
Torah and mitzvot — by harnessing all of one's faculties to
the service of G-d — the "animals bear." They bear the man
on the celestial throne to the level of the *Ein Sof Baruch Hu*,
for [42]: "He (G-d) is not a man" ("*ki lo Adam hu*").

As a consequence of the above, we know that the ultimate
goal of spiritual service is self-elevation to the level of "not a
man," which is higher than the level of "Man." This level is
attained in spite of the fact that "I created the earth and man
upon it"[43] which means that "*Anochi*"[44]—I, G-d—created the
world for the sake of "Man." It is also written, "And you are
My flocks, the flocks of My pasture, you are 'Man'."[45] Our
Sages explain, "You [the Jewish people] are called 'Man'."[46]
The purpose of "I created" ("*barati*"), having the numerical
value of 613—the fulfillment of mitzvot, which is one path
in spiritual service, the level of "Man."

The second path in spiritual service is elevation of the
level of "Adam" to a higher level, that of "not a man" ("*ki lo
Adam hu*"). Although spiritual service usually proceeds in the
manner of elevation from below upwards, the benefit to the

soul powers comes from above downwards. The service, that is, the preparation and rectification are from below upwards: first one needs to rectify action, and on the next higher level speech, then thought, then emotions, then intellect, then will, and then delight — for each one, besides its specific correction and preparation, is based on the level immediately above it.

However, the influence of one level on another and the capacity for spiritual service is only granted from above downwards: delight arouses the will (or the will arouses delight, for there is no positive proof as to which is higher). Jointly they have an effect, sometimes on the intellect, sometimes on the emotions and sometimes on thought. These three — thought, speech, and intellect — are faculties that have a constant effect, for just as thought elevates the speech or lowers it, to purify and sanctify it or to defile and profane it, similarly the intellect can have a positive or negative effect on the emotions. All this derives from the influence of delight and will, for all the soul powers depend on them: wherever a person's delight and will are most intensively focused determines the exact effect on the other faculties.

Actually, all of this is the method of spiritual service in the first path, to prepare and correct oneself in order to be "Man." This, however, is not the main objective — only a gateway to the true spiritual service, self-elevation to the level of "not a man." This means that a person's delight and will precisely match G-d's delight and will, so that there is no longer any sense of personal desire — because one is "*ois* Adam" ("no longer Adam"), having transcended the level of "not a man." A person's whole existence, from the lowliest faculty, the power of action, to the highest, the power of delight, is subjugated to G-dliness with actual self-sacrifice.

There are two kinds of self-sacrifice: potential and actual. Although both of them constitute true self-sacrifice, there is a distinction: in potential self-sacrifice the individual has some hope, some reason to think he may be rescued. Although he does not cease to offer up his life, there is, nevertheless, a spark of hope that he will survive. However, in actual self-sacrifice there is no such hope, and, moreover, the individual does not consider this at all.

Even more deeply: in the instance of potential self-sacrifice the individual sacrifices himself for a specific goal but his thoughts are focused on his own selfhood, that he gives up his soul and that he derives pleasure from this act.

Thus Rabbi Akiva, who gave up his life to sanctify the Divine name for the sake of Torah study, performed this act of self-sacrifice for Torah, yet derived gratification from the essential act of self-sacrifice. This is in contrast to the self-sacrifice of our Patriarch Abraham, who strove to promulgate G-dliness in the world. He exemplified actual self-sacrifice in this quest and did not think of himself at all. His practice of actual self-sacrifice adhered to the essential act of altruism, being totally devoid of any thoughts of selfhood.

Potential self-sacrifice is in contrast to this. Though the person actually gives up his life, this willing self-sacrifice does not adhere to the essential act. It is rather an aspect of his own selfhood that he is rendering up his life. However, the level of "not a man" in spiritual service is the absolute submission and dedication to G-dliness with all one's soul powers, powers from the lowest action to the loftiest delight in a manner of actual self-sacrifice.

With regard to self-elevation to the level of "not a man" in spiritual service, there are two modes: Firstly, in a soul of *Atzilut* an actual soul of *Atzilut* or in a soul of *Atzilut* of *Beriah, Yetzirah, Asiyah*[46] — and all the more so a collective soul[47] — it is in a manner of above to below: the *Yechidah*,[48] the loftiest level, of the soul has an effect on the various levels of the soul. However, in this second mode, for the average person, elevation to the level of "not a man" in spiritual service is achieved by accepting the yoke of Heaven, thus reaching the highest levels, something every person is able to accomplish. We see this manifestly in the superiority of those who excel in spiritual service over those who excel in intellectual comprehension.

By way of illustration, I explained briefly the difference between the "two cedars of Lebanon" of Chabad *Chassidism,* Izik of Gomel and Hillel of Paritch. They both excelled in intellectual comprehension of Chassidus and in spiritual service. The distinction, however, was this: while Izik Hommler excelled in spiritual service, he was primarily a *maskil,* an intellectual, while Hillel Paritcher, though he surpassed the former in intellectual comprehension, was mainly an *oveid,* one who stresses spiritual service. I then explained the superiority of spiritual service over intellectual comprehension.

When I saw the rapt attention of the gathered and their desire to hear more, I concluded that this time and place provided an opportunity to arouse them publicly about the present situation and said:

We perceive the surprising significance of accepting the yoke of heaven in this time, when the *Yevsektzia* persecutes observant Jews. Through self-sacrifice we accept G-d's yoke, meaning that not only are we unaffected by the *Yevsektzia,* but that we must stand firm against their agents as they illegally destroy all the institutions of Judaism. We must publicize the government laws concerning the religious education of children: that five children are permitted to learn with one teacher and that every father is permitted to hire a teacher for his children. Similarly, every congregation of thirty is permitted to maintain a synagogue and a *mikveh* at its own expense. It is necessary to make these laws known to everyone.

All Jews, our brothers who are natives of this country, carefully and zealously obey the law of the land. It is fitting to do so, for we all remember the adversity and cruelty we suffered under the old regime. Our Sages urge us to pray for the welfare of our country — providing, of course, that the ruling power does not touch our religion and our Torah — and all the more so if it helps us.

Many, if not most of our brothers the Jewish people, err in thinking that the group which calls itself the *Yevsektzia* was established by the government, or even that it has some power superior to that of the government. The *Yevsektzia* was established by a few people who harass the Jewish religion, who hate religious Jews, and who gather against them the most ignorant young men, ones who love idleness and who pursue fleshly pleasure, since lawlessness suits them. And with these soldiers the *Yevsektzia* persecutes observant Jews.

The leaders of the *Yevsektzia* are the outcasts of the human species: liars, false and cruel, and without doubt their disgraceful theft and treachery will be revealed. Eventually, each one will slander his fellow to bring him to destruction, because he himself is in trouble, and the other will counter by revealing the first one's deviousness and bring him also to the same fate. Until they are blotted out, they are a grave threat to the strongholds of religion.

We must all arise in unison against this group which harasses our Torah and our religion, the cursed *Yevsektzia*, may its name be blotted out, and we are all obligated to publicize the complete truth regarding the law of the land in connection with learning Torah and keeping *mitzvot*:

1. The *Yevsektzia* is a private group and it has no power superior to a government institution.

2. The *Yevsektzia* is based on force, which is against the principles of civil liberty.

3. In every city and settlement in which the *Yevsektzia* targets all religious matters, observant Jews are to consult the Jewish community in Moscow.

This declaration evoked a fiery response in all those present. They asked me to recite a *ma'amar*, which I promised to do tomorrow, Thursday, after *Ma'ariv*.

Yesterday at our gathering at the house of A.R., Rabbi K. asked me to visit him in his home, and I promised to do so today, Wednesday, at eight in the evening. From the synagogue I went straight to Rabbi K's house. My visit was friendly and he spoke of a chance meeting with my father in Marienbad after the great conference in Vilna, 5668 (1908).[50] The Polish *chassidim* and the *mitnagdim* jealously acknowledged that the Rebbe of Lubavitch was the only one who pursued community needs with diligence and wisdom. Rabbi K. was a man of intense feelings and his talk made an impression.

At 9:00 the *chassid* Rabbi Boruch Shalom came with a message from Mr. A.L. Fuchs, relating that G.P.U. agents had called him and asked him about me. He thought I should leave the city since they were stalking me, and even before Rabbi Sh. had finished speaking, the telephone rang with the news from *chassidim* that the G.P.U. wanted to speak to me from Leningrad and that the conversation would take place in another quarter of an hour.

The news of the call from Leningrad made an impression on me at that time. I don't know why. I am only able to describe it as follows: The good mood —*di gute shtimmung*—

and the joyousness of the two or two and a half hours beforehand, when I spoke in the synagogue concerning my opposition to the *Yevsektzia*, dissipated the moment I heard that
the G.P.U. wanted to speak to me. My spirit fell—*a shlechte
shtimmung*, a bad mood—with an inner agitation.

Rabbi K. and Rabbi Z. intensely debated the question
whether the telephone message was destined to come soon.
Concluding that it was something relevant to me, Mr. N. G.
sat next to the telephone and waited.

My dejection gradually increased and at that moment I
appreciated the explanation of the difference in sound made
by the angels called "*ofanim*" as opposed to the sound made
by the angels called "*serafim*." The song of the "*serafim*" is sung
with "pure speech" and "sacred melody,"[51] while the song of
the "*ofanim*" is sung with a "mighty sound." Since the *serafim*
stand in the world of *beriah*, a world of understanding, and
since the *serafim* can completely comprehend the Divine
light, their song is sung with "pure speech." The *ofanim*, however, marveling at the song of the *serafim* but realizing that
they are incapable of understanding it, sing their song with
"a mighty sound," analogous to a man who hears something
but does not know what it is. He makes a tumult, for who
knows if it is a favorable or unpleasant thing — or even
something dreadful! The mind rules over the heart, but when
a person knows something without fully understanding it, he
feels intense agitation, or is, to say the least, disturbed.

The telephone rang, and I heard the voice of Mr. N. G.,
who took the telephone to listen, and the room fell into a
profound silence. The men near the telephone stared with
wide eyes and open mouths at Mr. N.G., whose face changed
from red to white, and from which I understood that it was
adverse news.

Mr. N.G.: "Last night they visited the house of Rabbi Morosow and searched the whole night, but found nothing. The next day at noon they came a second time and conducted another search for over five hours, and again found nothing. Before they left, they took Rabbi Morosow to prison. Mr. B. Ch. has already departed — he will arrive tomorrow morning; they want to consult with him because the situation is serious."

The faces of Rabbis K. and Z., Mr. G., and Rabbi Boruch Shalom darkened and certainly my face was like theirs, although I did not have a mirror before me to confirm this. Actually, I calmed down to a certain extent after the news, and I am amazed that I was able to do so.

Mr. A. and Mr. Sh. looked at me pityingly — a very hateful thing to me — and the Rabbis K., Z. and N.G. sat with bowed heads and low spirits. The only one to offer encouragement was Rabbi Boruch Shalom, who said the following:

"A *chassid* is required to be strong in the ways of spiritual service; all the more so a Rebbe, son of a Rebbe, grandson of a Rebbe, whose pedigree goes back to the Alter Rebbe and who is ultimately a physical and spiritual descendent of Moses.

"I will tell you what I heard from the Rebbe[52] on the 19th of *Kislev* 5657 (1897) when he stayed in the dwelling place of Mrs. Miriam and her sons, the brothers Maneszehn in Kalpatchni Faulik. The Rebbe recited the discourse '*Padah Bashalom Nafshi*' and afterwards spoke of the unique qualities of *chassidim*: a *chassid* is naturally clever and firm in his convictions, a *chassid* has fire, a *chassid* has the power of self-nullification, a *chassid* has a 'sense of smell' — he knows intuitively the difference between good and evil. These are all splendid qualities if a person uses them for spiritual service according to the Torah. These very same qualities the Rebbe bequeathed to the *chassidim* with his spiritual service. Abraham with his self-sacrifice 'made' Jews; and the Rebbe with his self-sacrifice 'made' *chassidim*.

"Today, over a hundred and twenty years have passed since the Rebbe[53] publicly revealed the path of *Chabad Chassidus* — 5534 (1774) — and with his great self-sacrifice educated and directed the *chassidim* until he established, thank G-d, a 'generation of knowledge.' All the good qualities of intellect and emotions, all the good acts of service in Torah and *mitzvot*, and the 'service of the heart' which the *chassidim* have accomplished during these one hundred and twenty-three years — all that the *chassidim* will do from now until the coming of Mashiach — is the Rebbe's achievement. One cannot even conceive of the Rebbe's reward or his merit! It is certain that if a *chassid* proceeds in the path of our Rebbes, if he learns a few lines of *Tanya* for the sake of actual practice; if he calls out, 'Rebbe, I need a blessing or heavenly aid in this matter' — he must specify these matters briefly — then G-d will most assuredly help him in the merit of our Rebbe."

The words of Rabbi Boruch Shalom made a profound impression on the listeners. They responded with words of encouragement, saying that surely G-d would help. Even though it was pleasant to hear a review of my father's talk, I needed no encouragement when I remembered my father's exhortation for self-sacrifice.

I asked the assembled to keep the news of the arrest a secret, and I told N.G. to have Bentzion and Avrohom Yosef be ready to meet tomorrow at 11 o'clock. Then I received parting blessings and returned to the Stara Varvarsk.

The following evening, the Rebbe held a Farbrengen at a Moscow synagogue in honor of Purim Katan[54]. *The following let-*

ter illustrates some of the obvious risks undertaken by the Rebbe in his one-man war with the Yevsektzia:[55]

I came to Moscow at the end of *Adar I*, he, Mr —, one of the heads of the Jewish community, told me that during the time the Lubavitcher Rebbe was in Moscow, at the beginning of *Adar I* he, Mr —, was called before the G.P.U. and they asked him:"Is it true that Rabbi Schneersohn is now in Moscow and is collecting huge sums for strengthening Torah institutions? That he organizes hundreds of young men-of-learning with their leaders, and sends them throughout the country to strengthen all religious institutions? And that many hundreds of institutions, whether of *Chassidim* or not, obey him and honor him?

From their words, Mr. — gathered that the central G.P.U. was extremely interested in the activities of the Lubavitcher Rebbe, and that the situation was serious. Therefore he replied:"I know Rabbi Schneersohn very well as a man who, for many years, has done a great deal of good for the Jewish community. I also knew the father of Rabbi Schneersohn who also did much good for the welfare of the Jews in the land. But, in all truth, I am not at all aware of any activities of Rabbi Schneersohn on behalf of Jewish religious institutions. Of one thing I am certain, however: Whatever he has done, the Lubavitcher Rebbe would not undertake anything illegal. I know that he arrived in Moscow, but I am completely ignorant of his purpose in coming here."

When I came home, I called one of the relatives of the Rebbe, informed him of the questioning, and advised him to leave Moscow that very night.

The following day I met a man who worked closely with the Rebbe and asked him whether the Rebbe had left. He answered vaguely and I realized to my great sorrow that my advice had not been followed.

On the next day, towards evening, we passed the synagogue of the Lubavitcher *chassidim*. It was brightly lit and
crowded, and the crowd was overflowing into the halls and
stairways right onto the street. "What is all this?" I asked. I
was told that the Lubavitcher Rebbe was preaching from the
pulpit. When I heard this, I began to tremble.

We entered the synagogue to listen to the sermon. We
found the Rebbe standing on the *bimah*. In a loud and clear
voice he addressed the people who were crowded into the
House of Worship. The text of his sermon was an explanation of the miracle of *Purim* as a product of the strong faith
of the Jews who lived in Persia in those days: that they had
refused to assimilate with the Persian people, in defiance of
the will of the Persian government; that they were saved in
the merit of the 22,000 students of Mordechai who, when
they heard of the prohibition against the study of Torah, told
Mordechai: "We are with you to the death." These young
men and boys won the victory against the prince of evil,
Haman. This was a spiritual war, an eternal war that does not
happen only once, but which comes round again in every
generation, and which can only be won by strengthening
and maintaining the study of Torah by every generation of
Jewish children.

I observed some people in the synagogue and strongly
suspected that they were spies.

After a week I met Litvakov, the head of the *Yevsektzia*,
who engaged me in conversation and complained to me that
Rabbi Schneersohn was organizing all the religious functionaries, the rabbis, *shochatim*, teachers and heads of yeshivot throughout Russia. On top of this he complained that
Rabbi Schneersohn was encouraging and strengthening
their work, helping their institutions and *mikva'ot*, and pro-

viding their synagogues with preachers and their schools with teachers.

"Wherever we turned," he told me, "not only in Russia, but also in Little Russia, in the Interior of Russia, and even in the far provinces of Georgia, Turkestan, etc., there too, could be found the emissaries of the Lubavitcher Rebbe, Rabbi Schneersohn, working to strengthen the institutions of Torah study and religious activities." And he told me a great many details about the work of these Chabad *chassidim* on behalf of the Jews of Georgia.

Notes

1. *Sefer Hasichot* 5580–5587, pp. 128–158. For more information regarding this trip, see *Igrot Kodesh* Vol. 1, pp. 616.
2. Of the *Va'ad*. See prologue.
3. Praying at length and with great concentration.
4. Noson Gourarie.
5. A coded message that the Rebbe was well (see p. 205).
6. Evidently, on the way back from the Rabbinical Commission in Petersburg, May 6-August 27, where he was arrested numerous times (*The Tzemach Tzedek and the Haskalah Movement*, Kehot, 1969, p. 46).
7. Isaiah 38:19.
8. The numerical value of the word "*chai*," spelled "*yud*"– "*chet*," is 18.
9. This is traditional phrasing; the custom is not to literally prostrate oneself.
10. Rabbi Menachem Mendel, the Tzemach Tzedek.
11. Rabbi Shmuel, the Rebbe Maharash.
12. This last expression appears to mean that S. will thrive by following the dictates of expediency. An obvious possibility for the identities of T., L. and S. is Trotsky, Lenin, and Stalin. Lenin was incapacitated by strokes in 1923. Two years later he succumbed to progressive paralysis of the brain. Trotsky was assassinated in Mexico City in 1940. But

this is speculation on the part of the editor.

13. In Koritz 1782 edition, this is p. 929.
14. *Ta'anit* 29a.
15. Unified State Political Administration.
16. *Sanhedrin* 42.
17. City Government Council.
18. His name is given below.
19. The Hebrew version of the name "Velvel"—"Wolf."
20. Rabbi Shalom DovBer, Rabbi Yosef Yitzchak's father.
21. The station serving Lubavitch.
22. Proverbs 18:16.
23. Ecclesiastes 11:1.
24. Reactionary, anti-revolutionary, and anti-semitic groups formed in Russia after the Russian Revolution of 1905.
25. A "head" for Talmud study.
26. Menachem Mendel Gluskin, Rabbi of Minsk and *Va'ad* Member.
27. Yaakov Klemes, a Rabbi in Moscow and *Va'ad* Member.
28. One of the "Rabbi M.'s" is probably Eliyahu Aharon Milovsky, Rabbi of Kharkov and *Va'ad* Member.
29. Dr. Josef Rosen, the Joint Distribution Committee representative in Russia.
30. Rabbi Shlomo Yosef Zevin.
31. Ezekiel 8:12.
32. Mr Yitzchak Saleivitch Orenson. Prominent Moscow attorney, chairman of a legal action committee established by the Rebbe in Moscow to defend Jewish causes.
33. Apparently the next several paragraphs describe events that took place earlier that day, before they visited Dr. Rosen
34. Proverbs 16:11.
35. Vladimir Haffkine, a well-known community activist and Alliance representative from Paris (See *Igrot Kodesh*, vol. 1, p. 541).
36. 1 *tchervantze* = 10 rubles.
37. Rabbi Yosef Yitzchak himself.
38. Bentzion Shemtov, one of the ten people who made a covenant to uphold Judaism. (see p. 21) An activist who traveled in Ukraine as the Rebbe's Emissary.
39. Rabbi Abraham, the son of the Maggid of Mezritch.
40. The well-known *chassid*, "Itche the Masmid."
41. Ezekiel 1:26.
42. Samuel I 15:29.
43. Isaiah 45:12
44. Denoting G-d's inner will (*Likkutei Torah, Pinchas* 80b).

45. Ezekiel 34:31.

46. *Yevamot* 61a.

47. I.e. souls of spiritually lofty individuals, whose souls originate in these different "worlds" or levels. For a general discussion of the concept of the four "spiritual words" of *Atzilut, Beriah, Yetzirah,* and *Asiyah,* see *Mystical Concepts in Chassidism, Tanya,* Bilingual Edition, p. 860, Kehot, 1981.

48. I.e. a Rebbe, whose soul includes and unifies all the other souls of the Jewish people.

49. Jewish mysticism identifies five different terms used in Scripture to refer to the soul as five levels of the soul, of which the highest is *Yechidah.* It is completely united with G-d and its name derives from the Divine attribute of unity. See *Tanya,* Bilingual Edition, *Iggeret Hakodesh,* p. 413, note 53, Kehot, 1981.

50. The actual year of the conference was 1909. For further details, see letters of Rebbe Rashab, Vol. 1, p. 38 ff.

51. Siddur Tehillat Hashem, p.44, Kehot, 1998.

52. Rabbi Shalom DovBer, the Rebbe's father.

53. Rabbi Schneur Zalman of Liadi, the founder of Chabad.

54. In a Jewish leap year when the month of *Adar* is observed twice, Purim is celebrated in *Adar II.* On *Adar I, Purim Katan* ("small Purim") is observed.

55. Printed in *Outlines of the Social and Communal Work of Chabad-Lubavitch,* Kehot, 1953.

APPENDIX 7

A Chassid's Memoirs
The Letters of Reb Eliyahu Chaim Althaus

*The following account is from two letters by a close confidant of
the Rebbe, and one of his closest chassidim, Reb Eliyahu Chaim
Altaus, to a group of fellow chassidim. The chassid's perspective is an
invaluable source for details of events before, during, and immediately following the arrest.[1]*

*The letters, from Iyar, 5688 (May, 1928) were written by Rabbi
Althaus to relatives who remained in Riga. In 1937 it was
reworked with more details, and sent to Warsaw for publication in
the* Hatamim *Journal. Added details from the second version appear
in our text.*

Those *chassidim* among us who were close to the Rebbe
were apprehensive from the beginning of the year 5687
(1927). Although at the time we could not be certain, ominous events were taking place. On the first day of *Rosh
Hashanah*, as the Rebbe recited the verses before the blowing of the *shofar*, he called out from the prayer book: "Be a
Guarantor for Your servant's good," and cried out with great
bitterness "*ay gevald!*" and then completed the verse, "Do not
let the wicked despoil me."[2]

This scene did not go unnoticed. We knew the great care
the Rebbe took in choosing his words, even regarding mundane matters. We had never heard the Rebbe speak even one
word of exaggeration, and for him to act this way on the first
day of *Rosh Hashanah*, and in the verses before *shofar* blow-

ing, was all the more troubling. Surely there was some portent in this, and each one of us drew his own conclusions.

Much later I learned that our holy Rebbe himself was fearful from the beginning of 5687 (1927), as Rabbi Michoel Dworkin and I had heard from the Rebbe in Kostroma before the liberation. These were his exact words: "Before 5687 (1927) I was very afraid. I did not speculate about what my own fate would be. I was thinking about *chassidim*."

Having said this, he told me that he remembered that one year (he did not recall which one specifically), his father of blessed memory had told him, "You should await with caution the end of the year 5687 (1927)." Then the Rebbe added, "Before I instructed that Psalms be said, it was very, very hard for me to give the directive." I asked him when this was, and he replied, "On *Simchat Torah*."

As we all know, on *Simchat Torah* of that year the Rebbe instructed that Psalms be said, as divided up for the days of the month in the various prayer assemblies. This was to be observed in all cities every day, followed by *Kaddish*. In general he appeared distressed that *Simchat Torah*. Heartbroken, he spoke until nightfall, unable to conceal his bitterness.

I then recollected that during the *Kiddush* of that day he had entreated his *chassidim* at length. This occurred at the time of the *Kiddush* festivities held in the room of his righteous mother. He asked that they should accept upon themselves the recitation of Psalms as divided according to the days of the month, to be said by all public prayer groups after the morning prayers. I asked him if I could fulfill this obligation with my normal practice of reciting Psalms daily before my prayers, and he replied thus, "The Psalms recited before the prayers are related to *Tikkun Chatzot* (midnight penitential prayers)." In general, all of the Rebbe's discourses during that *Simchat Torah*, lasting from daytime till night, were delivered in a mood of great bitterness and oppression of heart.

I am convinced that the well-known note, found in the private study of the Rebbe on the day of his imprisonment (may we be protected from such adversity), regarding the recitation of Psalms was also written in the month of *Elul*, 5686, or the month of *Tishrei*, 5687 (1927, 1928). The note was written in pencil, in his own handwriting, but there was no notation as to the day it was written. At the bottom of the note the Rebbe writes his blessings for "A joyous year." The blessing for a good year is usually stated at the conclusion of a year [in anticipation of the coming year], or at the beginning of the new year, hence my impression as to the time it was written:

Listen, *chassidim*, and all Jews who await *Mashiach*; give over in my name to all *chassidim* in the world that I have instructed them to recite a portion of Psalms as divided for the days of the month in all *chassidic* synagogues after the morning prayers every day, *Shabbat* included. This should be done with a *minyan* (prayer quorum) and followed by *Kaddish*. All merchants and businessmen who are not *chassidim* should attend synagogue services and be present for classes in *Ein Yaakov* — G-d will help their livelihood abundantly. *Chassidim* should be told that such is my instruction, and other Jews should be told that I am asking them, for the sake of *Ahavat Yisrael* (love of the Jewish people), and concern for Jewish welfare, to fulfill my request — and G-d will provide a prosperous year spiritually and materially, and we will merit a complete redemption through *Mashiach*, amen.

The entire winter of 5687 (1927) felt particularly dismal, and a feeling of dread pervaded the Rebbe's household. The Rebbe worked relentlessly, pursuing the activities he had undertaken seven years earlier in 5680 (1920), when he ini-

tially accepted the position of Rebbe. He had labored might-
ily to strengthen religion in the entire country, opening
schools for children and *yeshivot* for older students, as everyone knows. And not a day went by without harassment from
that band of evil people, who sin against G-d and who have
separated themselves from the Jewish people through their
evil deeds: the *Yevsekztia*! They alone harassed him, and at
every step these fiends made libelous accusations about him
to the government. But the "G-d of Abraham and the Fear
of Isaac" stood at our side constantly to save him from his
persecutors.

After extensive inquiry by government officials and testimony by secret agents, it was quite clear that the Rebbe had
no connection whatsoever to groups opposed to the government and that he was not its adversary. His sole concern
was Torah and *mitzvot*. No law existed forcing individuals or
communities to violate their religion. If not for the *Yevsektzia*, which afflicted the Jewish people like a plague, all would
have been tranquil. The government itself allowed us to teach
G-d's Torah and to perform His *mitzvot* proudly and publicly.

These evil people realized that they could not contend
with him, and that G-d was with him every step of the way:
whenever they destroyed a study hall, a *mikveh*, a *cheder*, a
yeshivah, he would pay no heed to them and immediately
begin to rebuild. So they resolved to remove him from this
world completely, G-d forbid. Mustering their strength to
carry out their scheme, they leveled against him outlandish
accusations and caused much damage[3] to his community.

That winter of 5687 (1927), their activities became even
more apparent. As we were to learn, they held several meetings to scheme against the Rebbe, and amassed libelous accusations for the campaign against him. Because of a separate
libel, the Rebbe's secretary, our friend Elchanan Dov

Morosow, was arrested and imprisoned that same winter, along with other *chassidim*.

On 19 *Kislev*, during the festive meal, their spies were stationed in the house, waiting within the crowd to hear if the Rebbe would give his customary talk, hoping perhaps to catch traditional words of encouragement on the subject of serving G-d, which they could then twist into something incriminating. They kept the house under close surveillance, watching everyone who entered and left, literally counting the Rebbe's every step. We were later to learn that they had a record of almost every syllable he uttered.

The Rebbe, in his purity of spirit, sensed all of this. We did, too, and were fearful. In the winter, during *Adar I*, as he was traveling to Moscow in connection with his community work, I escorted him to the train station. When I entered his compartment to bless him and receive his blessings, he said to me in a bitter tone: "A chapter of Psalms will not cause any harm: say a chapter of Psalms for me."

Dread took hold of me when I heard those words, and I understood then the fears with which he lived. He knew he was endangering himself but felt obligated since there was no one else to rely on. Those of us observing his efforts saw clearly how he had singlehandedly rebuilt Judaism in our country, and how if not for him, the Torah would have been erased from the memory of the Jewish people.

Inspired by his self-sacrifice, all of the *chadarim*, their supporters and teachers, stood firm. Repeatedly I heard him say, "I am involved with matters that do not pertain to me. My role is to study and teach *Chassidus*; this is what I was appointed for. Regarding all general community matters we require a special committee of the rabbis and community leaders. The task belongs more properly to them, and it is their responsibility."

A number of times during the seven years of his leadership, he convened the rabbis of the largest cities; turning to them, he begged that they undertake this holy work. He promised to work with them when necessary, but asked them to shoulder the responsibility for helping our needy brethren, and to concern themselves with the *yeshivot*, *chadarim*, and *mikva'ot*. The Rebbe had not merely asked them to accept the work: he had even promised them complete anonymity, no one would know of their connection to these matters.

To his great sorrow, not one of them stepped forward. Truth to tell, it is hard to fault them, because they were afraid to assume such a task, knowing the grave threat the cursed *Yevsektzia* posed to their lives.

At the end, and at great risk, the Rebbe himself had to assume the entire burden. This was undoubtedly not what he wanted, as he explained the difference between the self-sacrifice of Abraham our Patriarch and that of Rabbi Akiva, the Talmudic sage. Abraham, on the one hand, wanted only to promulgate G-dliness and to fulfill G-d's commands — and to that end, self-sacrifice was accepted as his life mode. Rabbi Akiva, on the other hand, actively sought an opportunity for actual self-sacrifice. It seemed the Rebbe was implying that, like Abraham, he was unhappy with the situation, but was reluctantly prepared for self-sacrifice to achieve the proper objective.

On *Purim Katan* 5687 (1927), while in Moscow, the Rebbe expounded on the concept that in *galut* (exile), when darkness covers the earth, concealing holiness and hindering the study of Torah, the Jewish people are strengthened from above to transform the darkness into light; this is achieved through the power of "the children G-d has given,"[4] when we assemble them to study Torah publicly. This is the foun-

dation upon which all else rests, and which must be served
even if it entails literal self-sacrifice. This is the ultimate purpose of the darkness of exile: to overcome these challenges.
You, my friends, surely remember our emotions at that time,
and our fear after that discourse, when we heard the Rebbe
say "literal self-sacrifice."

At the end of summer 5685 (1925), H. Gurevitch, the
chairman of the Leningrad community council approached
the Rebbe with a proposition. He told the Rebbe that he
wanted to halt the decline of Judaism in our country, since
he saw "that there were wholesale defections from the religion, that everything that pertained to religion was deterio-
rating daily, and that even the remnant was imperiled."

Gurevitch was from a prominent family, with a Jewish
education until 15 years of age. At that age, he entered a secular high school, and assimilated there with anti-religious
youth. Afterward he moved on to a Leningrad college where
he received a degree in law. He was a hot-headed Zionist,
vehemently anti-religious. In 1925, he was elected chairman
of the Leningrad community council. The Rebbe was not
acquainted with him until he approached the Rebbe.

Most energetically this chairman undertook to travel to
all of the large cities in our land to meet with the rabbis and
leaders, ostensibly to "awaken them from their slumber." He
would arrange, he told the Rebbe, for a government permit
to hold a rabbinical conference in Leningrad, for "the law in
the Constitution allows for this," evidenced by the fact that
the priests and ministers in Moscow have already received a
permit and gathered to make many improvements in their
own religion. "And we, the Jewish nation," he continued, "on
account of our great apprehension, are sitting with folded
hands and doing nothing for our religion!"

Referencing the fact that he was not personally Torah observant, he declared, "Don't look at that fact that I have no beard; I may eat non-kosher as well, but in theory I agree with everything, I believe in G-d and His Torah, and whole-heartedly love my people and my religion. My heart is with you." To prove his sincerity, he emphasized that he had been elected chairman of the Leningrad community, which was considered 'religious,' and that he always agreed with Rabbi Katzenelenbogen, may he be well, the head of the Leningrad community.

Moreover, given that he was a lawyer who was well versed in the laws of the land, the chairman was of the opinion that this conference should take place not in Moscow, whose central location made it the appropriate site, but in Leningrad, which enjoyed longstanding precedence in all matters Jewish in Russia. Additionally, such a choice would honor the elderly Rabbi Katzenelenbogen, the chief Rabbi of Leningrad. With these words, the "chairman" hoped to deceive the Rebbe, as he had done Rabbi Katzenelenbogen.

Rabbi Dovid Tuvia Katzenelenbogen, the Chief Rabbi of Leningrad, besides being well-versed in Torah, was a pleasant, truthful, and kind man with a love toward every Jew. Not only did Jews of all stripes respect him; religious and non-religious, Zionists, *chassidim* and non-*chassidim*, but non-Jews as well respected him. But due to his straightforward, trusting personality, and his gullible nature, the "chairman" was able to prey on him through his deceptive words.

The Rebbe, with his many years of experience in work for the community, beginning in his early years by assisting his father, the Rebbe, Rabbi Sholom DovBer, of blessed memory, listened patiently to the "chairman's" presentation. Discerning something amiss, the Rebbe replied kindly: "By nature I trust everyone, and while you say that this is with good intent, my initial reaction is disapproving. Nevertheless,

I will not be as outspoken as my father, and I will weigh this important matter seriously." And the Rebbe told him a story that occurred in Warsaw:

A meeting took place many years ago,[5] among three Rebbes: The Gerer Rebbe,[6] the Rodzminer Rebbe,[7] and my father,[8] of blessed memories . . . The three of them were conferring on a question, the *tzenz*[9] that was being forced upon rabbis in Poland. Before the [Lubavitcher] Rebbe heard all the arguments in favor of acquiescing to the *tzenz*, he said that he was absolutely against it. After he was asked to explain his disapproval, he replied, "I do not desire it." To the Gerer Rebbe's question, "Lubavitcher Rebbe, is this the basis of your opinion?" the Rebbe answered, "Yes, I base myself upon my first reaction, not wishing."

From his youth the Rebbe accustomed his body, and every one of his 248 limbs, to abhor what is prohibited by Torah, so that every limb should be ready to fulfill the *mitzvah* with which it is associated. And as his limbs grew accustomed to fulfilling G-d's will, his body could function in accordance to his nature; and when it 'did not wish' for something, it was not to be desired.

The Rebbe continued modestly, "I am not on this level, but even simple logic dictates that it would be a great danger in our country to hold a public conference. I see more potential danger than benefit in holding this conference. It would be good for the rabbis and community leaders to meet and discuss strengthening *Yiddishkeit*, but let it be without fanfare and without formality."

Several days later, H. Shachnevitch, another member of the community council, approached the Rebbe. He suggested the Rebbe join with the council to decide these matters. The Rebbe replied, "I have never involved myself with affairs of the city where I reside; it is not my role. In Rostov, too, where I dwelled until now, I had no involvement with the local community.

He also asked the Rebbe to publicly denounce the "*Azet-*colonies." This organization built villages for Jewish farmers. As a Zionist, he opposed the idea of any colonization whatsoever. The Rebbe was unhappy to say the least, that the "*Azet*" colonies had no synagogue, *cheder*, rabbi, *shochet*, or *mikveh*. They raised pigs and violated Shabbat and the festivals publicly. He did, however, see potential for improvement. He worked very hard to improve their situation and accomplished a great deal. Besides *shochatim*, he sent emissaries to build the synagogues, *mikva'ot*, and *chadarim*. However, he was often thwarted by the *Yevsektzia*, which reached out its evil tentacles to make the colonists "forget Your Torah and violate the decrees of your will."[10]

On the issue, the Rebbe replied that he was not aware of the full intent of the colonies. With that Shachnevitch left.

Subsequently, the Leningrad community council began to actively oppose the Rebbe, may he be well. The Rebbe, of course, always conducted himself in a forthright manner, while his adversaries acted deceitfully with the rabbis and community leaders. Publicly they proclaimed their intent to strengthen all matters of religion, *kashrut*, *mikva'ot*, etc. However, the program, drawn up by the commission headed by Shachnevitch, stated clearly their goals to establish a seminary with a new ideology, to institute new synagogue rules and a new prayer book, and to make other innovations prohibited by the Torah.

When their plans were revealed, the community council split into two factions — the chairman with thirteen delegates on one side, and the remaining delegates, the ten G-d-fearing ones, on the other. Thus the two sides battled constantly.

The religious members knew that as the minority within the council, they could never accomplish anything, since in religious matters decisions were determined by the majority, who would decide everything against Torah law. Furthermore, their very presence in the community council might deceive G-d-fearing Jews into believing that all the resolutions passed by the community council were in accordance with Jewish law. At that point, all of the G-d-fearing delegates decided to leave the council. Henceforth, the remaining delegates would not be able to deceive everyone by designating the board as 'religious.'

The withdrawal of these delegates, and with them the G-d-fearing members of the community, soon became public knowledge. Their first action was an attempt to salvage the honor of Rabbi Katzenelenbogen. They sent a delegation of three to him, to attempt to apprise him that his name was being used to prey upon innocent Jewish souls. They spent a long while with him, explaining to him what the full import of the council's actions might be. He promised to conduct a full investigation, on condition that they immediately return to the council, and announce, prior to the inquiry, that the council was legitimate. Of course, the delegates couldn't agree on this condition.

Before departing, they told him:

Rabbi of Leningrad, we have fulfilled our responsibility. We found it imperative to defend your honor and inform you that the anti-religious elements are deceiving you. They are using your Torah-knowledge as a spear to pierce the Jewish heart. We are here to save our souls and your soul. Now, do as you see fit. May the merit of the Torah stand for you, in time. Be well.

Following this, at the end of *Cheshvan*, 5686 (1925), the ten delegates held a mass assembly in one of the synagogues in Leningrad. They notified the congregated people of the events transpiring in the community board and the reasons compelling them to leave:

We, the ten delegates, elected by you, the G-d-fearing Jews of Leningrad, those who are here and those who are not, must express our gratitude for the great honor entrusted to us to be your representatives to the honorable Leningrad community board, with "the presumption that a messenger fulfills his mission."[11] You relied upon us, knowing that as long as we were at our "holy posts" in this city, nothing offensive would take place. Now to our great sorrow, we are compelled to leave the community council, because all of the chairman's actions are directed against G-d and His Torah. We disassociate ourselves from them in any matter concerning religion. And since they, the majority, are thirteen, and we, the minority, ten, we did not wish to violate G-d's will and "be included with the majority for evil."[12] We vindicate ourselves by mounting the strongest possible protest, but we are compelled to warn you of the impending danger that this "General Assembly" stands to cause the Jewish nation to "forget Your Torah and violate the decrees of your will."[13] And now, act in a manner conforming to Jewish law.

Those assembled discussed the situation. The decision was unanimous. After thanking their representatives, the community decided to set up an authentic "Religious Community Council." They voted on a temporary acting commission to arrange a program and attempt to obtain the necessary permit.

At that time, the law was that every twenty Jews may establish a prayer quorum, with the government's sanction, but they may not convene gatherings. But fifty people had permission to pray, as well as to hold meetings, without need for a special permit each time.

On the basis of this law, our late friend Rabbi Shimon Lazaroff submitted to the government a document with fifty signatures, and received a permit to establish a synagogue called "Tzemach Tzedek."

It was a beautiful, spacious building in the city's center, and many prominent individuals in the community frequented it. It was truly a holy assemblage. The Rabbi was a G-d-fearing scholar, with a kind demeanor. He led his congregation peacefully. Each Sunday, members of all local *chassidic* congregations gathered there to discuss issues pertaining to the secret *chadarim*, fixing *mikva'ot*, and job placement for Shabbat-observant Jews. The community was a true pride for anyone who beheld it.

Covertly, the synagogue also served as a front. Many children's teachers in Leningrad received their pay from the Rebbe, and there was also a functioning *mikveh*. There were classes in Talmud at each *minyan*, all supported by the Rebbe.

This entire situation infuriated the chairman. In retaliation, he and several of his group, including Mr. Rabinovitch (who wrote under the pseudonym "A Jewish Man" and edited *Hamelitz* and other publications) took an oath. Understanding how dear to the dissenters was our holy Rebbe, they attacked both him and his *chassidim*, openly and secretly. They attempted to obscure this controversy by invoking the historical one of *chassidim* and *mitnagdim*, now wholly a matter of the past. In this way they successfully deceived many Jews, including pious ones.

They maligned the *chassidim* in the presence of the elderly Rabbi Katzenelenbogen, telling him the *chassidim* hated him, persecuted him, and shamed him behind his back. Rabbi Katzenelenbogen, may G-d grant him long, pleasant years, became a pawn in the conflict, believing the guileful

words of the chairman's group. In this way, the latter succeeded in opening up a rift between him and the Rebbe.

For decades the Rebbe and Rabbi Katzenelenbogen had
been of one opinion on any matter involving religion, but
the guile of the secularists succeeded, temporarily at least, for
"the ways of the wicked prosper,"[14] and the argument continued unabated. The rabbi's associates were jealous of the
Jews' love for the Rebbe — of his good work, of the fruits
of his labor, of the thousands of dear children G-d enabled
him to educate, in the *chadarim* he founded and continues to
found, of the hundreds of sweet students, may they ever
increase, who study G-d's Torah, *Gemara, Ein Yaakov, Midrash*
in all of the study halls, of building of *mikva'ot* in all places.
So the strife between the community council and the G-d-
fearing ones spread, but these two groups were unequally
matched, as were the weapons with which they did battle.

The G-d-fearing ones, the minority, lacked the power —
and above all the governmental authority to do anything
publicly. They had neither money, nor a permit to raise it.
Also, they were instructed by the Rebbe, may he be well, to
pursue peace and to distance themselves from any argument.
They were not to exert even the slightest effort without first
consulting with three others, and greeting those on the other
side pleasantly—with the hope that this would cause their
opponents to abandon their evil ways. So it was that the
entire "power base" of the G-d-fearing ones inhered only in
their separation from the secularists.

The old council, however, acted differently. The members
had government authority to appoint rabbis, collect charity,
publish public protests in writing and thereby wage war
against the G-d-fearing ones. As if these powers were not
enough, they commenced libel and slander.

The entire matter, with all of its details, became known to the *Yevsektzia*, who promptly joined forces. In the beginning the *Yevsektzia* helped the council secretly. Then, it became known that these people had passed the matter on to the "*Polit Atdel*" (the "Political Division") of the G.P.U., who could also aid them in secret.

Many rabbis in various cities were summoned by the Political Division and were urged to take part in the General Assembly of Leningrad and "not to follow Rabbi Schneersohn." Some of the rabbis who couldn't afford the trip were even offered travel expenses. The rabbis were then asked to swear in writing, on pain of death, not to disclose what had been discussed with them, on pain of death. The Christians, or "Nazarenes," had already set up a program to reform their religion. The council and the *Yevsektzia* had the same desire . . .[15]

But the *Yevsektzia* was also apprehensive, knowing that the rabbis were still far from subverting the Jewish religion. Furthermore, if the intentions for the "General Assembly" became common knowledge, it would be shown to be anti-religion. After learning who supported this goal and the degree to which our Rebbe opposed it, the Moscow community, led by genuinely religious people, withdrew. In addition, the community of Minsk wanted no part of it, seeing the danger behind the proposed conference. But many people in the cities where word of the "General Assembly" reached, mistakenly believed the Rebbe had indeed agreed to the chairman's trip, for the chairman had visited with him. Indeed, the chairman himself assured the people that the Rebbe had approved of the "General Assembly." But not trusting his words, many people inquired of the Rebbe himself, may he be well, via correspondence. Many sent letters to the Rebbe containing blessings for success and asking him to notify them of the program and of the time it would take place.

Our Rebbe kept silent. He did not even issue a public objection. In the month of *Sivan* 5686 (May, 1926), the Rebbe arranged a great meeting of all the rabbis of the country. During this meeting he also refrained from taking a leading role or even revealing his opinion. Instead, he asked the rabbis to deliberate upon the matter earnestly, and afterwards present the pros and cons so that he could render his opinion.

The meeting continued non-stop for three days and nights, and after much discussion with the secularists, everyone agreed that the assembly, although "it was best if it had never been created," would, after the fact, occur. At this point, opinions differed. The pious rabbis, recognizing the danger, G-d forbid, of this assembly, resolved to absent themselves and do whatever possible to stop it. Those who were uncertain decided that, since the religious conference would take place anyway, they may as well determine that the majority be G-d-fearing rabbis and that only valid propositions be accepted. "To the contrary," they argued, "it is a greater danger to boycott the assembly. The secularists will affiliate with the community council and, with the authority granted by the government, pass, G-d forbid, blasphemous and heretical resolutions, and the onus will be also upon us, the religious ones, heaven forbid, to implement them."

Our Rebbe, the last one to speak, then revealed his holy opinion:

Undoubtedly, I concur with those who say that it would have been better had the conference not been created in the first place. I also have the firm belief that G-d will not let it come to be. But if, Heaven forbid, it is convened, we may not take part in it . . . One who fears for his soul should distance himself from them. I am strongly opposed to those who say that we should try to be the majority so that the resolutions will be in accordance with our rules and wishes. It is very dangerous to rely on something so uncertain. In a case of uncertainty concerning a law of the Written Torah we have a halachic principle:[16] "We do not nullify a prohibition at the outset; a creature is never nullified, not even one part in a thousand."[17] (i.e. The secularist's ambitions are a sure thing. Our ability to overcome them is questionable.) It is almost certain that no one who enters this assembly will leave with his piety intact."[18]

I heard the following from his holy mouth as the three of us traveled in his compartment from Kostroma to Leningrad, on Friday morning, 16 *Tammuz* (July 16), in his compartment: the Rebbe, may he be well, his son-in-law, and myself. At that time, when it seemed that the assembly was about to be held, he said the following: "I hope it will not take place since it will cause great confusion. But if, G-d forbid, it does take place, whoever comes into contact with it will not be able to purify himself."

When the meeting took place in his house, our Rebbe, sincerely pursuing peace, asked the rabbis to go to Rabbi Katzenelenbogen, may he be well, to speak with him at length, to show him the imminent pitfalls in the assembly, and to convince him of his mistake in following the advice of these evil people. The rabbis did so, but to their chagrin, not only were they unable to correct him, their visit actually proved harmful. The elderly rabbi was irked when he saw how the Rebbe was able, in this dark period, to assemble the great rabbis of the big cities, and how revered were his activities throughout the community. Nevertheless, for their sake Rabbi Katzenelenbogen arranged a meeting in the community council between the rabbis and the secularists.

I can picture this meeting as vividly as though it were taking place today. The scene was awesome—the rabbis requesting from them the plans for the "General Assembly" issue. Without a program and a prior meeting, they argued; "We cannot endorse this assembly. We need first to know your motives, and we are beginning to understand that it is not 'kosher meat' and '*mikva'ot*' alone, as you have written. In truth, every G-d-fearing rabbi can administer this in his own city. For this we do not need any major conventions. We request that you tell us that which has hitherto been concealed."

Hearing these heartfelt words, the chairman's associates could no longer restrain themselves. Contrary to the chairman's wishes, they revealed the true intent of the assembly: "It is not kosher meat and *mikva'ot* that concern us, for that is a private matter; let everyone eat what he wishes, kosher or non-kosher. This is not our concern, and it does not bother us. Let the *mikvah* be kosher with forty *se'ah*[19] or with one less. Our main goal is the education and the schools; for this we are creating the 'General Assembly.' We wish to reform the children's education in accordance with contemporary spirit. With this we will be able to save the Jewish children from the *Komsomol*. In these times it is hard to continue with the old methods of education, those our parents favored, with doddering *melamdim*, rather than professional educators or curricula. Ours is a new era, and there are new people, new teachers, a new Torah."

No sooner had he finished speaking than the most respected of the rabbis[20] cried out: "Now we clearly see the danger which lurks in the 'General Assembly.' You wanted to force our attendance, and only now have we learned how to oppose it." He then announced to all of the gathered that the new program "would destroy all of the Jewish youth and bring them to assimilation — the Jewish people, the Torah, and the Holy One Blessed be He, are one and eternal![21] Abraham Our Father was one man alone!"[22] As he spoke these words he began to cry bitterly until he actually fainted.

This outcry caused a great commotion among the assembled and the chairman hastened from his place to bring the rabbi some water. Because of the impact the rabbi's words had made, the meeting ended without any resolution.

After the meeting, the rabbis again warned Rabbi Katzenelenbogen of what they had heard from those sinful men and of how the association of his name with the assembly would mislead many people. If he was not able to restrain these men, the rabbis suggested, then the assembly should not be called at all. In that way, the Rabbi could save his own soul by distancing himself from these men, in accordance with the principle "You shall not place a stumbling block before the blind."[23]

The Rabbi retorted that the statements at the meeting were made from a personal perspective and without the assent of the council. As further justification, he pointed out that the chairman was not the one who spoke. "The community council is not responsible for words spoken orally," he added, "for personal opinions it does not actually agree with."

Out of deference to his position and old age, the rabbis continued to honor him. However, they begged him at least to hold a meeting of rabbis as he saw fit, to determine with them whether the assembly was worthwhile, whether the timing was correct, and whether the loss would exceed the gains.

Again, the Rabbi answered: "Will the rabbis respond to my call? When the Lubavitcher Rebbe called you, you came immediately — but if I were to call, would you come?"

With this they parted from him, and each returned to his home.

In every city where these conflicting rumors reached, two sides immediately formed: the "G-d-fearing ones" and the "freethinkers." In the middle of it all stood the rabbis, shocked and confused.

"The Great Assembly" of the Leningrad community, with Rabbi Katzenelenbogen at their head — one needed only to mention the name, and all who heard thought that great good was being done and that it would result in great success.

But then they began to reflect: Why are the "G-d-fearing ones" standing on the side? Where is the Lubavitcher Rebbe? Why do we not see or hear any mention of him? Isn't he the leading figure in our country now, who bears the shattered Jewish nation on his shoulders, along with its Torah and mitzvot? Is not he the one who places his life in constant danger to build *yeshivot* and *chadarim* in every city? And if his strength is so great from a distance, how much more so in the city where he resides. And why are only the "freethinkers" and the government enthusiastic about this assembly?

These questions spread through the entire country, sowing confusion among all Jews whose hearts were touched by the fear of G-d. The few who wrote to the Rebbe, requesting direction, did not merit his revered reply for the aforementioned reason: He desired only peace and brotherhood. Perhaps he would persuade Rabbi Katzenelenbogen to return from his erring path. The Rebbe trusted in G-d that the assembly would not occur and that it would be nullified at its source.

At the beginning of the winter it was learned that special representatives were being sent to the large cities to speak publicly on behalf of the assembly. Several of the rabbis began to urge the Rebbe to state his opinion on the matter, at least for the benefit of some of the larger cities. For the proponents of the assembly were misleading the communities that were far from Leningrad, saying that he too, may he be well, was in agreement with them. Unless the Rebbe revealed his opposition in writing, the rabbis could not single-handedly fight the Leningrad community council. They feared that their voices would go unheard and that representatives would be sent from their own cities.

On 5 *Tevet*, 5686 (1926), the Rebbe agreed, and wrote the following letter:

By the Grace of G-d,

Tuesday, 5 *Tevet* 5686, Leningrad

Greetings and Blessings!

Paragraph One of the bylaws of the Leningrad community states that it may participate in the general conference of any religious community, and that it may call a general gathering of the religious communities. The chairman therefore proposed before the members of the community council to apply this rule to convene a general conference, and to contact other communities to ascertain their opinions at the conference; and his proposal was accepted.

I was informed of this, and I responded that I was opposed to a general gathering of any nature, for whatever goal. Such a general conference might cause harm, G-d forbid. I am sure that the many who, thank G-d, are loyal to G-d and His Torah and religion, with true love for our brethren, will clearly be opposed to a general gathering.

With the spread of rumors of a general gathering, many letters have reached me from various places, the majority of which express fundamental doubts about the event, and they have all reached the determination that this conference should best not take place. Although my opinion is firm and clear in opposition to this gathering in any form, I did not find it necessary to state my opinion publicly. This was because it appeared there was no momentum building for the proposal.

Now, however, I have read many letters, written naively, asserting that since the call for a general gathering is coming from the Leningrad community, then it is certainly with my participation or agreement. I have also been told that the person responsible for this project has, on many occasions, stated that I concur with his opinion. (I am very surprised how such serious conclusions can be decided upon by conjecture, and I am distressed to hear the citing of my name by people with whom I do not concur, neither in spirit, nor in fact.)

Therefore, the pure truth for the good of our brethren, the Jewish people, may G-d be with them, requires me to declare my opinion publicly: it is perilous to call this gathering, and its source is impure. I am categorically opposed to calling any gathering (even to calling a meeting about the general gathering), and I see potentially negative results from it, Heaven forfend.

I therefore request that all who read these words or hear them will relate them to their friends and acquaintances — and they in turn to their friends — for the populace to know: I have no connection with the Leningrad community council, the original proponents of the general gathering. My opinion is against any type of general gathering, and the council may not take this responsibility upon itself, and doubtless all religious communities are against a general gathering.

The Leningrad community is now trying to obtain a permit for a joint summit of members of various community councils, in order to decide whether or not a general gathering is needed. I recommend that every community elect members who are appropriately qualified in spirit, goals and deeds, who will represent the good of the Jewish community. If the permit is granted for the aforementioned summit they must fulfill their responsibilities impartially and render a clear opinion, like any knowledgeable person, that we do not need a general gathering, that even the discussion about it was gratuitous, and that no trace should be left of it at all.

Any wise person, loving his nation and his religion, who knows something about community work for the good of the Jewish people, will understand on his own whose opinion to reject and whose to accept.

"May G-d grant His nation strength, and bless His nation with peace."[24]

With much blessing to all Jews spiritually and physically.

With threefold blessings.

[Signature].[25]

Although we couldn't print the letter, for lack of a permit, knowledge of the Rebbe's objection spread rapidly as the letter was passed from hand to hand and mouth to mouth. The letter strengthened the resolve of all G-d-fearing people to openly oppose the "General Assembly," and also to persuade others to reject it.

But at the same time, as with any conflict, the opposition also intensified its efforts on behalf of the faction in the Leningrad community. Letters were sent urging people to reject "Lubavitcher *Chassidus*" and instead to rely on Rabbi Katzenelenbogen, may he be well, "who is the eldest of the rabbis and who is with you in your pain; this is only the old conflict of *chassidim* and *mitnagdim*."

Thus it was easy to "place a stumbling block before the blind," and the disagreement spread to the entire country, until certain individuals in every community learned that the *Yevsektzia* was standing behind the community council, extending its long arm. Only then was the dark secret known, not publicly, but privately, to the community leaders and prominent rabbis. The *Yevsektzia* prohibited them from publicizing this fact, adding threats and forcing them to state their agreement.

Thus this most important matter remained unresolved until *Sivan,* 5687 (June, 1927). The community council circulated letters to all of the communities in the country, exhorting them to prepare for the upcoming assembly once the permit materialized and they were notified of the exact time. They finished with the *Shehechiyanu* blessing and openly blessed their counterparts in the communities at large.

At the very same time, the chairman and several others sent secret letters to nonobservant individuals in every local community to let them know whom to elect from their city as delegates. Publicly, they spoke of kosher meat, rabbis, *shochatim, mikva'ot,* and other religious matters, elaborating upon the need to strengthen religious Judaism. Privately, they disparaged traditional Jews — "their quaint customs which were out of touch with the times, and their 'extremist leader.'" They called for a "new education," and "many reforms."

Meanwhile, something else occurred, which, truthfully speaking, still remains an enigma. If it weren't such an important part of the events I am describing, particularly concerning the questions and allegations directed at the Rebbe when he was in prison, I would omit it.

On the evening of *Shemini Atzeret* 5687, before *hakafot*, a gentile messenger came to the Rebbe's house and told the Rebbe that a Professor Baratchenko wished for a private audience, and that he had traveled especially from Moscow to see the Rebbe. The emissary was told that it was a festival and that on those days the Rebbe did not deal with mundane matters. He refused to accept the answer, thinking it was merely an evasion, and pleaded to be allowed to present his case before the Rebbe. Because of the professor's honorable name, and because we were a little apprehensive, one of us went to the head table and told the Rebbe of the guest. The Rebbe, unperturbed, asked his secretary, Mr. Lieberman, to beg the guest's pardon and to explain that since it was a Jewish festival the Rebbe could not receive him. If the emissary wished, he could return after the festival (two days later) when the Rebbe would gladly meet with him. The professor answered that he was pained over his wasted time, but because of the importance of the matter he would remain in Leningrad until after the festival, which he did.

When he returned after the holiday, he was received immediately for a lengthy private audience. We did not know the professor's aims or the nature of his business with the Rebbe. Later on, we learned that he was the Baratchenko who dealt with the occult (which was also based on mathematics) to reveal mysteries and predict the future. And, supposedly, it had some kind of connection to Kabbala. He had already organized a group in Moscow to pursue this study, for which they received a government permit. They were joined with keen interest by many leading scholars. Baratchenko, having learned that the leader of the Jews lived in Leningrad and was well-versed in Kabbala, and that "the paths of the heavens are illuminated before him,"[27] went to him to "seek out G-d" and to learn that which was hidden (for according to the professor, the key to his study was knowing the oneness of G-d).

All that was learned of the Rebbe's answer is this: "*Chassidus* has no relation whatsoever to foretelling the future, and in that matter we are prohibited from seeking out that which is beyond us." The Rebbe was prepared to help Baratchenko with whatever the latter needed to know of Kabbala and *Chassidus*, but his time was precious and he personally could not do it at that time. He added that he also could not do the necessary translation. When Rabbi Menachem Mendel Schneerson[28] would arrive shortly from Yekatrinaslav, the Rebbe would ask him to find what the professor needed from Kabbalistic sources and to translate it into Russian. It would then be sent to Baratchenko's address. Rabbi Menachem Mendel knew the language of Kabbala well, the Rebbe explained, and could also translate proficiently.

Satisfied, Baratchenko thanked the Rebbe and went on his way. We also learned that the Rebbe was unsure and suspicious of this professor's true intent. In the first few minutes of talking with him, he had speculated about the professor's sanity, but Baratchenko sensed this and pulled out a certificate signed by several of the most respected professors in Moscow, testifying that he had a lucid mind and that he was not insane in the slightest. Baratchenko was also concerned that the Rebbe would think he was a spy, so he showed many certificates from the *Sovnorchaz* government agency, where he held a respectable position.

After some time, a sum of several hundred golden rubles unexpectedly arrived for the Rebbe from Baratchenko. In the attached note, he wrote that he was sending the funds for the travel and other expenses of Rabbi Menachem Mendel. The Rebbe immediately sent back the entire amount, without even deducting the return postage.

Baratchenko, after receiving the money, could find no peace for his troubled soul and sent a lengthy letter to the Rebbe, expressing his humiliation. He had tried his utmost to show the Rebbe his purity of motive and simple sincerity. From the fact that the Rebbe had returned the money, he wrote, it was obvious that the Rebbe was unjustifiably suspicious of an innocent man. To remove any trace of suspicion, the professor would need to visit with him again face to face.

And so it was: he returned again in the winter and met with the Rebbe in his room, and the Rebbe introduced him to Rabbi Menachem Mendel.

All that year the professor exchanged letters with Rabbi Menachem Mendel, who also visited his house, and the Rebbe forgot all about the professor and his doings. In the end, the matter was entirely forgotten.

That winter on February 16, 5687 (1927), a terrible thing occurred in the Rebbe's household: the Rebbe's chief secretary, Rabbi Elchonon Dov Marasow, was arrested and sent to the worst prison in Leningrad, "*Das Fremd Varitelnaya Zeklutshenil,*" locally called "*Spalerka.*"

Rabbi Marasow's imprisonment caused anxiety in the Rebbe's entire household. He was being jailed with the worst political criminals, and we were all sure it was because of the Rebbe's work.

The Rebbe was then in Moscow for two days; we therefore sent him a message urging him to remain there for some time, until further notice. The Rebbe, though shaken by the news, did not for a moment consider hiding, and he hastened home.

It was learned that Reb Elchonon Dov was being held in dark and solitary confinement under heavy guard. He was allowed no food from home; his family received no answer to their inquiries or their requests to give over at least the medications that he needed. (He was quite weak in general; all the more so at this time.) The prison officials refused to communicate with family members and had them ejected from the prison. They even denied the prisoner his *talit* and *tefillin*. All the efforts to ease his situation were of no avail, although one organization[29] did manage to provide him with kosher food and some clothing. But it proved impossible to clarify the charge upon which he was arrested.[30]

It was initially surmised that Reb Elchonon Dov had been arrested as a consequence of the Rebbe's efforts in behalf of the *chadarim* and *yeshivot* in all the towns across the country. Reb Elchonon Dov kept the addresses in a special book, hidden constantly in his portfolio. The fearful situation initially had a very bad effect on the Rebbe's health.

It was assumed that the comprehensive list of *yeshivot* and their addresses which Reb Elchonon Dov kept hidden in his portfolio were confiscated during the search. Later we learned that at the exact moment the G.P.U. agents arrived with search and arrest warrants, Reb Elchonon Dov managed to hand over to his eleven-year-old son[31] the Rebbe's entire correspondence on *chadarim* and *yeshivot*. The boy already knew what to do: he hid the documents in a bag and went outside. The officers, paying no attention to him, let him leave. Blessed is G-d, who sanctifies His name in secret as well, and through this child thousands of schoolchildren were saved. This miracle happened "in these days and in our time."[32]

The news of the arrest spread quickly throughout the country, and every teacher who worked in the hidden *chadarim* feared for his own safety. But not one of them stopped his holy work, for they had been prepared, from the day the *Yevsektzia* was formed, to sacrifice their lives to

enable even one Jewish child to learn G-d's Torah, and to save him from these "agents of the Inquisition."

The Rebbe himself was told that he was the cause of Reb Elchonon Dov's arrest. The Rebbe was also told of the first question the G.P.U. asked upon entering Reb Elchonon Dov's house: Was Reb Elchonon Dov, in fact, the "chief secretary of Rabbi Schneersohn?" This question seemed to be a clear proof that his relationship to the Rebbe was his only crime; nevertheless, the Rebbe told us clearly that Reb Elchonon Dov was arrested for another reason which had no connection to him or to his work. At first we thought the Rebbe was saying this just to lessen the fear of those working with him. But later we learned that the Rebbe, may he be well, was right.

Reb Elchonon Dov's "crime" did in fact have no connection at all to his work for the Rebbe. He was arrested for a different matter, a libel concocted about him and a group of *chassidim* from Nevel, who supposedly helped someone to cross the border illegally. In truth, he was totally innocent, even according to the law of the land. He is so far from such matters that merely to level such a charge is ludicrous, comparable to the blood libels a century ago in the era of the fanatical priests.

But G-d had decreed that Reb Elchonon Dov, too, drink from the bitter waters of the terrible year 5687. And, to our great distress, his suffering has not yet ended. He and his friends lie in misery, dwelling in the darkness of one of the remote cities of exile in Siberia. They are alone in "a dry and weary land."[33] May the L-rd who metes out judgment upon our enemies have pity on the imprisoned and save them from darkness and "the shadow of death" and speedily free them from their shackles.

In the winter of that year another mysterious incident occurred, this one involving the Rebbe's dwelling. It has led to another unpleasant matter, which we still have not been able to clarify.

In every major Russian city there is a special commission, a *Kamchaz*, which has tight jurisdiction over all the local dwellings. This commission appoints a *Zshakot*, Residential Action Committee, which in turn controls all the dwellings under it. It can build and demolish, allow anyone it wants to dwell in a house, or evict anyone it pleases.

According to its rules, tenants are divided into four categories by status and honor. The highest and most respected is the "*rabotchi*," the simple worker. He is above anyone's authority, and he himself has authority over others. In every courtyard, nine *rabotchis* are chosen to direct the affairs of the courtyard: to fix, assign apartments, evict, and manage all the financial affairs. Above all, they are appointed to protect the workers, and at the very same time to persecute any "non-workers," known as "*nye tradavai element* (non-working element)." Befriending the worker and harassing the non-worker is an identical imperative. He who has greater ability to pursue the "non-worker" and make his life miserable is made a leader. Essentially, the *rabotchis* are immune to any reprisal, and anyone who dares lay a hand upon them is severely punished.

The lowliest in rank among the four levels is anyone having any connection to religion, be it ours or, *lehavdil*, any other. It is particularly virtuous to humiliate a rabbi or priest and their assistants. And it is forbidden to show them any pity. If anyone does so, his infraction is proclaimed at the yearly meeting and he is forced to leave the group.

In the Rebbe's courtyard there were about 60 dwellings. His dwelling exceeded the combined income of all these dwellings, for the rent was determined by the tenant's status according to the above-mentioned four levels. Anyone who was not a simple laborer had to pay one hundredfold; how much more so if he was counted among the "believers" whose profession was related to religion, as in the Rebbe's case. The taxes of the entire courtyard were to be paid by this one person's dwelling. You can imagine how the Rebbe's household endured the burdens laid on them by the authorities.

It is impossible, here and now, to tell you of the hundreds of miracles that transpired before the very eyes of those who lived in the Rebbe's environs throughout the three and a half years that he was in Leningrad. A *minyan* was established in his house three times a day, and on Shabbat over one hundred people came, may they ever multiply. Even more came whenever he delivered a *chassidic* discourse. And for *Rosh Hashanah, Yom Kippur, Sukkot, 19 Kislev, Purim, Shavuot* — all the holidays — guests from cities far and near arrived, up to 500 people besides the local *chassidim*, who were equally numerous.

You must remember that we *chassidim* differ in garb and appearance from the general population. We stand out in our prayers and our joyfulness on the holidays. Yet all of the large rooms filled with hundreds of people; the vigorous dancing and loud voices singing *chassidic* melodies reverberated through the street, not to mention the entire courtyard.

Below the Rebbe's dwelling was located a large store belonging to the G.P.U., formerly the *Cheka*. Adjacent to the Rebbe's dwelling, on the other side of the wall, lived an important G.P.U. officer, *"natchalnik"*. As the door to his dwelling faced the Rebbe's, not a day would pass without somebody mistaking his door for the Rebbe's. Many of the Rebbe's visitors came from the villages, where their primary vocation was Torah study, and their provincial ways might have irritated the local inhabitants. Now, a village person's way of ringing the doorbell is quite different from a city dweller's: the villager pushes his finger into the bell as far as it will go, and he will not release the bell until the door actually opens before him. Each time this happened, the G.P.U. officer respectfully explained that a mistake had occurred, and courteously showed the visitor the door he was seeking. The two floors above the Rebbe's dwelling consisted of neighbors not of our *chassidic* community who probably didn't appreciate the constant tumult caused by visitors.

The Rebbe's dwelling was located on the corner of two of the most prominent streets in Leningrad: Machovaya 22 and Fantilamanskaya 12. Anyone familiar with this city is aware of the erstwhile prestige of these two streets. In the time of the Czars, it was an exclusive area and no Jew was ever allowed to set foot near that corner, which was reserved for barons and ministers. The previous tenant occupant in the Rebbe's dwelling had been the Baron from Kass, the Governor of the Besravia region. This Baron, in his own handwriting, had signed over the dwelling and much of its furniture to the Rebbe. In *Sivan* 5684 (1924) the Baron was compelled, according to Soviet law, to leave Leningrad and was banished to one of the remote "cities of exile." Until this day many of the Baron's furnishings remain in the Rebbe's dwelling. It is, thank G-d, a spacious and beautiful dwelling, with seven windows looking onto Fantilamanskaya Street, ten onto Machovaya Street, and one overlooking the corner, at an angle. The room where we prayed and where the Rebbe would say *Chassidus* was expansive, similar to the second hall in Lubavitch.

There was no "official permit" for prayer assemblies, because every time they would apply to the *Ispolcom* Executive Commission, they would be summarily rejected. All of the congregants and locals presumed, however, that a permit did exist, for thank G-d, many arrived to pray and without any attempt at concealment, just as in the largest synagogues. The police, who were aware of the prayer service, were certain we had a permit. The "*Opravlenia Doma* Housing Authority*,*" were also sure we had a permit, since it was required by contract. Yet, given the open manner of prayer, it did not occur to them during those three years to ask to see an official permit. Of course, the entire thing was sustained by a miracle. Truthfully, even those of us who knew, couldn't begin to fathom the self-sacrifice it must have entailed.

As I write these lines, I picture the last *Rosh Hashanah*. I am overwhelmed when I think of the many guests, in various styles of dress, their beards, their long sidelocks, over one hundred students who arrived from the Rebbe's *yeshivot* for a month's stay. I can picture the way it looked — just as it was thirty years ago in Lubavitch — visitors wandering through the streets, asking where the Rebbe lived, the *Oprovdom* (the officer of the *Opravlenia Doma*) standing in the street with the policeman, looking at these odd creatures and showing them the proper door to find the Rebbe, all with the greatest deference and respect. Through G-d's kindness everything was peaceful until the winter — and this was literally miraculous.

In January, 1927, it was "revealed" that the *Oprovdom* manager of the building, had stolen a large sum, about 4,000 gold rubles, from the *Opravlenia Doma*. When he was called for interrogation and asked where the money was, he did not at first know what to answer. On account of his great simplemindedness and most of all his drunkenness, he was at a loss to explain the deficit. He had no understanding of anything related to reckoning, nor any recollection of this matter.

The truth is that he was not the thief. It was the book-keeper, who could calculate very well. An evil, scheming person, he had stolen the money, hidden it, and blamed the whole thing on the *Oprovdom*, knowing the latter was a drunkard whom everyone would believe to be the culprit. In order further to conceal his crime, this bookkeeper found it most convenient to implicate the Rebbe, may he be well, claiming that the entire missing amount was owed by the Rebbe. The man added that "in the 'holy house,' where it was known that the *Oprovdom* was a drunkard, the residents had surely obtained receipts from him for more than what they actually paid." He added that the receipts held by the one who handled the payments for the Rebbe's dwelling were forged, and he told this story to the *Oprovdom* as well.

The authorities were delighted with this explanation, for now they had a pretext to find something amiss in the house of the "holy man." Suddenly, a warning letter arrived from the directors of the courtyard. It stated that if the full amount, several thousand rubles, were not paid within several days, the matter would be turned over to the courts which would order him both to pay the amount and vacate the house.

The person in charge of paying the Rebbe's rent and dealing with the landlord was a highly honest, but volatile, individual. He received the letter from the *Opravlenia Doma* with the demands and warnings, knowing that in truth they were owed nothing and that it was an empty libel. He also sensed what was going on.

He stormed into the office and showed them how the accusation was false and how the bookkeeper had fabricated the whole story. He demanded that all the books be brought to the director's house and for the director, and only the director, to make the calculations in order to evaluate the situation.

These words, spoken with such intensity, accomplished their purpose. The director acquiesced. As I mention the latter, I cannot be unappreciative and neglect to describe him favorably. He, too, is a simple man. Formerly a baker, he is now the director of a large factory. During the several years' interim he was prominent among the *Cheka*, and he is rumored to remain secretly connected to them. As one of the righteous Communists, he merited to defend the innocence of the Rebbe's household.

He realized the integrity of the *chassidim,* although he never saw the Rebbe the entire three years the Rebbe lived there. He did, however, observe and know the people around him and those who came to visit him. He also heard the prayers and the singing coming from the house and knew clearly that the Rebbe had no connection to politics. Indeed, the Rebbe toiled only in Torah day and night, drawing Jewish hearts closer to their Father in Heaven. The founding of *chadarim* and *yeshivot* did not bother the director at all, since he did not belong to the *Yevsektzia.*

Let us praise[34] the gentile Communists who have no involvement with anything connected to the Jewish religion. The distress is only in the mind of the *Yevsektzia*, from the "mixed multitude"[35] who left Egypt with us and whose wicked ways persist. In the past we studied Torah publicly and Judaism was whole. As we know, the Communist Party cannot tolerate the *Yevsektzia*, either. As the "great Luchatcharske" himself said at one of the general assemblies in Moscow, the *Yevsektzia* is "a thorn in the flesh of the party."[36] Once he even joked from the podium that the *Yevsektzia* is "a blemish in the eye of the party." But the non-Jews are different.

This also applies to this chairman I mention, a simple man, a Communist in the fullest sense of the word. He did not pursue imagined honor, nor did he glory in his free-thinking religion and his denial of everything, nor did he coerce others into denial. He was not a "paper Communist," like the typical *Yevsektzia* member, who, when he finally, after much intense effort, receives his party card, scurries about, shouting to all that he is a Communist, knowing they are likely to think otherwise and be suspicious. Since he is only a "paper Communist," he rings the doorbell all day and all night to publicize his opposition to any matter of holiness, to harass anyone who fulfills *mitzvot* and studies the Torah.

He and his kind confiscate synagogues belonging to thousands of Jews, and turn them into clubs and theaters. In the place of the Holy Ark, they place a statue of Lenin and the like. Not long ago, in G-d's house, one of the synagogues in Minsk, on the first night after taking control, they placed a pig in the Holy Ark, wrote on it "Paschal Sacrifice," and laughed derisively. Currently, they are digging up Jewish cemeteries, removing the bones of the deceased to turn the sacred places into parks. This is one thousandth of their terrible deeds, may G-d judge them. These villains do such things every day, and only to show the party their devotion, and win their trust.

This chairman of whom I speak is different. He has never believed in G-d, but he will not interfere with his fellow's beliefs, nor will he laugh at Judaism and its tenets. He honors religious people; he will not mock a Jew who believes in what he denies, and he will not make a display. Every time someone of the Rebbe's household came to him with a request to build a *sukkah* in the courtyard, and a big one at that, not only did he permit this, but he ordered the watchman to guard it against youths who might damage it.

So it was with this situation. After he learned of the theft and the underlying intent to blame it on the Rebbe's household in the hope of ruining his reputation, the director took all of the record ledgers to his home, trying to avoid any publicity until he could personally investigate and evaluate the entire business. During one of the long winter nights, we sat in his home — he, the bookkeeper, two people from the investigation committee, the manager from the Rebbe's house, and myself. Patiently, we sat and pored over the calculations until the morning, scrutinizing the accounts from the entire three years. It was obvious the Rebbe and his followers were honest and that the accusation was groundless.

The chairman stood up angrily and, in front of us, shouted at the bookkeeper: "Now the whole matter is clear and we know who committed the theft! What do you say now? Now I know Rabbi Schneersohn's honesty and your dishonesty, and I will know what to do with you!" The two investigators left the house with bowed heads.

The manager of the Rebbe's household and I, thanked G-d for clearing the Rebbe's name and saving him from the desecration of G-d's holy name. On the contrary, His name was sanctified publicly, and with many thanks and blessings we parted triumphantly from the chairman.

The chairman did not let the matter rest. He quickly wrote a full report of what had transpired, signed it together with the investigation committee, and forwarded it to the "Serious Offenses Commission." Only a few days passed, and the *Oprovdom* was arrested and imprisoned.

The Rebbe received a summons from the prosecutor to appear as a witness, since he was the one whose name was cited in the report and the person accused. The thought of the Rebbe himself having to appear troubled us greatly, for it did not befit his honor. I requested of the chairman to ask the prosecutor to have the Rebbe excused from appearing since he had been unaware of the daily transactions. Only I and the manager knew, and we offered to go in his stead.

The chairman consented, thank G-d. He phoned the prosecutor, whom he knew personally, and he also gave me a letter to submit to him. With Divine help all went well, and the prosecutor wrote on the summons that I could appear in the Rebbe's place. I gave thanks to G-d that the investigator was not a member of the *Yevsektzia*, but a simple gentile.

He interviewed me respectfully, I answered all of his questions truthfully, and I left in peace. The planners of this snare were themselves ensnared.

As a result of this whole incident, the officer of the Serious Offenses Commission learned that this chairman had helped the Rebbe. Bear this in mind, for it is connected to another story I shall later relate.[37]

Purim of last year was totally without precedent. What we saw and heard during the Purim festive meal was unlike anything we had ever seen or heard in our entire lives; nothing comparable to this had been witnessed by our fathers or our fathers' fathers. True, it did not come upon us without warning. From the beginning of the year, to our great wonder and sorrow, we felt there were disturbing events occurring with greater frequency, obstacles which distracted the Rebbe from his holy work, literally at every step. He suffered not only from the left, the cursed *Yevsektzia*, but to our dismay from the others as well, as had the Alter Rebbe in his time — things that should not be spoken of publicly. The time has not yet come for all of these matters to be made available in written form, not to add fuel to a fire still aflame and whose sparks, it is reasonable to assume, could produce an even greater conflagration than what existed before. In every generation there is no Jacob without a brother Esau, who "hunts" and, after the blessings are given, cries out bitterly that his brother came in secret and stole them.

The great conference in Karastien in the province of Vohynnia-Padolia[38] was a major cause of the Rebbe's arrest. One hundred rabbis had gathered, and at the opening, with much fanfare, the Rebbe was chosen as the Honorary Chairman, notwithstanding the fact that he was not even in attendance.

The Rebbe dispatched a reply:

Thank you for the honor you have bestowed upon me. With this you demonstrate that you are proceeding in the ways of Rabbi Schneersohn of Lubavitch[39] and Rabbi Chaim of Brisk,[40] loyal to the ideals of our unforgettable teachers. The entire Jewish nation is anticipating that you will continue in your ways without compromise. Wish the participants well. Best wishes for success.

When the Rebbe's reply was received in the middle of the conference, the entire assemblage stood up while the telegram was read by Rabbi Zamsky.[41] This greatly angered the *Yevsektzia*. Many times during the conference directives arrived from the Rebbe. The place teemed with G.P.U. agents, and after the conference, the danger to the Rebbe increased greatly.

The appointment of the Rebbe as Honorary Chairman came as a surprise, as there are almost no *chassidim* in that area. Even the Rebbe's predecessors had little influence there. However, the Rebbe began to exert major efforts to promulgate *Yiddishkeit* in that region. In the years 5685-5687 (1925-1927), he was informed of the eradication of Judaism in these places and of the general abandonment of religion, with the result that many Jewish towns were left without a children's teacher. The *Yevsektzia* was even more powerful in those parts, and the observant Jews' fear of the *Yevsektzia* was even more intense. In those regions the *Yevsektzia* included many of the judges, officers, and policemen; even some of the prison guards came from their ranks. Naturally, any Jew who valued his life was afraid, not only to be a teacher, but even to send his child to learn.

Despite all this, the Rebbe sent secret special representatives and directed them to institute a cheder in every city in that area, large and small. He would pay for it anonymously. The representatives would remunerate every teacher for one or two months and distribute copies everywhere of the sections of the Constitution stating that it was permissible to study with three children. If teachers encountered any difficulties from the *Yevsektzia* or any other mishap, they were to report immediately to the *Va'ad* that the Rebbe had formed in Moscow. He also ordered his emissaries to speak from the pulpits of the synagogues and study halls in every city, to strengthen the hearts of the Jews and bring them closer to their Father in Heaven by teaching *Chassidus*, *Ein Yaakov*, and *Mussar* between afternoon and evening prayers. They strove to uplift the people spiritually from their downtrodden state.

With G-d's great kindness, the Jewish people were not left like abandoned orphans, and in every city the emissaries found Jews who agreed wholeheartedly with them and who eagerly joined their ranks. Hundreds of *chadarim* and *Ein Yaakov* groups were rapidly formed, may they ever increase, bringing boundless joy to the Rebbe. To our great despair, however, the *Yevsektzia* also learned of these developments and had many of the emissaries arrested, so that in 5687 their work was brought to a halt. They were exiled to the towns of Siberia, may G-d have mercy on them and deliver them from captivity to freedom.

With the passage of time the source and inspiration of all these emissaries became known in these areas: the Rebbe's holiness and self-sacrifice became revealed, and his great name was spread. It was on the merits of this work that the Rebbe was chosen as Honorary Chairman of this conference. However, the fame bred more hatred among the anti-religious, who feared that if his influence became too strong in those regions, it would completely nullify the remnant of their own supporters.

The "chairman," the arch-zealot promoting the Leningrad Conference, endeavored covertly to thwart the Rebbe's goals. While acting benevolently in direct dealings with the Rebbe, he plotted behind the Rebbe's back. May G-d frustrate his terrible plans and cause him to return from his crooked path, and remove the blindfold from his eyes. Those of us who were close to the Rebbe knew of his terrible suffering from within and without, and of all the misery which the Rebbe encountered. In private, his soul cried out day and night; he could not rest.

Hence, at that Purim feast, we expected him to share his inner concerns with us, as Purim was usually a time of revelations. We felt he would finally pour his heart out to us. Instead, what we saw was totally unanticipated, unlike anything we had ever seen.

The Rebbe spoke openly, sharply, and intensely. He wept, his face flushed with emotion, and in his voice was an anger one had never heard before. We actually witnessed an outpouring of soul, so intense were his feelings.

In the midst of the Purim feast, the Rebbe abruptly stood up, pulled at his shirt to reveal his heart, and pounded hard with his fist on his bare flesh, calling out, "Elye Chaim, Elye Chaim! I told you to write harshly last year, but you did not listen, and this is why there has been so much suffering all year. After Shabbat you shall write a letter to all the cities and villages with these words: 'We possessed a Rebbe,[42] and he left us his son to guide us, and the son has instructed us to write in his name that anyone handing his child over to the school of the *Yevsektzia* will be severely punished by Heaven, Heaven forbid.' Will you write this? Remember well what I say to you!"

He repeated these words again and again, pounding upon his chest. He called me again, and with a radiant countenance declared, "When you see the body consumed, have no feelings of pity. Concern yourself solely with protecting the head."

The *chassidim* were greatly alarmed by the Rebbe's open defiance of the *Yevsektzia*. One of the elderly cried out, "Rebbe we cannot stand to hear such words. We need a Rebbe of flesh and blood."

The Rebbe answered, "I asked my father, 'in the manner of Nikolai?' And he replied, 'like Nikolai!'" Seeing our confusion, the Rebbe explained:

Nikolai the First was sent as a youth by his father, Czar Paul, to conduct maneuvers to test his capabilities as a soldier. Nikolai had received military training during his adolescence and distinguished himself during these war games. Exhilarated by his achievement, he sealed with his ring a decree which bestowed lavish presents on the officers and soldiers who had participated with him. He did this without consulting his father and the royal treasurer.

When the father learned what had happened, he was gratified by his son's success but enraged at his bold actions and lavish expenditures, which were beyond the means of the treasury. He summoned Nikolai to the palace and commended him on the military skills he had displayed during the maneuvers. However, as penalty for his spending without first consulting his father, the prince was to be banished from the capital city for two full years.

The Rebbe concluded by repeating, "I asked my father 'in the manner of Nikolai?' and he replied, 'like Nikolai.'"

Our fear reached an even higher intensity. We could not bear to hear such things — firstly, because of the dire events he was foretelling; and secondly, because we were acutely aware of the spies in our midst, as they had been at every *chassidic* gathering since our arrival in Leningrad. Because the Rebbe's home was open to all, he usually took care as to how he spoke in our presence. We begged the Rebbe to stop, but he faced them directly and cried out: "*Yemach shemam*! [May their names be blotted out!] I know that they are here; I am not afraid of them."

We gazed at the agents, and their faces, flushed with anger, deepened our concern for the Rebbe's welfare. I hastened to the elderly Rebbetzin, the Rebbe's mother, Shterna Sarah, to ask her to approach her son and try to prevail upon him. I entered her room and related all that had taken place. She hurried to the large room, to the relief of the *chassidim*, for they understood her purpose, and they quickly made a path for her.

Before she could speak, the Rebbe turned to her with great deference and said, "Mother, please return to your room. Say Psalms and weep in prayer to G-d; that will help." As he spoke, tears flowed from his eyes. Seeing this, the Rebbetzin began to cry, too. Thus they stood, facing each other in silence and tears. The scene moved us deeply, and we all wept. After these harrowing moments the Rebbe spoke, "I do nothing on my own. I consulted with Father."

The open defiance implicit in the story of Nikolai, and the direct confrontation with the agents, provoked much alarm among the *chassidim*. They were also distressed by the Rebbe's remarks to a *chassid* named Zalman about the care that should be taken to protect small children from the falsehoods of the *Yevsektzia* educational system.

"Zalman," he said, "if they should ever make a great bonfire and confront you with the choice of yielding your child to their schools or casting yourself into the flames, do you know what should be done? I am telling you, Zalman: let yourself be cast into the flames to prevent your children from being given over to their schools!"

The Rebbetzin begged the Rebbe not to overtax himself, but to find a room where he could rest. She continued to speak gently in this vein until, from weakened health and sheer exhaustion, he fainted. He was carried from the room and, after some effort, revived. We waited until his return for the recitation of Grace after the Meal . . .

After that Purim we were very afraid. We discussed the Rebbe's words, the meaning of the narrative about Nikolai. "Didn't the *Yevsektzia* agents, who were standing right there, take in every single word?" We knew it was only a matter of time before something awesome happened. We each concealed our feelings, in order not to frighten each other even more. It is no exaggeration on my part to say that fear was written all over the faces of some of the *chassidim*. We began stopping by the Rebbe's home twice every day to see if all was well. Those who lived farther away would call by telephone to find out how he was.

There was good reason to be apprehensive. The General Religious Assembly was once again on the verge of convening. The organizers knew that the Rebbe opposed the conference and that his influence extended throughout the country. He was well connected to all the Rebbes and community leaders, who themselves knew that at any moment he might ask them openly to do everything in their power to forbid the conference. He only had to make an open declaration — at which point the Jewish people would forthrightly state their objections, and the organizers would lose everything.

Consequently, the organizers took a different path. In one of the meetings around Passover the chairman stated that if the Rebbe would not retract, then he would be coerced into doing so. After Passover the *Leningrad Diska Pravda* newspaper unexpectedly printed the following anonymous article:

The famous tzaddik Schneersohn from Lubavitch recently arrived in Leningrad and settled at Machovaya Street, number 22. His powerful influence extends not only to the rich bourgeoisie, but also to simple people, the working class.

Although brief and anonymous, the article was significant to those of us who knew a little about their methods. We saw it as a partial warning, and a partial prophecy of what was to come. As we would soon learn, we were not in error.

Another incident was connected to the Rebbe's arrest: In Leningrad there is a *Yevsekztia* institution called "*Shul un Buch*," which was created to spread *Yevsekztia* literature. In 5687, seemingly without reason, membership and morale fell sharply. So too, their newspaper *Emes*, which had until recently sold thousands of new subscriptions, was slashed to fewer than one thousand in Leningrad. And since their revenue had dropped so drastically, they were in danger of closing. They turned to their Moscow headquarters for help.

At that time, the *Yevsektzia* sent a special representative from Moscow to determine the cause of these events. As he began to investigate, he asked the local officials if they knew any possible reasons for the trend. They answered in one voice: Schneersohn, who had recently arrived in town — through his influence the synagogues had begun to fill with prayers. He had established Psalm recitation, study of the Talmud and more. The man from Moscow announced, "So we will have to get rid of him."

We saw well enough what they were up to. After the arrest, we discovered that this man had stayed in Leningrad specifically to implement their intentions. After the Passover festival, the community council of Leningrad decided to actualize its plans for the General Assembly, and they had already prepared the convention's entire program and established a time to convene it: 23-25 *Tishrei*, 5688 (October 19-21, 1927). They commenced sending invitations, along with secret speakers, to every city — to the rabbis and communities.

Our Rebbe, may he be well, realized that their plans were about to go into effect, and his heartfelt words to the community explaining the great danger that the assembly posed did not have the desired impact. He therefore composed a letter. Before circulating it, he again sent three rabbis along with his son-in-law Rabbi Gourary, to Rabbi Katzenelenbogen, who was vacationing in Tzara Sela, to sway him from his skewed path. Should their soft ways have no effect, they were to lodge an official objection in the Rebbe's name.

To our great chagrin, Rabbi Katzenelenbogen again failed to heed the Rebbe's word or turn from his path. He asked the delegation to return in three days and advise the community board. Three days later, on 15 *Sivan* (June 15), the rabbis returned to our Rebbe and forlornly relayed the elder's disagreement. They stated that, in their opinion, all of his entreaties were to no avail, and that the Rebbe had already extended himself gently and peacefully again and again. He had been to a great extent self-effacing.

Afterwards, the Rebbe wrote an open letter addressed to "The Entire Jewish People." The organizers, seeing that their entire conference was about to be nullified, finally put their plan into motion. They approached the G.P.U. with all of their evidence and explained that it was imperative to arrest the Rebbe immediately before he could put a stop to the conference.

One page of the Althaus document is missing here — the one concerning the Rebbe's betrayal, at the hands of informants bearing false accusations.

On the night of the 15th of *Sivan*, the police came to arrest the Rebbe. The Rebbe, who was having his dinner, did not stand up, but quietly requested a cup of coffee. Then he requested *mayim achronim*,[43] said the after-blessing, and went into his office where he sat, again calmly.

The Rebbe's daughter Moussia was alone in a room. Through the open window she called to Menachem Mendel Schneerson, who was approaching, "Schneerson, guests have come to visit us!"

He understood, and immediately ran out of the courtyard to inform the close *chassidim*. I was lying in bed awake. The moment I heard the first knock I took fright. I ran to the door and called out, "Who is it?"

"Mendel Schneerson."

Before I even opened the door, I knew something terrible had happened to the Rebbe. I woke up my sons, and we all hurriedly got dressed. We went outside, and we were so anxious we were uncertain what to do. My son and Mendel Schneerson went to the home of Mr. Lieberman, the Rebbe's secretary, to wake him up and help him destroy the many documents he possessed pertaining to the *chadorim* and *yeshivot* throughout the entire country, as well as all of the financial records, and to prepare him for the search that would undoubtedly soon take place in his home. I went to the home of R.P.G. to wake him up and inform him. Together we proceeded toward the Rebbe's house. Before we arrived at Fontilamanske Street from Litino, we saw a group of "angels of death" from the G.P.U. walking across the street. They pointed at us, and we immediately turned around.

When I reached the Rebbe's house I beheld a most terrible sight, a tragedy in the making: Our holy Rebbe was sitting in an open automobile between two armed villains, who glared at me like animals ready to consume me. And the Rebbe, may he be well, his eyes full of kindness and his countenance full of love, gazed at me and nodded. Later, in Kostroma, the Rebbe told me: "When I saw you from the automobile I was at peace, knowing that a friendly person would be in the house. And I recalled how we saw one another twelve hours ago, and under what circumstances we see each other now."

When I realized that in a moment the Rebbe would be out of sight and in the hands of these murderers, I jumped into a nearby wagon to follow him and see where they would take him. However, the Rebbe's eldest daughter prevented me and, tears streaming down her face, asked, "What are you doing? Why? What will we gain? Let us go inside and decide on a course of action without losing a moment."

The Rebbe's younger daughters were also outside, and we stood, lost. The fright made our hair stand up. It was a little after two in the morning when we went inside. The first sight I beheld was the old Rebbetzin standing on a bench next to the Holy Ark, the top half of her body bent within, and calling out bitterly, "Master of the Universe! It was for Your Torah and Your service that my son was taken! Help me, dear G-d, and save me from these enemies! 'May G-d be with us as he was with our holy ancestors, to not abandon nor forsake us.'"

I tried to tell her that it was enough. I saw she was weak, but she didn't hear me through her cries. I left her to find the others, and when I saw the door to the Rebbe's office, which was usually closed, open wide, I trembled. His holy chamber was left open for all who wished to enter — a profanation of holiness, devastation in the House of G-d! This room, outside of which we would stand for hours hoping to have the merit to enter (and even then, not all of us were so fortunate), and now, I thought, what has become of it?

When I entered, I saw a second scene: The Rebbe's son-in-law and Gourary[44] were standing and wailing near the Rebbe's holy desk. All the drawers had been thrown wide open, and on the desk and below it bundles of letters and manuscripts lay upside down, mixed up, strewn about — chaos and havoc. At the sight of me, their pain doubled and they wept without uttering a word.

I stood like a stone. For a while we just remained there in silence while they looked to see if any incriminating papers were still left. They feared the enemy might return.

As they organized the desk they made two piles: the "kosher" one and the dangerous one. Among all these papers they came across a small, undated note pencilled in the Rebbe's sacred handwriting, concerning the recitation of Psalms in every congregation throughout the country. I will later transcribe this note. (In Kostroma I asked the Rebbe when he wrote it, and I received no response.)[45]

After some time we began to speak, and I learned about the search and arrest. In general, the G.P.U. agents treated the Rebbe in a respectful manner. They did not speak to him over harshly; nor did they make light of his honor. The search was relatively lenient. For example, they were about to take the manuscripts of the Rebbe's father of blessed memory when the Rebbe asked them to desist, and the manuscripts were immediately returned. The Rebbe was even allowed to walk from room to room unmolested. After being informed of his situation, he told them, "Think very hard whether you will gain from this — won't you lose from the great uproar my arrest will create?"

One of them replied that the G.P.U. would accept responsibility for everything, and that all of its actions were carried out with forethought. It was not worried about the consequences.

The Rebbe answered: "Nevertheless, I request that you repeat my words by telephone to your superior and consult with him. Perhaps you will change it to a house arrest."

Heeding the Rebbe, they telephoned their superior, but to no avail. Afterwards he asked them for his *talit* and *tefillin*, and was promised not only the *talit* and *tefillin* but also pen and paper, as much as he desired. At the time we didn't know they were lying, and we considered these significant concessions.

When they suggested proceeding by foot to the notorious prison "Spalerka," the Rebbe replied that he was weak and that walking was difficult. He asked for an automobile. Though automobiles were scarce that night due to the hundreds of arrests going on, the agents telephoned and an automobile was sent.

More than an hour passed, however, before the automobile arrived. As they were finally leaving, one of the agents said to the Rebbe, "Let me take your bag for you. I will take it outside and bring it to the automobile for you. Let me aid you as my father attended to your father." For his father was a *chassid*.

He took the package from the Rebbe's hand, but the Rebbe told the aide to take it back from him. "True," he answered, "your father had the privilege of serving my father of blessed memory; your father followed in the ways of my father. But you want me to proceed in your way. You did not, and never will, merit this. I will not go in your ways."

Many other such words were exchanged between them, all calmly and respectfully. As the Rebbe was being led away, his son-in-law asked him, "What shall we do? Should we publicize it, or perhaps it would be better to keep this quiet, not to provoke them with the publicity?"

The Rebbe answered, "First you must send *pidyonot*[46] to the *Ohalim* in Haditch, Niezin, Lubavitch and Rostov, not via telegraph, and not via special messenger, but through special express post." Concerning publicity, the Rebbe said he preferred to avoid it. He stated only that I should meet with H. Goren.

The news of the Rebbe's arrest spread quickly, and by six in the morning the house had filled with *chassidim* and others. In that brief time the entire city was thrown into turmoil over news of the arrest. Every Jew who lived there feared the G.P.U., and now even more so, knowing that the Rebbe was uninvolved with politics or business matters, things which normally would have provoked punishment. The state was taking a great man hostage. But why? And for how long?

Several hours after the arrest there was still no opportunity to deliberate and formulate a plan of action. For, after the Rebbe was taken from us, we were lost. Not even his family or closest associates knew where he was being held. Was it Spalerka, as they had said, or somewhere else? Had his food and belongings been given to him? Especially his *talit* and *tefillin*, because prisoners were not allowed to receive these religious objects.

We wandered from room to room like sheep without a shepherd. Who would decide what path to take? For any contact with the G.P.U. was perilous. During a good part of those first hours I pondered how to proceed.

Finally we agreed that R.M.E[47] and R.F.G[48] would be in charge. It was difficult for me to assent, for it was fully against my nature or mode of doing things, as I preferred to act independently, but I did not take one step without first consulting with them. I initially suggested that I, alone or with someone else, go to the head of the G.P.U. to clarify the reason for the arrest. But the others had a different strategy. While I wanted to contact *chassidim* around the world, to generate a great clamor, they planned the opposite — to do everything discreetly.

Hence, on the first day, we decided that the Rebbe's son-in-law, Rabbi Gourarie, should go to Moscow and function through the community there. And we searched for channels to the head of the G.P.U. in Leningrad.

During those first days we put all our efforts just into determining clearly whether "Yosef is still alive"[49] and to clarify where the Rebbe was, and whether his *tefillin* had been given to him. To our great anguish, it wasn't till Friday, the third day of his arrest, that we learned he was alive, after the prison accepted food for the Rebbe, may he be well (for according to law, the prisoners receive food from home once a week). Nevertheless, we rejoiced at this sign.

From Moscow we were informed by telephone that the large communities throughout the country, such as Moscow, Minsk and Kharkov, had sent telegrams in the name of the entire Jewish nation to Kalinin, asking him to grant the Rebbe freedom, and guaranteeing that he had not sinned against the state. They also suggested that we go to the chairman . . .

Finally, the chairman gave us a telegram, and on the first Shabbat of the imprisonment, I personally sent one to the G.P.U. in Leningrad and a copy to Moscow. We later met at the home of Rabbi Katzenelenbogen, in the resort town of

Diska, to discuss a strategy. On the one side, there was myself with the Rebbe's son-in-law Rabbi Gourarie and Rabbi Menachem Mendel Schneerson; on the other, Rabbi Katzenelenbogen, the "chairman" Gurevitch, Mr. Lehsman and Mr. Ginsburg. We planned for a delegation from the Leningrad community, led by Rabbi Katzenelenbogen, to meet with the head of the G.P.U., face to face, requesting the freedom of the Rebbe, and offering themselves as guarantors. Meanwhile, news of the arrest spread throughout the country, and in all the synagogues, fast-days were decreed and Psalms recited after morning prayers.

The news also traveled abroad, especially to the United States. On the third day of the arrest, telegrams arrived from Chicago and other large cities, but we did not respond to them. Overseas, the significance of our silence was understood.

From America, protests by the hundreds were sent to Berlin, and the German Secretary of State, Dr. Strehzman, was entreated to pressure Moscow for the Rebbe's release. We, in Russia, were unaware that so much of the world was agitated. Indeed, many countries were protesting. We later learned that the German Secretary of State, Dr. Strehzman, led the efforts through Ambassador Krestinsky, who notified Moscow that the arrest had generated agitation all over the globe. He advised that, to still the outcry, the Rebbe be immediately released.

All of our efforts in the immediate locale — through friends and the anxious Moscow community — were to no avail. The scholars from Vitebsk came to their aid; Rabbis H. Mendelov and Gluskin from Minsk remained in Moscow the entire period until the first release was obtained.

In Leningrad the details of the Rebbe's arrest, his health, and the clarification as to whether he was still alive at all were still being kept from us, and we devoted our efforts to obtaining any glimmering of information. Through unrelenting work, after ten days and nights, we finally received word from a certain doctor that the Rebbe was still alive.

On Shabbat, 25 *Sivan* (June 25), we obtained the first receipt the Rebbe had signed. Our joy that day was overwhelming. The receipt was passed from hand to hand among hundreds of people, who regarded it as miraculous. It put new heart into us.

On Wednesday, *Erev Rosh Chodesh Tammuz* (June 29), at ten o'clock in the morning, the telephone rang. I picked up the receiver to see who it was, and I heard the voice of an anxious girl speaking in a tone of bitterness. She knew my name and said that we were not unknown to each other.

"Why are you sitting at home and not going to see Rabbi Schneersohn?" she demanded. "Prepare him food for the way immediately, and come to see him! The entire family should immediately come to Spalerka to see him, for today he will be exiled to the Solovaki Islands for ten years of hard labor. Before he departs, the family has permission to give him food for the way and to wish him goodbye." When I heard these words, I trembled.

The sentence was reduced to three years exile in Kostroma. On his way to Kostroma, the Rebbe was allowed to stop at home for several hours.

In the few hours the Rebbe was home,[50] we learned of the accusations against him. It was for these that his blood was spilled: 1) He is the leader of all *chassidim* in the world. 2) He founds *chadarim*, *yeshivot* and fosters various religious activities in the country. 3) He is the authority of the orthodox in the entire land, the intelligentsia, and the bourgeoisie both here and abroad. 4) Through his efforts, sizable sums arrive from abroad for those who study Torah. There were many other details which I would prefer not to state.

And these were the first words we heard from him:

"Now I have seen clearly that 'You are the L-rd'[51] All of the stories told of the Alter Rebbe were now very clear to me. Not a quarter hour passed that I did not see my father. Now many new insights into the profundity of *Chassidus* will be added. If I knew that this would lead to the open study of the Torah, I could endure all of my sufferings."

He said much more, which cannot be spoken. It was too powerful. Eighteen and a half days he sat in fasting, and in every prayer he said *Aneinu* (the prayer added for a public fast-day). He practiced literal self-sacrifice until his *talit* and *tefillin* were given to him on the third day. He said and wrote much *Chassidus* there. At present we know of two *Ma'amorim*: *Min Hameitzar* ["From the depths I call out to you, O L-rd"][52], and *Havayah Li Be'ozrai* ["G-d is among those who help me"].[53]

We arrived at the city of exile on Monday night. The following morning we appeared for the weekly registration, and the local Jews received the Rebbe there, with much respect. On Tuesday, 12 *Tammuz* (July 12), we came once again to that place, and the authorities, immediately upon seeing us, informed us of his unconditional release. On Wednesday we received the official release and on Thursday morning we arrived home, thank G-d. "And the Jews had light and joy and gladness and glory."[54] The light of the Torah illuminated our paths, and the joy of the *mitzvah* opened our hearts. May it be G-d's will that we no longer endure anxiety, and that the Jewish flame not be extinguished, and may the wellsprings of *Chassidus* spread forth.

But my dear friends, after all we have seen with our own eyes, we must take to heart the Talmudic adages oft repeated

by our Rebbes that "a miracle does not occur every day" and that "one does not rely on a miracle."[55] We are not yet tranquil, and our joy is incomplete.

There is still a sadness buried deep in our hearts. We are not aware how the salvation suddenly arrived, from here or from there, and why it suddenly turned for good. Therefore, the terrible fear from the past will continue to haunt us for the coming days. For who knows what a new day will bring? Who knows which way the wind will blow, which side of the political world will turn upon the Rebbe? Although he has absolutely no connection to politics, enemies have learned who this great man is, and they saw his great esteem in the eyes of the Jewish people who are spread out in all corners of the world, who revere him and the very mention of his name; and we are afraid lest an evil eye take hold of him — lest they set upon him and treat him like a plaything for, G-d forbid, some terrible purpose.

Therefore, a holy responsibility rests with us, and with our brothers and friends, to fulfill the teaching of our Sages: "A wise man needs a guardian, and should not walk alone in the dark."[56] Stand prepared at your posts to know always if the Rebbe is well and what his situation is. Do not turn from the "crown of our heads and the delight of our hearts" for one moment. Stay in unison with our life-source at all times and with *chassidim* around the world in general. For his sake beg mercy from our Father in Heaven day and night. May the merit of his forefathers, our holy Rebbes, guard him against all evil, so that he shall not be suspected for that which he has not trespassed, and that all of the winds in the world shall not move him from his place, G-d forbid.

Notes

1. The first version was printed in Mimeograph form in *Reshimot*, Israel, 1972, and printed in part in *Biton Chabad*, vol. 18, p. 26. It was reprinted in full on page 1358 of *Likkutei Dibburim* (Hebrew Edition), vol. 5, p. 1358.

The latter version was printed in part in the footnotes to Collection of Letters on Psalms, and partly in *The History of Chabad in Soviet Russia, 1918—1950*, Kehot Publication Society, 1989.

2. Psalms 119:122.

3. Compare Isaiah 11:9.

4. Isaiah 18:8.

5. In 1911. For more details about this meeting, see *Igrot Kodesh Admur Harashab*, Kehot Publication Society, Vol. 2, p. 565 and Vol. 5, p. 37.

6. Rabbi Avraham Mordechai Alter of Ger, the "*Imrei Emet.*"

7. Rabbi Aharon Menachem Mendel Guterman.

8. Rabbi Sholom DovBer, the fifth Lubavitcher Rebbe.

9. A proposed law allowing only individuals possessing academic decrees to hold rabbinical posts.

10. *Siddur Tehillat Hashem*, Kehot Publication Society, p. 59.

11. *Eruvin* 31b.

12. Exodus 23:2.

13. *Megillat Esther.*

14. Jeremiah 12:1.

15. Ellipses in original.

16. Whereas the normal ratio is 60 to 1, here, in the case of "a creature" — an insect form — no ratio whatsoever will suffice to nullify its power to prohibit the mixture in which it is found.

17. *Chulin* 100a, *Tosafot*. The mere fact of outnumbering the secularists will not nullify their ability to do damage. [When non-kosher substances are combined unintentionally with kosher food, there apply at the time laws of nullification rendering the food kosher and permissible. However, in the instance of a "creature," and/or any similar insect, no ratio — even a thousand parts or more to one — can accomplish nullification.]

18. For a description of this meeting in the Rebbe's own words, see *Igrot Kodesh* vol.1, p.130.

19. A halachic unit of measurement. Forty se'ah is the minimum quan-

tity required to render a *mikveh* kosher.

20. Presumably, his name is concealed to protect him from dangers very much present at the time that this is written.

21. *Zohar* I 24a; II 60a.

22. Ezekiel 33:24.

23. Leviticus 19:14.

24. Psalms 29:11.

25. Another, more detailed, letter in the matter of the "General Assembly" was penned by the Rebbe on 13 *Sivan*, 5687 (June 13, 1927), two days before the his arrest. It was still on the Rebbe's desk at the time of his arrest. The letter can be found in *Igrot Kodesh* vol.1, pp 327–330.

26. "Who has granted us life, sustained us and enabled us to reach this occasion," a blessing said upon hearing good news.

27. See *Berachot* 58a.

28. The Rebbe's future son-in-law and successor.

29. From the description of the organization in the source, this is presumably the Red Cross.

30. Marasow, who was later freed, was re-arrested two years later and sent to Siberia, where he perished. For details on the arrests and executions of many of the Rebbe's *chassidim* and emissaries see *Toldot Chabad in Soviet Russia*, Kehot Publication Society, 1989.

31. Mendel Marasow.

32. See *Siddur Tehillat Hashem*, Kehot Publication Society, p. 59.

33. Psalms 63:2.

34. The following passages, while sadly true with reference to the *Yevsektzia*, may have been written for the benefit of the Communist censors.

35. Exodus 12:38.

36. "*Tzara'at Adamdamet*" in the original; see Leviticus 13:24.

37. In the text available to us, Rabbi Althaus does not seem to return to this subject.

38. A conference of rabbis from the Zhitomir region. In the end, rabbis from across the USSR participated.

39. The Rebbe is referring to his father, Rabbi Shalom DovBer of Lubavitch.

40. Rabbi Chaim Soloveitchik, Rabbi of Brisk.

41. Rabbi Avraham Yehoshua Heschel Zamsky, Rabbi of Rostov.

42. The Rebbe is referring to his father, Rabbi Sholom DovBer of Lubavitch.

43. Ritual washing of fingers at conclusion of meal prior to recitation of Blessings after a meal (*birchat hamazon*).

44. Unknown. Perhaps Rabbi Refael Gourarie.

45. The note is transcribed on p. 257.

46. Requests for intercession in prayer.

47. Perhaps Rabbi Moshe Mordechai Epstein.

48. Perhaps Rabbi Refael (Faleh) Gourary.

49. See Genesis 45:28.

50. The narrative concludes from the first letter, p. 1354.

51. Psalms 91:9.

52. Psalms 118:5.

53. Psalms 118:7.

54. *Esther* 8:16.

55. Jerusalem Talmud, *Shekalim* 6:3; Jerusalem Talmud, *Yoma* 1:4.

56. *Berachot* 54b.

Excerpts From the Rebbe's G.P.U. File

Among the many recently-released documents of the former Soviet Union are the following, a small part of a once hefty dossier concerning the Soviet Government's various investigations, arrests, and interrogations of the Rebbe.

Although it is difficult to determine how much the contents may be distorted by Communist bias, careless or selective recording, etc., these documents have intrinsic interest as primary sources, and some of the intensity of the Rebbe's confrontation with the Soviet authorities does come through.

I
Excerpt from Interrogation of Witnesses[1]

Investigator's Name: Lulav.
Family Name: Schneersohn.
Name and Father's Name: Yoseph Sholomovitz.
Citizenship: U.S.S.R..
Nationality: Jewish.
Place of Birth: Lubavitch.
Date of Birth: 1871.[2]
Age: 56.
Education: Home, finished yeshivah.
Mother's Name and Father's Name: Shterna Yehosefpuvna, 72.
Wife's Name and Father's Name: Dina Avromovna, 42.
Family: Mother, wife, three daughters.
Party affiliation: Unaffiliated.

Occupation: Rabbi lecturer.
Occupation Before Revolution: Rabbi.
Occupation After Revolution: Rabbi.
Government Employee: No.
Private Employee: No.
Connection to Army: None.
Arrest Order: #1653.
Place of Arrest: Machovaya 22, apartment 12.

From when do you know the Rebbe Schneersohn?
In summer of 1920 I saw him every day until he went to Moscow in September 1921. I know that in summer 1921 Rebbe Schneersohn was called to *Cheka* and they told him of plans to exile him to the north of Russia.
What special occurrences took place in summer, 1921?
In summer 1921, there was a public trial against *Yeshivah Tomchei Temimim*, and they closed the *yeshivah*. Rabbi Schneersohn split the students into two groups: One group he sent to Poltava, and the other one to Kharkov.[3]
Until when did the *yeshivahs* exist there?
Until 1924.[4] Then they moved to Nevel.[5]
From where did the Rebbe Schneersohn have the money to support the *yeshivahs*?
He would receive money from the Jews of Russia, and also from *abroad*.[6] Every month he would receive these monies from all over the U.S.S.R., and also from *abroad*.
Who would raise the money?
In every large city in the U.S.S.R. there was an appointed person for the monies, and he would send the money to Leningrad or wherever the Rebbe Schneersohn wanted.
Do you know who the appointed people were?
Yes. In Moscow – Yaakov Zurbitzermakalik; in Kharkov – Shmuel Bezpalov; in Kremenchuk – Hirshel Katzav;[7] in

Vitebsk — Rabbi Medalya.[8]

Do you personally know of letters between the Rebbe Schneersohn and abroad?

Yes. I know that he used to send mail through Jews from Latvia. I know of letters he sent to Goren in Riga, to Schneersohn in Paris — his uncle,[9] and to Gourarie in Vienna.

When did he send these letters?

In summer 1921.

Do you know of any letters from later on?

Yes. I know of several letters that he sent through the Polish diplomatic mail in 1922. And in 1924 he sent letters through the Estonian embassy with the help of a Jew named Shlomo Trainin.

Do you know of businesses in which the Rebbe Schneersohn was involved?

I know that in 1923 he traveled twice to Moscow to help Gourarie's business.

How did he help him?

He used to meet with a Jew in Moscow who worked in the government office responsible for tobacco production. Afterwards, Gourarie received a government position in Rostov in a factory that processed tobacco.[10] I don't know more details, but I do know that there was a great loss, and they almost took him to court, and the Rebbe Schneersohn saved him from the case with the help of a Jew from Moscow named Meir Jacobson.

★★★

Who turns to the Rebbe Schneersohn?

Many Jews turn to him. They ask his advice.

What type of Jews?

Many of them are hiding from the G.P.U.. The Rebbe Schneersohn tells them to stay underground and not to go to the G.P.U.

When they turn to him by mail, where do they write to him, to his home?

No. The Rebbe Schneersohn receives all of his letters to two addresses: 1) Chonye Morosow. 2) Aharon Althaus.[11]

★★★

Did you also know the Rebbe Schneersohn's father?

Yes.

What were the circumstances?

In the end of 1896 I was a member of the *Bund*, and afterwards I was the party representative of the "Jewish Socialist Workers Party" to the *Sejm*.[12] In 1906 I was sent to Lubavitch. There I got to know the Rebbe Schneersohn − the father and the son.

Why were you sent to Lubavitch?

To solve a problem with a student of the Yeshivah who was a member of our party.

What happened?

In the Yeshivah they realized that he was a member of our party, and when he returned from a meeting they stopped him and placed him in a locked room. The party members took up arms and went to free the student. The Yeshivah students were there with sticks but we fired into the air and they ran away. Schneersohn, the son, passed the information on to the police and the police stopped the party members who went to save the student.

How did you come into the picture?

After this incident they sent me to Lubavitch to deal with Schneersohn, the son. I had three demands: 1) To free our party members. 2) To absolve the excommunication imposed on the student's family. 3) To give 5,000 rubles to the party.

What was Schneersohn's response?

He agreed to the first two conditions but not to the third one.

What was your response?

We began various types of threats to Schneersohn. We also threw stones through his windows.

★★★

What do you know about the Rebbe Schneersohn's relationship with Professor Baratchenko?

He wrote letters to Rebbe Schneersohn. Once he also visited him. He tried to convince the Rebbe of his theories.

Are you familiar with Rebbe Schneersohn's position regarding the Conference of Rabbis?

A negative position.

Why?

He held that at the conference there could be resolutions against religion.

Why did he think so?

Because at the conference there were supposed to be participants who were not so religious.

★★★

Do you know of an underground movement operating in Leningrad in the last years?

Yes.

Who is in this movement?

Jewish *Chassidim* who have underground *chadorim* and *yeshivot* throughout the U.S.S.R.

Who stands at the head of this movement?

Rebbe Yosef Schneersohn.

What is his position?

He is considered one of the leaders in the religious orthodox Jewish movement.

With whom does he have contacts?

He has a network of contacts with many Jews abroad. He communicates with Jews in Poland, Latvia, Estonia and in other lands. And he has connections with Jews in *all*[6] of the cities of the U.S.S.R.

Who are his main helpers?
Morosow and Lieberman.
How can his doings be proven?
In Morosow's home there are many letters from which it can
be seen that the underground group continues to function
and that the Rebbe Schneersohn heads the group, and also
that he receives large amounts of money from Jews abroad
and from Jews in the U.S.S.R.

II

PART OF THE REBBE'S FIRST INTERROGATION
Date: 6/16/27

Investigators name: Lulav.

When did you arrive to Leningrad?
1924.
From where?
Rostov.
With what do you occupy yourself?
With the studies of *Chassidus* – the knowledge of G-dliness.
What is your position in all *chassidic* circles?
A professional in *Chassidus.*
Do you receive letters by methods other than mail?
All of my letters I send and receive through mail. I have no
other ways of sending letters.
Do you have any connection to *yeshivot*?
That is not my job.
What is your position on *yeshivot*?
I am in favor of them.
**From whom do you receive money for your activi-
ties?**
I receive no money for religious purposes.

In this interrogation we would like to hear from you about your relationship with Professor Baratchenko.

In 1925 a certain person who is involved with philosophy turned to me. I did not know his name.

What did he want from you?

He asked me several questions about the Star of David.

What did you answer him?

I answered him I had not seen anything in *Chassidus* on this matter and that I could not answer him on this subject.

Why was the professor interested in this?

The philosopher said that it interested not only him, but his entire group.

Why did he continue to send you money?

After three months I received about 150, 200 or 250 rubles from this person.

Why?

For research. He wanted people who study *Chassidus* to find answers to his questions about the Star of David.

What did you do with the money?

I did not take it. I sent it back to him.

Is that all?

I wrote to him that I would not do any research, for it didn't interest me. I also wrote to him that I was sure that others who learned *Chassidus* also had no answers to his questions. After that I had no contact with this person. To this date I do not know who he is at all.

Why were you against the rabbinical conference?

I was against the entire idea because before a conference of rabbis is organized, a conference of the *leading* rabbis of the U.S.S.R. is needed, and they—not you, the government—need to decide whether or not to hold a conference.

Why do the leading rabbis need to decide this?

Because only they can be relied upon to decide whether to hold the conference or not. And if they would decide to hold it, they would need to decide what the topic is, and not the government. I did not agree that all of the rabbis should decide what the topic of the conference is. I do not agree that the rabbis should hold a conference according to the directives of the government.

Notes

1. Apparently at least one of these persons was an informant specifically assigned to make the case against the Rebbe.
2. The Rebbe's true age differs from that in his official papers. The Rebbe was in fact four years old in 1871.
3. Both towns are in the Ukraine.
4. In 1924 the Rebbe was forced to leave Rostov.
5. See *Toldot Chabad of Soviet Russia*, Kehot, p. 262.
6. Italics in original
7. Probably a nickname for Reb Yechiel Tzvi Hirsh Gourarie.
8. Rabbi Shmarya Yehuda Leib Medalya.
9. Rabbi Menachem Mendel, brother of Rabbi Shalom DovBer of Lubavitch.
10 Presumably a reference to the Rebbe's establishing of vocational work for Jewish communities, including a cigarette factory in Rostov. See p. 220
11. Presumably an erroneous reference to Rabbi Elye Chaim Althaus.
12. Polish Legislature.

Refusal to Travel on Shabbat

A Talk by Rabbi Menachem Mendel Schneerson

The following talk by the Rebbe's successor, Rabbi Menachem M. Schneerson, provides some additional details of the incident of his predecessor's refusal to travel on Shabbat. The Rebbe's refusal raises the halachic question of whether one is allowed to remain in danger to avoid violating Shabbat. The discussion of this question leads to important insights into Rabbi Yosef Yitzchak's approach to self-sacrifice.[1]

I

On Thursday, the first day of *Rosh Chodesh Tammuz*, shortly before noon, the Rebbe was informed that he would be released from prison and exiled to the city of Kostroma for three years. He was also told that he would be freed that very day, and he would be able to spend six hours with his family; that night he was to commence his journey to Kostroma.

Since it was Thursday, the Rebbe inquired when he would arrive in Kostroma and was told, on *Shabbat*. Only through great effort to influence the higher levels of government was permission obtained for the exile journey to be delayed until Sunday, the third of *Tammuz*.

One of the officials who had conducted the actual arrest of the Rebbe stated that if he would not leave at the scheduled time and arrive in Kostroma on *Shabbat*, then he would not release him from the prison. The Rebbe replied that he was prepared to remain in prison for a long time, but under no circumstances would he travel on *Shabbat*.

This requires clarification: in rebuffing the instructions to travel immediately to Kostroma, the Rebbe was placing himself in certain mortal danger. Was such behavior permissible under Torah law?

Initially, the Rebbe had been sentenced to death. Extensive efforts on the part of his devoted *chassidim* and admirers, who successfully organized international declarations of outrage and protest from countless individuals, including many distinguished world leaders, were successful in having this terrible penalty rescinded. The sentence was first diminished to ten years of hard labor, and then further reduced to an exile of three years in the distant city of Kostroma. The situation was nevertheless fraught with great peril, for those who had initially issued the decree still adhered to their original harsh view. They were compelled by higher governmental sources to change their plans, but still retained their original position and authority. The fact that the Rebbe was still in their jurisdiction obviously entailed great danger for him. Indeed, the Rebbe's rejection of the intended *Shabbat* journey was a source of great provocation. He had acted contrary to their dictates. His affirmation of *Shabbat* in their sphere of authority was a challenge to their prestige.

On the other hand, there were other mitigating factors which would have perhaps *halachically* justified his leaving the prison. Since he would be released immediately, the possibility of transgression of the holy *Shabbat* would not occur during his prison stay. Moreover, there was an element of doubt, indeed many factors of uncertainty, whether the journey would actually occur. For once he was freed on Thursday, there would have been greater freedom for endeavors under the Rebbe's personal guidance to defer his scheduled departure that night. Even presuming he would leave at the set time, there still remained a complete day of traveling, during which those concerned with his welfare could exert themselves to effect the interruption of his journey. Thus, the

Rebbe might be enabled to observe the entire *Shabbat* under *halachically* permissible circumstances.

Superficially, we are faced with a very profound problem. Why did the Rebbe take so tenacious a position when it entailed the possibility of immediate peril? The more pragmatic response would have been to immediately leave the danger of prison confinement and then formulate strategies to avoid the *Shabbat* journey.

II

Indeed, this stance of heroic self-sacrifice in the face of great peril was an all-pervasive quality that characterized all of the Rebbe's activities, even prior to his arrest for the promulgation of Torah and the strengthening of Judaism in that land.

As discussed many times in the past, the Rebbe's stance of self-sacrifice in that era encompassed not merely those instances where it was necessary to act in this way; he acted this way even when it was a matter of choice, with other less dangerous possibilities available. Moreover, as discussed at length,[2] the Rebbe chose such acts of self-sacrifice in cases where eminent Torah scholars were of the opinion that it was not necessary to endanger one's life.

Viewed from the perspective of general communal responsibilities, this posture is understandable. The Rebbe was fully aware of the precarious situation of those times, conscious of the fact that the very existence of Jews and Judaism was being threatened. Thus, to assure that the "flame of Israel" would not be extinguished, mindful of his role of spiritual leadership and motivated by a sense of responsibility for the survival of the entire Jewish people, he acted boldly and displayed self-sacrifice, undeterred by the reckonings of limitations, of pros and cons.

In this specific case, however, it would appear that the journey affected only him personally, and not the welfare of the general Jewish community. Why, then, did he choose so dangerous a course? Indeed, this act could have endangered his whole life work.

III

One answer to this problem is to view the entire matter in the context of the twin concepts of *Kiddush Hashem*—sanctification of G-d's name—and *Chilul Hashem*—profanation of G-d's name. The goal of the Rebbe's tormentors was to nullify his multi-faceted endeavors for the promulgation of Torah Judaism. Had the Rebbe not resisted their directives, this would have been, in effect, a victory for them: The Rebbe had agreed to travel on the *Shabbat*! Most of those learning of his acquiescence would be unaware of the many mitigating factors mentioned previously. Jewish law is explicit that in the area of *Kiddush Hashem* and *Chilul Hashem*, the primary concern is the possible misconception of those viewing the act, who may see it as a violation of Jewish law, regardless of the actual severity or laxity of the conduct itself.

This concept of *Kiddush Hashem* is the link between the third day of *Tammuz* and the Torah reading of *Chukat,* which is usually read on a *Shabbat* proximal to the third of *Tammuz,* the day the Rebbe was released from prison. That Torah reading describes "the waters of conflict," which resulted in the punishment of Moses and Aaron by the Divine decree "You will not bring this assemblage (of the Jews) into the land (of Israel)."[3] Moses' offense was that he was instructed to speak to a stone so that it would miraculously give water. Instead, he struck the stone in anger.

At first glance, that punishment is problematic. Why was the sin considered so severe that it would prevent Moses from entering the land? We are told of other instances when Moses, as it were, was held to account, yet never was so severe a punishment accorded to him. Only in this case, the difference between *hitting* the stone rather than *speaking* to it resulted in the awesome, harsh decree that he could never enter the land of Israel?!

The rationale for this is indicated in the Torah: "For you did not believe in me to sanctify Me before the eyes of the Jewish people."[3] Rashi explains that when Moses argued in a previous incident, "Shall flocks and herds be slaughtered for them?"[4] (implying, as it were, that G-d could not provide meat for the entire Jewish people), he was not punished for this.

As Rashi comments, "This is because the event occurred privately and he was spared. But in this instance (the striking of the stone), since it occurred in the presence of the entire Jewish people, he was not spared, because of the sanctification of G-d's Name."[3]

Thus, when the factor of the sanctification of G-d's Name is present, or its reverse, then the primary focus is how the occurrence will be perceived by others.[5]

IV

The Rebbe's conduct can be explained on an even deeper level. The Rebbe's response to his captors was not only in relation to matters affecting Judaism; he had firmly resolved that he would act firmly and steadfastly in any matter. He endured much physical punishment for this stance, even though his response was not related only to matters of the sanctification of G-d's Name or the promulgation of Torah.

What is the explanation for such bold courage? The name of the Torah portion *Chukat* conveys the primary concept. The Alter Rebbe explains that the word *"chok"*—usually translated as a law with no apparent rationale—is to be understood here as deriving from the Hebrew *chakuk*—'carved and hewn'—in contrast to mere writing.[6] When one writes, the letters are added to the surface of the parchment. Though the letters are absorbed in the parchment, they and the parchment remain two separate entities. Therefore, the letters can be easily changed or totally erased from the parchment.

But hewn letters are not independent; they are intrinsic to the substance into which they are carved, an actual part of the stone. Thus, it is impossible to separate them, and any attempt to modify the letters invariably affects the stone itself.

Similarly, on a spiritual level, if the service of G-d is merely an added dimension to an individual's identity, then changes and variations in that service may occur under various conditions. Extenuating factors or compelling circumstances may cause an individual not to fulfill a particular aspect of the service of G-d, but his essence is not affected.

However, if the service of G-d is hewn into his personality, an actual dimension of his personal selfhood, then no differentiation can be made. To deprive such a person of the fulfillment of his service to G-d would mean to destroy his basic identity. This would be analogous to letters carved on a precious gem; any attempt to change the letters destroys the very gem itself.

Therefore, when the service of G-d is carved out on the very soul itself, then such a personality will undergo self-sacrifice for any detail of Judaism. No rationalization, however seemingly justified, will ever be given to explain any inactivity, any less-than-perfect service to G-d, because this person's identity is totally merged with any and all action related to such service. He and his actions are indivisible.

This was the life-mode of the Rebbe. Fulfillment of Torah and its commands was in the manner of "hewn letters," intrinsic to the essence of his identity. Therefore, his self-sacrifice was not a function of intellectual deliberation as to whether an action was obligatory or desirable. His response to existential challenge occurred naturally, because his service of G-d was the very core of his own existence.

Notes

1. *Likkutei Sichot*, vol. 28, p. 124
2. *Likkutei Sichot* vol. 18, p. 302.
3. Numbers 20:12.
4. Numbers 11:22.
5. See Maimonides' *Mishneh Torah, Hilchot Yesodei Hatorah* 5:11 for one view on this matter.
6. *Likkutei Torah, Bamidbar* 56a.

Important Dates in the Life of Rabbi Yosef Yitzchak Schneersohn

5640 (1880): Birth of the Rebbe on 12th of *Tammuz*.

5655 (1895): Begins communal work as personal secretary of his father, and participates in the conference of communal leaders in Kovno.

5656 (1896): Participates in the Vilna Conference.

5657 (1897): On the 13th of *Elul* he marries the Rebbetzin Nechama Dina, daughter of R. Avraham.

5658 (1898): Appointed head of Yeshivat Tomchei Temimim.

5661 (1901): To lay the groundwork for establishing the Dubrovna factory, travels to Vilna, Brisk, Lodz and Koenigsberg.

5662 (1902): Travels to S. Petersburg for communal matters.

5665 (1905): Participates in organizing a fund to provide Passover needs for troops in the Far East.

5666 (1906): Travels to Germany and Holland, and persuades bankers there to use their influence to stop pogroms.

5668 (1908): Participates in organizing the Vilna Conference.

5669 (1909): Travels to Germany to confer with communal leaders.

5670 (1910): Occupied with preparing the meeting of Rabbis. Between 5662 and 5671 (1902-1911) he is arrested four times on different occasions in Moscow and S. Petersburg because of his activities.

5677 (1917): Participates in arranging the conference of Rabbis in Moscow.

5678 (1918): Participates in arranging the Kharkov conference.

5680 (1920): Accepts leadership of Chabad–Lubavitch.

5681 (1921): Arranges program of communal activities to strengthen *Yiddishkeit* in Russia; establishes Yeshivat Tomchei Temimim in Warsaw.

5684 (1924): Compelled by the *Cheka* (secret police) due to slander by the *Yevsektzia,* to leave Rostov. Settles in S. Petersburg and labors to strengthen Torah and *Yiddishkeit* through activities involving Rabbis, Torah schools for children, *yeshivot, shochatim,* senior Torah-instructors and the opening of *mikva'ot;* establishes a special committee to help manual workers be able to observe *Shabbat;* establishes Agudas Chabad in U.S.A. and Canada.

5687 (1927): Establishes a number of *yeshivot* in Bukhara. On 15 *Sivan* he is arrested and held in Spalerno prison. On 4 *Tammuz* he is exiled to Kostroma. On 12 *Tammuz* he is informed that he is free; the next day he is in fact released and at the Government's instruction he moves to Malachovka near Moscow. On the day after *Sukkot* 5688 (1927) he leaves Russia and settles in Riga, Latvia, and founds a *yeshivah* there.

5688-9 (1928-9): Campaigns successfully to have *matzot* sent to Russia.

5689-90 (1929-30): Visits *Eretz Yisrael* and the United States.

5694 (1934): Moves to Warsaw; establishes association of *Temimim;* establishes branches of Yeshivat Tomchei Temimim in a number of outlying towns in Poland.

5695 (1935): Begins publication of *Hatamim* journal.

5696 (1936): Moves Yeshivat Tomchei Temimim and his residence from Warsaw to the city of Otwock.

5699 (1939): Establishes world-wide Agudas Chabad.

5700 (1940): On 9 *Adar* II, he arrives in New York and settles in Brooklyn; devotes himself successfully to rescuing his pupils; establishes Central Yeshivat Tomchei Temimim.

5701 (1941): Begins publishing the journal *Hak'ria V'hak'-dusha;* founds Machne Israel.

5702 (1942): Establishes Yeshivat Tomchei Temimim with preparatory schools in Montreal, Canada; establishes Merkos L'Inyonei Chinuch; establishes Yeshivat Achei Temimim in Newark, Worchester and Pittsburgh; establishes Kehot Publication Society of Lubavitch.

5703 (1943): Establishes Otzar Hachassidim Library of Lubavitch.

5704 (1944): Establishes Nichoach group to collect and publish Chabad melodies; begins publishing the journal *Kovetz Lubavitch;* establishes Society for visiting the sick *(Bikur Cholim).*

5705 (1945): Establishes relief office for refugees, with a branch in Paris; establishes Eideinu Society for advanced Talmud study, and Shaloh (religious instruction for public-school students); initiates efforts to improve the spiritual situation of Jewish farmers and others in rural communities in America.

5708 (1948): Founds (Kfar) Chabad village at Safaria, near Tel Aviv, for refugees from Russia.

5709 (1949): Urges the organization of a commission for the education of children of *olim* to Eretz Yisrael housed in the *ma'abarot* (transit camps) and meets with success.

5710 (1950): In the weeks before his passing he lays the foundations and program for educational work and strengthening Torah in North Africa. As a result, a seminary for teachers, a *yeshivah*, a junior *yeshivah*, a Talmud Torah for boys, and one for girls, all under the general name "Oholei Yosef Yitzchak—Lubavitch," have been established. On *Shabbat parshat Bo*, 10 *Shevat* 5710 (1950) at eight in the morning, he passes away and is interred in New York.

Notes

1. From the *Genealogy and Brief Notes* printed in *Hayom Yom*, Kehot, Brooklyn, N.Y. 1988

Founders of Chassidism
and Leaders of Chabad-Lubavitch

THE FOUNDER OF CHASSIDISM
Rabbi Yisrael Baal Shem Tov
Elul 18, 5458—*Sivan* 6, 5520 (1698-1760)

SUCCESSOR
Rabbi DovBer, the Maggid of Mezritch
(Date of birth unknown)—*Kislev* 19, 5533 (?-1772)

FOUNDER OF CHABAD
Rabbi Schneur Zalman of Liadi, the "Alter Rebbe"
Elul 18, 5505—*Tevet* 24, 5573 (1745-1812)

SECOND GENERATION
Rabbi DovBer of Lubavitch, the "Mitteler Rebbe"
(Son of Rabbi Schneur Zalman)
Kislev 9, 5534—*Kislev* 9, 5588 (1773-1827)

THIRD GENERATION
Rabbi Menachem Mendel, the "Tzemach Tzedek"
(Grandson of R. Schneur Zalman; son-in-law of R. DovBer)
Elul 29, 5549—*Nissan* 13, 5626 (1789-1866)

FOURTH GENERATION
Rabbi Shmuel
(Son of Rabbi Menachem Mendel)
Iyar 2, 5594—*Tishrei* 13, 5643 (1834-1882)

FIFTH GENERATION
Rabbi Shalom DovBer
(Son of Rabbi Shmuel)
Cheshvan 20, 5621—*Nissan* 2, 5680 (1860-1920)

SIXTH GENERATION
Rabbi Yosef Yitzchak
(Son of Rabbi Shalom DovBer)
Tammuz 12, 5640—*Shevat* 10, 5710 (1880-1950)

SEVENTH GENERATION
Rabbi Menachem Mendel Schneerson
(Son-in-law of Rabbi Yosef Yitzchak; sixth in direct
paternal line from Rabbi Menachem Mendel)
Nissan 11, 5662—*Tammuz* 3, 5754 (1902-1994)

Index

Acknowledgments

I would gratefully like to acknowledge the following people and institutions:

Rabbi Yosef B. Friedman of the Kehot Publication Society for his painstaking review of the text, adding, amending and enlightening; Dr. Binyomin Kaplan, whose sustained and dedicated efforts in the editing of this work are deeply appreciated. His expertise in the English language, sensitivity to nuances in the original texts, and general capability significantly enhanced this project. Also Rabbi Elkanah Shmotkin of Jewish Educational Media, whose research skills, industry, and editorial judgment were invaluable; Chayah Sarah Cantor, for her editorial suggestions. Rabbi Aaron L. Raskin of the Chabad Research Center for his excellent insights and assistance; Rabbi Shalom Dov Ber Levin, head librarian of the Agudas Chassidei Chabad-Lubavitch Library and Archive Center; and Rabbi Meyer Rivkin for his initial impetus for this project.

Also the late Dr. William Brickman, University of Pennsylvania School of Education, for his introductory essay placing the events in historical perspective.

The Levi Yitzchak Library of the Lubavitch Youth Organization; the Yeshiva University Uptown Campus Library; the Stern College Library; the YIVO Library; and the Joint Distribution Committee Library, for making available their research sources.

Rabbi Yehuda Krinsky, of Lubavitch World Headquarters, a friend for more than four and a half decades.

My earliest teachers in Chabad Chassidus: Rabbis Dovid Raskin and Beryl Junik; Rabbi Mordechai Altein, an early mentor in the study of Chabad, and his wife Rebbetzin Rochel Altein, editor of the English section of *Di Yiddishe Heim*, the Chabad Women's Journal, where much of this material first appeared.

The late Dr. Abraham Duker, Dr. David Kranzler, Dr. Charles Bahn, all members of the faculty of the City University of New York, for their perspective insights, and comments.

Yeshiva University President Norman Lamm for his general interest in Chassidus and his particular focus on its existential ramifications; Dr. William Schwartz, Academic Vice-President of Yeshiva University; Karen Bacon, Dean of Stern College for Women, and Rabbi Dr. Ephraim Karnafogel of Stern College, for their general encouragement of scholarly endeavors.

My wife Yehudit Metzger for her constant support and suggestions. My departed parents Chayim Yitzchak Moshe and Tcharna Metzger, and my wife's parents, Rabbi Abraham Mordechai and Mintcha Hirschberg, whose dedication to the ideals of Judaism sensitized me to the heroic altruism of this narrative.

Rabbis Avraham Laber and Avraham Berns for painstakingly researching the precious historical documents found in the document section.

To many friends and relatives too numerous to mention, who aided in this work. All credit belongs to the above and the responsibility is solely mine for any oversight or limitations.

ALTER B. Z. METZGER